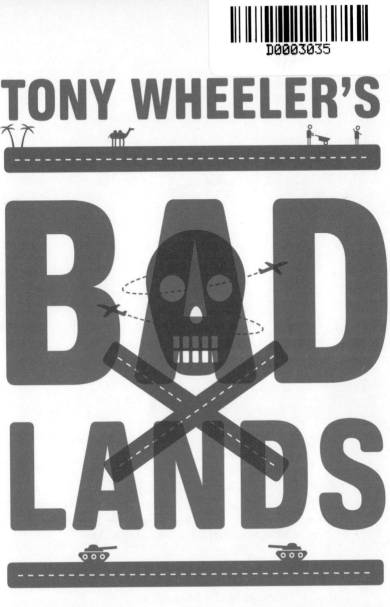

TONY WHEELER'S

BAD LANDS

A TOURIST ON THE AXIS OF EVIL

D0003035

Tony Wheeler's Bad Lands

Published by Lonely Planet Publications Pty Ltd

90 Maribyrnong Street, Footscray, Vic 3011, Australia
150 Linden Street, Oakland CA 94607, USA
2nd Floor, 186 City Road, London, EC1V 2NT, UK

First published April 2007
This edition published 2010
Printed through Toppan Security Printing Pte. Ltd.
Printed in Singapore

Edited by Nigel Chin, Alan Hurndall, Katie O'Connell,
Erin Richards, Angela Tinson
Internal design by Mark Adams
Cover design by Christopher Brand
Thanks to Jane Atkin and Brendan Dempsey

ISBN 978 174220 104 7
© Lonely Planet 2010

Photo credits:
All images Tony Wheeler except
Afghanistan 1, 2 – Mobin Jamshady
Afghanistan 6 – Wahid Jamshady
Afghanistan 8, Albania 2, Iran 1, North Korea 1, 8, Saudi Arabia 4 – unknown
Burma (Myanmar) 3 – Anders Blomqvist, Lonely Planet Images
Burma 8 – Maureen Wheeler
Iraq 1 – Husni Tutug

CONTENTS

INTRODUCTION

WHAT MAKES A LAND BAD?

It's got nothing to do with geography or topography. Rivers don't invade, deserts don't become corrupt and, while terrorists may hide out in a country's mountains and valleys, the land itself will have had nothing to do with why a Bad Land turned to the dark side. My travels through the Bad Lands took me through staggeringly impressive country – from endless desert dunes to snow-capped mountain peaks, from winding rivers to tropical beaches – but always in the background was the nagging realisation that these were countries that had gone wrong and that people, not nature, had made the wrong turns.

So while my travels do include a varied assortment of geographic and cultural marvels, it's delving into history and politics, much of it very recent, that illuminates how each country achieved Bad Land status. I could not have asked for a better cast of characters – medal-dripping dictator despots, fatally flawed national heroes, heroically doomed reformers, religious fanatics and Nobel Prize winners all played their part in the Bad Land stories. Genghis Khan, Mother Teresa, Osama bin Laden, Lawrence of Arabia and, of course, George W Bush all make appearances. The obsessive pursuit of power can also lead to some decidedly eccentric behaviour; for some Bad Land rulers, dressing up ranks second only to erecting statues and portraits in their personality-cult enthusiasms.

Of course, it's not just the locals. One country's terrorists are another country's freedom fighters, and ill-thought-out measures to discourage terrorists can actually encourage them. We don't even have to fund them directly – although some very respectable countries have done exactly that. For some countries, turning bad may be all their own work, but equally often outside influences from colonial meddling to big power-proxy struggles have played a disproportionate part in a Bad Land's sorry situation.

I've been travelling for a long time. Although I was born in England, I lived in Pakistan until the age of five and did almost all my high-school years in the USA. I've kept on travelling ever since, co-founding Lonely Planet Publications in the early 1970s, writing dozens of travel-related books and maintaining a keen interest in the world's weirder places. 'Where's your favourite place?' I'm often asked, and my honest answer is, 'The departure lounge.'

On the ground, walking the streets, you quickly pick up whether a place is safe or dangerous, and often have a far better idea of how well the average person is doing than expert economists can glean from any number of GNP and GDP statistics, or international journalists from meeting with government officials and spokespeople after parachuting into a five-star hotel.

I'm not the only person to feel that way. In an article in the *Columbia Journalism Review* in 2006, American writer Robert Kaplan commented that 'In the 1990s, when it was particularly hard to get visas to Iran – and much of the information about that country emerged out of seminars in Washington – the best thing to read on the subject was *Iran: A Travel Survival Kit*, by David St Vincent, published in the Lonely Planet series.'

How did I choose my Bad Lands?

A country doesn't even need to be a fully fledged Bad Land to have some bad marks on its scorecard. Even nice little Switzerland has its bad side; if an evil dictator from a real Bad Land wants a place to stash his ill-gotten gains, the Swiss are only too happy to provide a secure, anonymous, no-questions-asked bank vault.

The selection criteria were simple enough: how does a country treat its own citizens? Is it involved in terrorism? Is it a threat to other countries? The Axis of Evil was an obvious starting point. Iran, Iraq and North Korea went straight on to my list. Then I added Burma (Myanmar) because it's regularly cited as exhibiting appalling examples of human-rights abuses and its military government has kept a Nobel Prize winner locked up because she had the temerity to win an election. Cuba because the USA has been shouting for regime change there for over 50 years with a conspicuous lack of success. Libya because it's done absolutely everything wrong – oppressed its own citizens, funded and actually organised terrorism, worked on Weapons of Mass Destruction and even invaded a neighbouring state. And got away with it.

Afghanistan joins the list for harbouring the terrorist who can claim to be the biggest single factor in creating the War on Terrorism with which we're all caught up, whether we want to be or not. Saudi Arabia went in as the place that bred lots of terrorists – and, what's worse, rich terrorists – by mismanaging things at home. Finally I threw in Albania, not because it's a Bad Land at all anymore, but simply because it's a fascinating example of a tiny, peculiar little dictatorship that cut itself off from the outside world at considerable cost to its own people.

So what's changed in the three years since this book was first published? Remarkably little. Afghanistan still teeters between relative calm in the west and the north, the odd suicide bombing and Taliban attack in Kabul, and a war zone in the south. The Karzai government continues to be less than convincing, but a trickle of tourists still arrives, and these days they even travel all the way across central Afghanistan.

In Burma the military generals make occasional encouraging noises, and then balance sense with nonsense by building a despised new capital city at Nay Pyi Taw in the centre of the country. Meanwhile Aung San

Suu Kyi continues to languish under house arrest, another uprising was quashed with ferocity in 2007, and the disastrous Cyclone Nargis in 2008 gave the government the opportunity to prove, yet again, that they can score 10 out of 10 for oppression and economic incompetence, but zero when it comes to providing useful assistance to their people.

In Cuba, Fidel continues to pull the strings from his (long-running) death bed, while Obama promises to change the US' attitude towards the Caribbean nation, but doesn't actually do very much. Yet, at least. In Iran, the general population proves, once again, that they want democratic change, and Iranian families head towards a fertility rate comparable to the most advanced Western nations while the Ayatollah continues to believe the calendar is stuck in the medieval era.

In neighbouring Iraq, the British have withdrawn completely and the American troop numbers head in the same direction, while the Iraqi government takes increasing control of its own destiny. Intrepid tourists continue to visit the northern Kurdistan region, but also start to head south to Baghdad and some of the other main attractions of the country. Nevertheless, nobody would claim that Iraq is a safe place to visit; random acts of extreme violence continue to erupt and the jury will be out for a long time yet on whether the 2003 invasion was a good idea. Whether the end result is a step forward or a step back is also yet to be decided.

Libya? Gaddafi continues to prove on a regular basis that he's as nutty as a fruitcake; in 2010 his latest exploit was to declare a jihad on Switzerland. They weren't very polite to his equally nutty fifth son Hannibal, were they? Meanwhile in North Korea, Kim Jong-il underlines that there's more than one crazy out there, alternating between threatening rants and holding out his begging bowl to the same people he's been menacing. On the other hand there have been some faint signs of the North Korean population realising that their loving father figure isn't quite as astoundingly competent as he claims – a disastrous demonetisation scheme in 2009 prompted public outrage.

In Saudi Arabia women still can't get behind the steering wheel, but there have been some minor improvements in general human rights, and the much-hated religious police, the *mutawwa*, seem to have been reined in just a little. Pushing schoolgirls back into a burning building because they weren't properly attired to appear on the streets proved to be a little too much for even staunch Islamists to stomach.

So the overall report is minor improvements in some places, a step forward then a step back in others, but no new chapters in the history books. The generals still rule, the dictators still dictate, the crazies are still at the controls; peace has not broken out.

Having completed my Bad Lands travels I ran my Evil Meter™ across the countries. How bad is really bad? The Evil Meter™ decides.

Bad Lands is a tourist account – places to go, places to stay, places to avoid. It is certainly not a Most Dangerous Places. Although I sipped tea in the garden of the British embassy in Kabul while guns rattled outside the walls, mused on whether Pyongyang was real or a movie set and felt distinctly nervous when my taxi driver found himself in a dead-end alley in Kirkuk in Iraq, I'm careful, cautious and have a low tolerance for pain. I had an extraordinarily interesting time visiting my nine Bad Lands. Only in Afghanistan and Iraq was I even slightly concerned for my own safety and I always ate well, slept comfortably, stayed healthy and, as a bonus, made some good friends.

It's worth reminding ourselves of Benjamin Franklin's immortal words: 'They that can give up essential liberty to obtain a little temporary safety deserve neither liberty nor safety.' Franklin's words about foolishly trading short-term expediency against the long-term good followed me on my Bad Lands trails, but so did the Persian poet Hafez. I visited his tomb in Iran, but I also remembered his words in another country where he is held in high esteem, Afghanistan:

Although the road may be dangerous and the final destination far out of sight.
There is no route which does not come to an end: do not despair.

AFGHANISTAN

I make a pilgrimage straight to Chicken Street. Back in the 'hippy trail' era of the late 1960s and early 1970s, this was the Kabul epicentre and Sigi's restaurant, with its giant chessboard in the courtyard, was one of the prime attractions. I don't recognise a thing along the reincarnation of this hippy highway, although the shops probably have precisely the same collection of goods – antique weapons, carpets, gemstones and Kashmiri crafts – as they did all those years ago.

'You could probably kit yourself out in authentically mirrored Afghan hippy gear on Chicken Street 2006', I think as I round the corner and pass by the Mustafa Hotel. Maureen and I stayed at the Mustafa back in 1972 and, as soon as the Taliban departed, the family that owned the hotel reopened it, barely skipping a beat. The threesome – two young guys and a chick (in hippy-era speak) – tumbling out of the door and hoisting their backpacks on to their shoulders have scarcely missed a beat either. From the baggy trousers to the billowing kaftans, they're time-warped straight from the Flower Power era.

I cross the road and duck in to the Shah Book Company, the real-life home of Norwegian writer Åsne Seierstad's bestseller *The Bookseller of Kabul*.

I'm back in Afghanistan after a 34-year absence.

This ancient land has always been plundered, invaded and fought over, but even the worst acid-propelled bad trip could not have encompassed the chaos and turmoil since my last visit. Back then, the country was enjoying the final months of a long spell of stability, peace and relative progress. A year later, it all started to fall apart. King Mohammed Zahir Shah popped off to Rome on holiday and his cousin Daoud Shah took advantage of his absence to mount a revolution. The king must have thought Rome's title 'The Eternal City' was accurate – his holiday stretched on for 29 years. It was not until 2002, at the age of 87, that he would finally return. During that period Afghanistan suffered almost continuous conflict – the Soviet invasion, civil war, mujaheddin madness, Taliban tyranny, the War on Terror. As I packed my bags for Afghanistan in 2006 a third of the country was 'racked by violent insurgency' according to the UN Secretary-General Kofi Annan, suicide bombings were on the rise, foreign contractors kidnapped, police officers and government officials murdered. The Taliban were resurgent and NATO forces were taking ever more casualties.

There will be little peace and love, and few flowers in our hair this time around.

• • • •

Situated at the crossroads between Asia and the Middle East, Afghanistan has always been a mosaic of ethnic groups and cultures. Travellers have been lured there for years, attracted by adventure and the thrill of the unknown. In 1972 I arrived in a beat-up old English Mini, having driven across Asia from Europe. Today I fly in from Dubai on a Kam Air 737. I'm staying at the guesthouse of Afghan Logistics, a transport, travel and tourism business run by the Jamshady brothers. The six brothers appear to be perfect Afghan entrepreneurs. Dad had bought and sold cars, an activity that produced zero return during the mujaheddin violence and the subsequent Taliban years.

'The only way to make money was to be in the army or in a mujaheddin force,' recalled Mobin, the eldest brother, 'but when I told my father I wanted to become a soldier he said, "If you want to be a robber or kill people, then go ahead. If that's not what you want then do something else, but be patient, things will change"'.

Mobin had left to work as a car mechanic in Tehran, but then the carpet business rebounded during the Taliban era.

'For a while there was a lot of money in carpets', Muqim, the second brother, recalled. 'We had 80 or 90 people working for us, mainly women and children, and once they'd made the carpets we'd export them via Pakistan.' I had heard rumours that many carpets bearing 'Made in Pakistan' labels were actually Afghan products, the tags simply slapped on them to get around restrictions on exports from the Taliban-controlled nation.

'Then the carpet business collapsed, the Pakistanis stopped it, so I went to Iran', Mobin explained. 'And Muqim used the money I sent back to study English.

'When the Americans arrived, Muqim worked as an interpreter to journalists and NGOs,' he continued, 'and we soon realised that as well as interpreters they also wanted vehicles. So I left Tehran, went to Dubai, bought the first of our Land Cruisers and drove it back across Iran and through Afghanistan to Kabul. I had to grow a beard to get through Kandahar. We started our business under our family name until someone pointed out that Jamshady didn't roll off foreigners' tongues. So we renamed it something much more catchy: Afghan Logistics.'

15.

I'm staying at their office, which also includes a guesthouse and the compound where they keep their assorted cars and four-wheel drives. It's in the Shahr-e Naw area, adjacent to the embassy quarter, and the streets are surprisingly neat and tidy. Sure they're potholed and often falling apart, but they're also swept clean, even if a lot of the garbage simply goes into the streetside channel known as a jube. Mobin and I set off to look around Kabul, first of all wandering down Chicken Street and Flower Street and then heading off to the bazaar near the river.

There's plenty of mobile coverage, but my phone can't roam on the Afghan networks. I buy a SIM card from Roshan. They have the best TV ads, Mobin tells me, and their coverage is good. Unfortunately my phone doesn't want to know about the Roshan SIM card so we go in search of someone to re-engineer it. Unsuccessfully as it turns out, although a couple of young phone-shop hotshots pull out the appropriate lead to hook my phone up to their computer, surf the net to find the correct protocols to change, and try to download them to my phone. They're clearly cluey tech-heads even if they can't make it work. This street is wall-to-wall mobile-phone shops. Mix in the abundant supply of internet cafés and Kabul seems a long way from some sort of medieval outpost.

'To hell with it', I decide after the third failure and chuck over another $45 for a handset as well.

· · · ·

The next morning Mobin and I fly off west to Herat, perhaps the most beautiful of Afghanistan's ancient cities. The road routes are either downright dangerous (via Kandahar) or difficult and possibly dangerous (via Mazar-i Sharif or straight across the middle from Bamiyan via the Minaret of Jam). The Kam Air flight across the country is superb. It's a crystal-clear day and the mountains, still sprinkled or even thickly coated with snow, look terrific. Afghanistan is a landlocked country largely bordered by Pakistan in the south and east, China in the far east and

Iran in the west. To the north Afghanistan is bordered by Turkmenistan, Uzbekistan and Tajikistan, all formerly parts of the USSR. The largest of the 'stans', Borat's Kazakhstan, lies further to the north.

Herat has been a settlement for over 2500 years and a centre of Persian art and learning. In more recent times it was the scene of a bloody slaughter that provoked the Russian invasion of Afghanistan. Having extended his cousin's Rome vacation, Daoud Shah, despite his strongman reputation, proved notably ineffective as a ruler and in April 1978 he was killed in a pro-Communist coup, which immediately split into opposing Khalq and Parcham factions. The radical form of Communism the Khalq group tried to impose, and the brutality of their rule, soon had the Afghans up in arms. Less than a year later, in March 1979, Ismail Khan – at that time a captain in the Afghan army, Khan is legendary in modern Herat – mounted a revolt that resulted in the slaughter of Soviet advisers and their families. The Afghan Communist government responded, pulverising the city using Russian-supplied bombers and killing more than 20,000 Heratis, but Khan escaped to the countryside and assembled a rebel army, which was widely supported by the Herat population. It was a portent of the horrors to come. By this time the USSR was trying to rein in the wilder excesses of their Afghan clients and even the Khalq faction had split into opposing groups.

In December 1979 the USSR, exasperated with the chaos developing and fearful that it would spread across the border to their Central Asian republics, arrived in force and the real trouble started. It was an occupation that would last 10 years and cost countless lives.

All the things I remember from the last visit – the Masjid-e Jami (or Blue Mosque), the four magnificently askew minarets of Baiqari's long-lost madrasah, and the even more dangerously leaning minaret in Gowhar Shad's Musalla Complex – look better than ever. Herat even one-ups my last visit thanks to the Citadel, aka The Ark, which was off-limits back then. Now this ancient fortress is spookily empty and open with amazing views across the city from its collection of towers and lookouts. It's a fine sunset finale to a fine day in Afghanistan's western metropolis.

I've come to Herat mainly because I want to continue on to central Afghanistan to see the Minaret of Jam, and the next morning it's entirely appropriate that I should be heading there in a Toyota Hilux. In the cities the Toyota Corolla is *the* vehicle. Vast numbers of them have turned up in Afghanistan since the Taliban's departure, but once you're outside the cities Afghan roads require a sturdy four-wheel drive. In the immediate aftermath of the American-led invasion in 2001, it quickly became clear that the Hilux was the Taliban transport of choice. Back at headquarters pricier Toyota Land Cruisers were the top wheels (Osama bin Laden had a fleet of them), but, as one commentator noted, at a local level the country was run by anybody with 'a beard, a gun, a Toyota Hilux and at least a little authority'.

The ubiquitous presence of the Hilux prompted Toyota to deny that it had been supplying them, although Wade Hoyt, a Toyota spokesman in New York, noted that 'it shows that the Taliban are looking for the same qualities as any truck buyer: durability and reliability' (John F Burns, the *New York Times*, 23 November 2001). In Australia popular Toyota TV ads, ending with a freeze-frame of the owners jumping for joy beside their wheels, were spoofed with an imitation ad showing a group of gun-toting beards and their burka-clad partners airborne beside a Hilux, which has just emerged unscathed from the best the US Air Force could throw at it. As the supply of Taliban targets began to run low, even a Hilux was worth getting in your bombsights.

Motorcycles have flooded in to post-Taliban Afghanistan in even greater numbers than cars, most of them Chinese clones of popular Japanese brands. Since there are no Chinese motorcycle brands worth coveting, any name seems to be slapped on the two-wheelers as they roll off the assembly lines. As well as real Hondas you could ride a Hond,

Handa or Hondie. Or if you want something geographically appropriate, try a Pamir, Caspian or Great Kabul. And if you simply can't get enough of Toyotas, why not ride a Corolla or a Land Cruiser?

Despite the comforts of my Hilux, the road to Jam is seriously hard work. The first 150 kilometres through Obey and Chisht-e-Sharif are quite feasible even for a regular car. We see plenty of Corollas. Then the road deteriorates and our hardy four-wheel drive starts to come into its own. Occasionally the needle reaches 40 kilometres per hour, but 15 kilometres per hour seems the appropriate average speed. The trip takes 15 hours, but however tough the travel there's always someone doing it even harder. We cruise by a minibus packed with 16 people who've been going two hours longer than us already and the back-seat passengers have a couple of goats across their knees.

There's plenty to see along the way. A wide, flat valley dotted with villages for the first few hours; stops at *chaikhana*, traditional Afghan teahouses, for breakfast and lunch; a long-abandoned caravanserai and a decaying fortress; the beautiful ancient *gombad* (domes) at Chisht-e-Sharif; and finally a series of pretty little villages wedged into corners of canyons and valleys.

It's dark by the time we arrive at the guesthouse directly beneath the great minaret so my first sight of Afghanistan's first World Heritage Site is in the morning. The Statue of Liberty, Eiffel Tower, Taj Mahal and Sydney Opera House get thousands of visitors every day. The Minaret of Jam has to wait until late May for the year's first arrival: I am 2006's first foreign tourist!

Hidden away at the junction of two rivers and beneath towering canyon walls, the minaret is big, beautiful and mysterious. Although it dates back to the late 12th century it's so remote that it wasn't discovered by the outside world until 1943 and not visited and properly described until 1957. Until recently the Qutb Minar in Delhi was the only minaret that stood taller and, apart from its Pisa-like lean, the Minaret of Jam is remarkably well preserved. Yet why here and for what purpose? If it was a minaret, where was the mosque? And if it was a victory tower, like the Qutb Minar, why build it so far from any habitation? Recent research has indicated that this may have been the site of the lost city of Firuzkoh, destroyed by Genghis Khan when he smashed his way through the region.

We spend a day exploring the area around the minaret, climbing the surrounding hills for views from above, crossing the Hari Rud river on a flying fox to check the view from the other side, and finally climbing the spiral stairway inside the minaret. We lounge back at the top of the stairs admiring the views and sipping tea, which our driver, Abdul Ghani Ahsan, has thoughtfully toted up to the top. Even the climb is something of a mystery. There are two separate stairways, clockwise and anticlockwise, but they disappear below ground level. To get to the stairs you have to clamber through a head-high hole in the side of the minaret. This is clearly something for future archaeologists to investigate. The Lonely Planet Foundation helped to fund the Minaret of Jam Archaeological Project.

* * * *

We depart at 3am for the long drive back to Herat. I'm beginning to realise there's a curious do-it-yourself nature to *chaikhana* dining. From dawn onwards as we drive through each village, Mobin leans out the window and calls out to passing shops and stallholders, 'Any eggs?' The answer is always 'No', but clearly it's going to be eggs for breakfast if at all possible. At 7.30am, four hours and 60 kilometres from Jam, we stop at a *chaikhana* and Mobin tells the owner to 'get bread and send a boy down to the village to look for eggs. It doesn't matter what they cost, I'll pay'.

20.

Inside, Mobin immediately spots a pile of potatoes heaped on the floor, demands a knife and sits on the ground to peel them. A frying pan also appears, but the gas cylinder produces so feeble a flame that Mobin heads into the kitchen to produce his fry-up (the eggs have arrived) on a wood fire. There are enough flies in the *chaikhana* to make an outback Aussie feel comfortably at home. Fifteen minutes later we're tucking into fried potatoes, eggs and tomatoes.

The next day it's a total mystery what time the flight back to Kabul leaves. At first there's a rumour it will be at 10am or 11am. Later that stretches to 3pm. We depart for the airport at 1.30pm and sit on the floor of a dusty room full of flies until 2.45pm when somebody turns up and takes over the desk and chair, which are the only furniture in the small building. It appears the only reason we've been here is for a preliminary ticket check, but Mobin is clearly a master of this process and has seated himself right by the desk so that we're straight through. Quite what good that does us is unclear since we now find ourselves sitting outside the same building with more dust, although fewer flies. Getting there first does give us chairs to sit on until 3.30pm when the signal is given to leave this compound and head for the airport terminal. We recruit a young lad to wheelbarrow our bags the couple of hundred metres. He's so small that there's no way he can push the barrow even without our bags in it, so Mobin takes over and tells him to spend the money we pay him on education.

The terminal is grey, gloomy and windowless, and the only aircraft outside is a Spanish Air Force Hercules that soon departs. There is some flying still going on, however. Two swallows have attached their nests to the terminal ceiling and frantic chirping from the baby birds announces that a parent has flown in through the terminal entrance or exit door, executed a skilful turn around the whirling ceiling fan, deposited something tasty into an open beak and headed straight out again, whisking through somebody's hair (or turban or burka) if they happen to be standing in the doorway.

At 4.15pm there's a sudden surge for the boarding gate, just a narrow channel fenced in with wire. Perhaps 30 seconds later a dozen or so female passengers appear from some hidden location and are escorted straight out on to the tarmac. Another 30 seconds passes and the Kam

Air flight from Mazar-i Sharif touches down. Now we go through security, which, as in Kabul, is haphazardly hopeless. My nail clippers and a pair of tweezers were confiscated from my wash kit in Kabul, but my Swiss Army knife was overlooked. In fact I'd intended all three items to be in my checked-in bag, except it was never checked in. This time two AA batteries get confiscated and the Swiss Army knife is again overlooked. While it's being overlooked, the batteries roll on to the floor so I quickly pocket them.

At 4.45pm we finally board and any pushing to the front turns out to be pointless because they reverse the queue and board the last guy in the line first. The burkas are already all aboard. I still score a window and, just like the Kabul–Herat flight, the views are terrific. For the first 20 minutes we follow the road to Jam exactly, the trip that had taken us nearly as many hours by car. My GPS tells me we pass just eight kilometres north of the lonely minaret.

Mohammed, sitting next to me, could almost be a poster boy for the new Afghanistan. After 21 years as a refugee in Quetta, Pakistan, moving there as a young child, he returned to Afghanistan just three years ago to work as a techie with Roshan, my mobile phone company. He agrees with me that relations with Pakistan are touchy, but underlines, as so many others have done, that Afghanis owe a huge debt to their neighbour. Pakistan and Iran both took in huge numbers of Afghan refugees fleeing the fighting and hardships of the 1980s and 1990s.

The Soviets occupied Afghanistan for virtually the whole of the 1980s without ever bringing the countryside under effective control. They were opposed by a feral assortment of mujaheddin – 'strugglers' – all armed to a greater or lesser extent by the USA, who saw the Afghan turmoil as an opportunity to weaken the USSR. President Reagan praised the mujaheddin as freedom fighters and even the movie *Rambo III* portrayed them as heroic, but all these wild bunches were equally likely to squabble with each other if they weren't fighting the Russians. When Mikhail

Gorbachev took over in 1985, getting out of Afghanistan was high on his agenda. In February 1989 the last Russian troops withdrew, but the US and its allies lost interest in Afghanistan and did little to help rebuild the war-ravaged country or influence events there. The CIA had fulfilled its intention of 'fighting the Soviets to the last Afghan'; now the place could be forgotten. The USSR continued to support President Najibullah (formerly the head of the secret service, Khad), but without the support of the Soviet forces his pro-Communist government steadily lost ground to the guerrilla forces. Anyone with any sense had long since fled over the borders.

'My education was all in Pakistan', Mohammed explains in flawless English. 'We all have to be thankful for the help they have given us.

'Roshan only started in 2003, but already we have built 500 communications towers and provide coverage in 28 centres. And we have eight lakh subscribers,' he continues, proving his English came courtesy of the subcontinent, where a lakh is 100,000.

The Kam Air 737 seems to have had a previous life in Latin America. I should Mantenga Abrochado el Cinturon, it says on my tray-back, which also tells me that my Chaleco Salvavidas can be found Bajo su Asiento. Where else?

• • • •

Kabul has seen more than its fair share of bloodshed over the years. The huge quantities of arms left with the Kabul government by the Russians and supplied to the mujaheddin by the Americans allowed the opposing groups to inflict severe damage on the city.

Remarkably the Russian departure did not lead to an immediate mujaheddin takeover. The mujaheddin skill at harassing the Soviets did not translate into the ability to mount a campaign against an entrenched force, and Najibullah hung on in Kabul for three years until the Cold War ended and Ahmad Shah Massoud and Abdul Rashid Dostum's Northern Alliance, a military-political coalition of various Afghan groups, took the city in April 1992. The fall of Kabul still did not bring peace. Gulbuddin Hekmatyar, who for years had been the major recipient of the American arms aid funnelled through Pakistan to the mujaheddin, had established himself outside Kabul and 'Rocketing Kabul' became part of the vocabulary as he rained missiles upon the city. Then in 1994 Dostum decided to switch sides and join Hekmatyar against his former comrade Massoud. In that year 10,000 people were killed in Kabul.

Meanwhile in the south, a new group had developed – the Taliban. A *talib* is a student. Taliban is simply the plural. In late 1994 I remember first hearing of this 'student army' rising up around Kandahar and marching on Kabul, determined to defeat the ruthless mujaheddin who only seemed to stop looting and raping to switch sides and start the whole process over again.

The Taliban sought to impose a strict interpretation of Islamic Sharia law and the population faced massive freedom restrictions and human rights violations. Women were banned from jobs and girls forbidden to attend schools or universities. Those who resisted were punished. Communists were systematically eradicated, as was eventually the majority of the opium production. The Taliban took Kabul in 1996 and Najibullah, reluctant to escape from the city with Massoud's retreating forces, was hauled out of the UN compound, beaten, castrated, shot and hung from a lamppost. The Taliban destroyed dozens of statues and figures in the city's once-magnificent museum, which had already been comprehensively looted during the mujaheddin era.

• • • •

By the end of 2000 the Taliban had captured 95 per cent of the country, aside from the opposition Northern Alliance strongholds in the northeast, but more crises were developing. A terrible drought was exacerbating already severe food shortages. The Taliban government seemed more concerned about enforcing their religious strictures and continuing their battles with the remaining mujaheddin of the Northern Alliance than grappling with the problem of feeding the Afghan population. That, they seemed to feel, could be left to the UN and NGOs, while at the same time they made the work of those organisations steadily more difficult.

As the Taliban's international support, apart from Pakistan, shrivelled up completely, the power and influence of the Arab-financed extremists of Al-Qaeda became steadily more significant. Osama bin Laden had been a prominent mujaheddin organiser and financier, funnelling money, arms and Muslim fighters from around the world into Afghanistan.

In January 2001 the UN Security Council tightened the screws on the Taliban and demanded the extradition of Osama bin Laden. Pakistan found itself in the difficult position of agreeing to enforce the UN sanctions and at the same time wanting to look after its Afghan clients. Not all was going well for the Taliban, however. Ahmad Shah Massoud, the charismatic leader of the Northern Alliance, had visited Europe to rally support while Abdul Rashid Dostum had received support from Turkey and had led his Uzbek men against the Taliban. In the west Ismail Khan, the Herat strongman (remember him?), had established a new base with Iranian support. In April the last vestige of moderation within the Taliban ranks disappeared when the deputy leader died of cancer in Karachi. More strictures were placed on humanitarian workers and in May, in a move seemingly modelled on Nazi Germany, Hindus were required to wear yellow badges.

In August UN Secretary-General Kofi Annan pushed for more carrots and sticks to be used on the Taliban while at the same time pointing out that the numbers of Islamic radicals in Afghanistan, the majority of them Arabs, had reached record levels. The summer offensive against

25.

the forces of the Northern Alliance included 10,000 non-Afghans in the 25,000-strong Taliban force and it was these non-Afghans who often inflicted the greatest cruelty on the local population, particularly the unfortunate Shiite Hazaras.

By this time Afghans made up the world's largest number of refugees, the drought continued without a break and the UN's World Food Programme was faced with feeding 5.5 million people, up from 3.8 million just a year previously. August was also the month when Australia put up the 'no entry' sign for 438 mainly Afghan refugees picked up from a sinking Indonesian boat by the Norwegian container ship *Tampa*.

In short, by the beginning of September 2001 Afghanistan was an unholy mess, and took another step towards disaster with the assassination of Massoud on 9 September. It's theorised that the suicide killing, using a booby-trapped video camera, was planned and executed by Al-Qaeda, knowing that the September 11 attacks were only hours away and that disposing of the Taliban's number-one opponent would ensure the opposition's support when the inevitable American reaction hit. Now all it took was four aircraft hijacks.

• • • •

I wake up from a weird dream about staying in somebody's home, inadvertently leaving a door unlocked and getting robbed. In the middle of a discussion about how this happened the burglar alarm suddenly goes off, except it isn't a wailing siren, clanging bell or shrieking scream; it's just a very loud voice repeatedly enunciating: ALARM, ALARM, ALARM. It's so loud I wake up with a start, in time to hear the last 'Allah Akbar' boom out from a nearby minaret in the muezzin's pre-dawn call to prayer. I was getting up soon anyway. This morning Mobin and I are off to the Bamiyan Valley in central Afghanistan, the centre of the Hazarajat, the homeland of the country's Shiite Hazaras.

To my eternal regret we didn't visit Bamiyan back in 1972. My diary reveals that we decided the transport alternatives were either too expensive – 'US$15 round trip' – or too difficult – '12 hours from 3am on the local bus'. Now the giant Buddhas, which looked out over the beautiful valley from their hillside niches, are gone, destroyed by the Taliban. An ancient reclining Buddha image in Ghazni also fell to the Taliban's iconoclastic urges.

In retrospect the destruction of the Bamiyan Buddhas in March 2001 seems like an omen of what was to come in New York six months later. The Taliban leader, Mullah Omar, had promised to protect them. Now he reversed course, an indication it was Osama bin Laden and the Arab fundamentalists who were in control, according to Nancy Hatch Dupree, the American author of *An Historical Guide to Afghanistan*, first published back in 1970 and still the classic guide to the country. 'It was the hardliners' way of saying: "We have won. We call the shots. We don't give a damn"', Dupree explained.

The destruction of the Buddhas seems to me like the perfect example of religious intolerance: 'Our religion is the only correct religion. You're an infidel; we're going to treat your religion with zero respect. Get fucked.' Angry Muslims (anger is something Islam seems to do very well), however, had been working Bamiyan over long before the Taliban arrived on the scene. Faces of Buddha images had been hacked off centuries ago.

Unfortunately Islam is far from the only religion to play these games. Knocking your temple down to build my temple right on top of it seems to be a game most religions like to play. It was certainly a favourite with Christian missionaries in the Pacific. Once they'd stopped those lascivious hip-shaking dances and covered up the grass skirts and bare boobs with nice Mother Hubbard dresses, their favourite activity was flattening Polynesian temples and building churches on top. Christianity has also included bouts of iconoclasm. The 16th-century Reformation in

Europe featured plenty of destruction of 'graven images'.

The route to Bamiyan is not unlike the road from Herat to Jam. A rough and rugged road that took just 6½ hours back in the 1970s (according to Dupree) today takes us 11 hours. There's plenty to see along the way. Villages surrounded by green fields and walled orchards pop up regularly, just like on the Jam route, but there are also regular *kala* (fortified houses) and ancient caravanserais. Dupree's guidebook faithfully notes these ancient markers, but they've since been joined by much more recent Russian tanks looking as if their crews just parked them by the roadside and walked away. Once a tank has stopped it's clearly all but impossible to shift. We stop for lunch at a very busy *chaikhana* in Ghorband. From our seat on the upstairs balcony I can see two tanks abandoned right in the middle of the village.

Next morning I gaze up at the empty Buddha niches looking reproachfully out on the valley, but what a beautiful valley it is and there's plenty of interest apart from the missing Buddhas. Everything around Bamiyan reminds me of somewhere else. The valley itself takes me back to Ladakh, the Tibetan region of north India. There are the same gently folded hills, beautifully shadowed in early and late light, with lines of poplar trees providing a green contrast to the grey-brown earth. Then in the background are the snowy peaks. There's also a touch of Turkey: the caves that dot the hillsides, not just around the niches for the great Buddha images but all around the valley, have a definite flavour of Goreme, the Anatolian area of troglodyte dwellings. When we head out to Band-e Amir, the recollections turn to Tibet – the rolling, utterly treeless sweep of country, still with mountains on the horizon, but also with that Tibetan habit of diverting off on a totally new road route every now and then.

Overtaking a slow-moving truck is rarely a problem. You just take the other fork when the road divides and a kilometre later the roads rejoin and the truck is behind you. Plus there's an Ethiopian interlude every now and then – Russian tanks from the Soviet era are seen, abandoned by the roadside, just as often as in that African nation.

The Hazara people of the Bamiyan region were among the first to rise up against the Russian invaders and they succeeded in driving the Russians out of the Hazarajat region by 1981. The unfortunate Hazaras have always done it tough. Physically they look quite different to the other Afghan tribes. They're said to be descendants of Genghis Khan's Mongolian followers who remained behind after his destructive invasion from 1220. Furthermore they're the Shiite minority among the country's Sunni Muslims and as a result they've always been looked down upon and discriminated against by the other Afghan groups. Khaled Hosseini's bestseller *The Kite Runner* revolves around the Hazaras' unfortunate position in Afghan society and in particular the mistreatment they suffered at the hands of the Taliban. It was only in September 1998 that the Taliban finally captured Bamiyan, only to lose it again less than a year later. They finally regained it in 2000 and underlined their control by destroying the Buddhas and massacring large numbers of Hazaras, people they looked upon as little better than nonbelievers.

From Bamiyan it's only a couple of hours along a much better road to the beautiful lakes of Band-e Amir where we're suddenly in the American southwest with soaring pinnacles and plunging canyons, but a surreal southwest because of those otherworldly blue lakes. Writers are keen to announce that no description can ever prepare you for the sheer beauty of these lakes and they're right. Like so many visitors in the past I am awestruck by the incredible blue of the main lake – Band-i-Haibat, the 'Dam of Awe'. The lake has created its own dam over the years with the sulphur deposits now rising to more than 10 metres high and continuing to build up as the water spills over the edge. There's a touch of Australia in the language – in Australian English a dam means not just the device to hold back the water, but also the water behind the dam.

Also awestruck by the lake are François and Arnaud, two French motorcyclists who have arrived overland from Europe intending to

continue to Vietnam. It's great to see some tourists rediscovering the
country. There's also a small group of Japanese tourists, led by feisty
Michiko Suzuki, who has spent three years in the country and complains
that the Japanese government, like the Australian one, contends that the
whole country is a no-go zone. She's irate about this. 'My name is black
in Japan', she says. She manages to get adventurous tour groups like this
together anyway, even if the government doesn't like it. 'The Taiwanese
are the only people who come here and aren't worried about it', she
continues.

There's much more traffic on the way back to Kabul than there was on
the way out. The road seems to be crowded with goats, sheep, donkeys
and even camels, quite apart from vehicles. There's a disproportionate
number of the standard UN vehicles, white Toyota Land Cruisers, out
and about today and, as always with the UN, travelling way too fast.

'They don't own them', comments Mobin. 'If the drivers owned the
vehicles, they wouldn't drive like that.'

A surprising number of the Afghan minibuses and Corollas seem to
be driven by 10-year-olds, barely able to see over the steering wheel and
looking even younger among their grey-bearded, turbaned passengers.

Coming down the hill from the Shibar Pass, we stop to photograph a
particularly nicely situated abandoned tank, its gun barrel blocking part
of the road. To my amazement the tank commander suddenly pops his
head up from the hatch. Has a left-behind Russian been waiting all these
years? More likely it's the donkey herder taking a break from the wind
while his scatter of hee-haws graze up the hill.

Just before we reach the sealed Kabul–Mazar road, just north of
Charikar, there are a string of car-wash guys waiting to hose the dust off
before you get back on the tarmac for 60 Afs, about US$1.20, plus a good
tip. Every car seems to stop for this pre-big-city service.

• • • •

My third and final excursion from Kabul is up to Mazar-i Sharif, the northern centre close to the border with the northern 'stans', which were once part of the USSR. Back in 1972 Maureen and I drove across Afghanistan entering from Iran to Herat, looping south to the current no-go zone of Kandahar, heading north to Kabul and then turning east to cross the Khyber Pass into Pakistan. We never went to Mazar.

Mazar may be peaceful today, but the Taliban takeover of the northern metropolis was a microcosm of the entire country's quarter-century of absurd infighting and treachery. It was a 'bloody drama of betrayals, counter-betrayals and inter-ethnic bloodshed which was astounding even by Afghan standards' according to Ahmed Rashid's seminal book *Taliban*.

In 1997 the Taliban controlled their southern redoubt of Kandahar, the western centre of Herat and the recently captured capital, Kabul. Ahmad Shah Massoud was marginalised, driven back to his final stronghold in the Panjshir Valley. If the Taliban could capture Mazar-i Sharif, they had effective control of the whole country. The capture, however, required the defeat of the ruthless Uzbek leader Abdul Rashid Dostum, the strongest of Afghan strongmen. Dostum had managed to keep Mazar clear of the turmoil that had devastated so much of the country, but he had a weak point – his second-in-command, Malik Pahlawan.

Defeating Dostum was, for the Taliban, simply a matter of bribing Malik to switch sides. It's only about 50 kilometres from Mazar to the Uzbekistan border and Dostum managed to escape, although Ismail Khan, the Herat commander who had been cooperating with Dostum, ended up in the Taliban's hands. Malik quickly found that his deal with the Taliban was really a Taliban takeover, not some joint power-sharing, and within two weeks the whole deal unravelled. Mazar included a substantial Hazara population as well as its Uzbek majority and the Shiite Hazara rose in revolt and slaughtered the Taliban invaders and their Pakistani supporters. Naturally Malik took this opportunity to renege on his recent deal and also went on the attack.

31.

The Taliban survivors fled south only to find that Massoud had taken this opportunity to venture out of the Panjshir Valley to blow up the southern entrance to the Salang Tunnel, which links northern and southern Afghanistan, thus trapping the terrified Taliban forces in the north. Meanwhile the Hazara also rose up from their Bamiyan Valley stronghold and the straightforward capture of Mazar instead turned into a disastrous rout.

Nevertheless a strong Taliban force remained in the north and less than four months later they resumed their attack on Mazar. Of course, this was the signal for Uzbek supporters of Dostum and Malik to start fighting each other as well as the Pashtun Talibans, and at this point Dostum reappeared on the scene from exile in Turkey. Apart from battling with his untrustworthy former supporter Malik, he now found himself fighting to regain the city not from the Taliban, but from the Hazaras, who had established themselves in the city during the chaos.

The Taliban fled south for a second time, taking the opportunity to conduct the occasional massacre of Hazaras as they went, and the Uzbeks added a new definition to the term 'containerisation'. Taliban captives were herded into shipping containers in the desert where, under the fierce summer sun, they died from either asphyxiation or simply roasting to death. It was difficult to tell from their blackened corpses how they had died. Dostum and Khan are both major forces in the Afghanistan government today.

• • • •

It's just over 400 kilometres to Mazar and time-wise a good part of it is getting clear of Kabul. The dusty, potholed back roads to Jam and Bamiyan might be slow, hard going and crowded, but well-kept roads like this one are seriously scary. Drivers regularly pull out to overtake against oncoming traffic, confident that it will pull on to the shoulder to let them through. Sometimes a faster overtaker passes a slower overtaker and on occasions somebody else will simultaneously overtake on the inside, putting four vehicles abreast on a single lane. The signature Afghan overtaking technique is the 'approaching a speed bump' manoeuvre. As one vehicle slows for one of the far-too-frequent speed bumps, another vehicle pulls out but then also has to slow down to a near stop. Since it's quite likely that somebody is trying the same trick in the opposite direction the end result is total gridlock with two other cars also occupying the whole road width. Speed bumps are often made by simply draping a Russian tank track across the road.

Once we're through the Salang Tunnel, the four-kilometre-long tunnel built with Russian aid back in the late 1950s and early '60s, we zip along at 100 kilometres per hour. There's still snow around the tunnel exit on the northern side. We stop beside the Doshakh bridge, where the melting water from the mountains rushes past a meadow lined with a cluster of *chaikhana* set up to cater to the passing traffic. Unhappily the whole site is rapidly submerging under a blizzard of soft-drink cans, plastic bags and other assorted garbage. I don't say anything about it, but Mobin is so annoyed he goes off to lecture the owner of the main *chaikhana*.

Mazar has a single major attraction, the Shrine of Hazrat Ali. Ali is the Prophet Mohammed's son-in-law and a main player in the great split between Shiite and Sunni Muslims. The Shiites believe he is the true successor to the prophet; the Sunnis disagree. Both sides do, generally, agree that Ali is buried in Najaf in Iraq, but somehow an alternative theory developed that he's here in Mazar in Afghanistan. Either way it's an important site, beautiful and peaceful in the evening glow and home to a famous flock of white pigeons.

The Hotel Farhat in Mazar has 'old Soviet character', according to the guidebook. It's also packed full of huge overstuffed furniture and features the sagging carpet-on-top-of-carpet on the stairs, which seems to be a design norm in Afghan hotels with pretensions. My room also

33.

has neatly folded sheets on the bed in case I feel like making it, two suitcase-like containers with blankets in case the temperature drops, and an air-con unit, which might prove more useful. Sitting on a chair beside the bed is a big metal box with instrument dials. A cable snakes out of it in one direction and another cable coils all over one side of the room before disappearing, who knows where? Heart monitor? No, it's a voltage stabiliser for the air-con.

We dine in the Bahaar Restaurant, which is liberally decorated with nicely misspelled calendars from the Kefayar Hotel & Weeding Centre. Presumably after the ceremony the couple can get down to some serious maintenance of the vegetable patch. Back at the hotel it's late and quiet. All the guests' shoes are scattered around just inside the entrance to the building.

The next morning we drive to neighbouring Balkh, the region's other big attraction. Today it's just a village, but it was a great Buddhist centre two millennia ago and already dubbed 'the mother of cities' when Islam arrived on the scene. Genghis Khan put an end to that and when Marco Polo stopped by, there were only ruins to impress him. The remains of the city's great mud walls still stretch for 10 kilometres.

The ancient Masjid-e No Gombad once had nine domes, or *gombad*, and is crying out for an archaeological investigation. The intricately moulded stucco columns, which once supported the domes, disappear into the ground for half their height. What lies beneath the surface?

The tomb of Rabi'a Balkhi in the circular park in the centre of modern Balkh is a potent reminder of the hidden half of Afghanistan. Her poetry proves that Afghanistan's women do have a voice and that love can still exist, even in such a male-dominated society. Rabi'a Balkhi fell in love with her slave, was imprisoned here and committed suicide by slashing her wrists, writing her final poem on her prison walls with her own blood. I'm about to stroll to the shade of a tree to check my guidebook's description of this event when Mobin warns me off.

'Don't go that way. There is woman', he says in a tone reminiscent of those old nautical maps with their 'here be monsters' notations at the edges. Two women are indeed sitting under the tree and it reminds me that several times Mobin has taken care to steer me away from approaching too close to the forbidden half of this country.

• • • •

We're off early the next morning, heading south for a small pilgrimage up the Panjshir Valley, Massoud's power base and final retreat. First, though, there's a short side-trip. So many wonderful places in this world meet all our expectations while failing to surprise us. We've had so many previews, seen so many photographs, glimpsed them as backgrounds in so many movies, read about them so many times that there's no unexpected shock. We know what to expect.

Every once in a while we suddenly find ourselves looking at something for which there has been no advance warning. Something that has had no book-cover portraits nor even the odd black-and-white photograph on some museum wall. Something like Takht-e-Rustam, only a few kilometres off the Kabul–Mazar road at Samangan, a Buddhist complex featuring a cave monastery and a rock-cut stupa. It's the stupa that really blows me away. I thought I knew my way around the stupas of Asia, but I have never even seen a photograph of this two-millennium-old rock dome. Here's something too solid for even the Taliban to damage. Clearly it has similarities to the temples of Ajanta and Ellora in India, also cut out of solid rock, or even the cave temples of Petra in Jordan, but the place it really reminds me of is Lalibela in Ethiopia, where you also can stand at surface level and look down at the marvel at your feet.

We pause for lunch again at the beautiful Doshakh bridge collection of *chaikhana*. There's no sign of anything happening about the trash situation. At the other side of the Salang Tunnel we diverge up the Panjshir Valley to visit the tomb (a grand mausoleum is under construction) of Ahmad Shah Massoud, the 'Hero of Afghanistan', the 'Lion of Panjshir'. Massoud kept the Russians at bay and guarded the only region of Afghanistan not to fall to the Taliban until, just two days before September 11, he was assassinated by Taliban suicide bombers.

Back in Kabul that night we're accompanied at dinner by Mobin's small-screen obsession. It seems Mobin has a number of obsessions, starting with photography. His little digital camera works overtime and he gets good results. In part it may be because people are so enthusiastic about getting photographed. Mobin will haul a farmer out of the field and run him through a hundred poses as if Mobin was a fashion photographer and the hapless labourer was a high-fashion model.

Then there's food: 'We must have vegetables' has been a regular announcement. A bag of salad ingredients rides around in the back of the car and if the *chaikhana* can't provide a suitable salad Mobin will provide it for them, preparing it as well if necessary.

Genghis Khan – aka Jenghiz or Chenghiz in these parts – is a definite obsession. We run into him on a regular basis. Old Genghis was in a particularly destructive mood when he swept through Afghanistan, and Shahr-e Gholghola, the 'City of Screams' in the Bamiyan Valley, is a pretty good example of his handiwork. The screams came from the city's inhabitants as Genghis slaughtered every man, woman and child. Mobin totes around an Afghan history book (two volumes), which he dips into periodically.

'If I meet him after I die, I will kill him' is a typical Mobin pronouncement about Genghis.

Finally there's Indian soap opera. After two weeks in Afghanistan I'm beginning to suffer from Bollywood overkill. Every hotel lobby or restaurant I step into has a television tuned to India, picking up either Bollywood movies, Bollywood soap operas or Bollywood MTV-style music videos. The music videos feature the usual sashaying around, sultry looks and sexy moves, but without ever getting too explicit. Anything too raunchy goes fast-forward or out of focus, but the Taliban ban on music and dancing has clearly resulted in a pent-up demand that all of Afghanistan is working overtime to service.

'Nobody wants to watch anything from Pakistan,' Mobin explains, 'but Iran is OK.' The Iranian passion for torch singers may generate lots of cassette sales in the bazaar, but it's not going to work as a video clip. A filmy sari works much better than an all-encompassing chador and when it comes to dancing Bollywood's a clear winner.

'My Mother-in-Law was a Bride' is the Hindi-to-Dari-to-English translation of the soap that has Mobin in thrall. Most of Afghanistan as well it seems, from the number of times I catch the theme tune and see the (rapidly becoming familiar) characters casting anxious/angry/passionate/perplexed looks at each other. Over dinner at the guesthouse this soap, with the actors' Hindi dubbed in to Dari, was always the focus of attention.

'This programme is perfect for Afghanistan', Muqim explains. 'Exactly the same concerns face people in Kabul', he continues, explaining that the pretty young woman arguing with her husband was complaining that he wasn't making enough money to buy her sufficient jewellery.

'I can't sleep if I don't have a lot of jewellery', she whines.

Once her husband had mooched out she snatches up the phone to complain to her mother as well.

'There's no air-conditioning in the apartment and I have to fix my own breakfast', she wails. 'How can I live like this?'

'Get a life', her mother wisely responds.

'We have four TV networks now', Mobin observes. 'Guess how many we had under the Taliban?

'Zero.'

• • • •

I have a final visit in Kabul – the OMAR (Organisation for Mine Clearance and Afghan Rehabilitation) Land Mine Museum. Most of the operation is indeed devoted to mines and clearing them, but as well as those most horrific weapons of often very minor destruction, the museum has all sorts of military equipment. It's a gruesome little collection of warped ingenuity, a bastard marriage of neat design and ugly practicality.

Don't those stylish Italians turn out smart little pressure-sensitive mines, perfectly packaged to take a child's legs off? The Russian mine packing a thousand pieces of rusty iron – 'chopped rod' – around the seven kilos of explosive is nowhere near as elegant, but it's guaranteed to make a real mess of anybody nearby when it goes off. Some of the nastier examples include the 'bounding mines', which, when triggered, jump a metre or so into the air before exploding, high enough to take your legs off at thigh level or a child's head off her neck.

Have I been getting too blasé about this country? Emerging from the hotel in Mazar, Mobin ducks down to look under the wheel arches.

'Checking for bombs?' I enquire.

'I don't know how good the security is at this hotel', he announces. 'I'm pretty sure they're OK, but I tell our drivers they must always check their cars.'

He doesn't mean the water and oil levels.

'If they put a bomb under your car, it will usually be close to the fuel tank.'

Mobin is almost annoyingly protective. He always manages to manoeuvre himself between me and oncoming traffic as we cross roads. Getting across the road always entails a game of chicken with the drivers. There are no pedestrian paths and very few traffic lights. Indeed, were there any traffic lights at all? He isn't happy about my heading out on to the streets alone.

38.

'Relax,' I feel like saying, 'I can look after myself.' I don't say it, though, and it's not a problem. I'm quite happy to go along with being shadowed.

On that final full day in Kabul my tranquil attitude finally gets a wake-up call.

I drop round to the British embassy to talk to a contact there and, after an interesting discussion while lazing back in the warm sunshine on the embassy's patch of grass – sipping tea in a traditionally English fashion – I head back to the separate arrivals building, hand in my visitor pass, retrieve my passport and phone Mobin. The guesthouse is only a kilometre or two away and he said he'd zip round to pick me up as soon as I call.

I can't get through. The lines are congested or there's some sort of problem with the connection. I sit down, wait a few minutes and call again. Still no luck. Five minutes later I'm about to try again when my embassy contact reappears to announce that something is happening out on the streets and the embassy is being locked down. We wander back by the dining area, grab another cup of tea and retire to the garden again. The British embassy has a lot of guys around with security written all over them, in appearance if not words. The Land Cruisers are armoured and so are some of these guys. Gradually the rumours start to percolate and the very first one is pretty close to the truth: there's been a car accident between a foreigner and an Afghani. Somebody, presumably the Afghani, has been killed and there's trouble.

Soon alternative rumours pop up. It's been a collision between an American army vehicle and one or more cars and when the crowd became threatening the Americans fired into the crowd. Or they didn't and the angry reaction to the accident is simply the resentment already seething from a recent raid in the south, which – choose your standard report – got a lot of Taliban bad guys or got a lot of innocent civilians. Quite possibly both. A sudden burst of gunfire coming from just outside the embassy wall confirms that whatever is happening is more than just a rumour.

By this time the news is coming through on the TV: scenes of Hummers racing by angry rock-hurling crowds, a government office and something else – a restaurant? a hotel? – being attacked, a car on fire.

The angry crowds are moving towards the parliament building in the south of the city. The embassy quarter, where I'm holed up, is in the north, but then the TV reports say that they're moving north towards the city centre, looting as they go. A hot new rumour suggests that the German embassy, virtually next door to us, is under attack. Obviously the American embassy is being threatened, but it appears the military are keeping the protesters well away from that tasty target.

We have lunch and talk some more. None of my embassy contact's afternoon appointments are going to turn up so I don't have to feel guilty about stealing his time. Barbara Stapleton, a European Union representative, is also marooned at the embassy and unable to phone out to find out what's happening. We were both in Cambodia in 1993, at the time of the first post–Pol Pot elections, and we swap tales about that sad but lovely country.

I mention Frank Zappa's definition of what it takes to be a country: 'You can't be a real country unless you have a beer and an airline – it helps if you have a football team, or some nuclear weapons, but at least you need a beer', and we show our age by remembering some classic rock concerts at the old Rainbow Theatre in London. Barbara recalls a Bob Marley concert where the mood turned uglier and uglier as the crowd waited for the reggae master to finally come on stage. And then it turned completely as the audience linked arms for another dose of redemption.

We also talk about the drug situation. The British are about to commit more troops to policing the Taliban-controlled Helmand province, site of much of Afghanistan's huge opium production. The Taliban did clamp down on opium production when they were in power, but that policy was reversed once they were out of power. Not only does the money from opium support the Taliban and spread violence, it also causes huge problems all the way from poppy field to some junkie's veins in New York or London. Naturally some leaks out along the way so Pakistan, the old Russian Central Asian republics and Iran all face increasing problems with drug addiction and all the crime, corruption and carnage it brings. Russian journalist Artyom Borovik pointed out in *The Hidden War*, his fine account of the Soviet war in Afghanistan, that money to support the mujaheddin didn't only come from the CIA; plenty of Western junkies were also doing their unintentional best to support capitalism's war with Communism.

We're told we can stay the night at the embassy if necessary and we both joke that in places like this you should always bring your toothbrush along. Things aren't so friendly out on the streets and when Barbara can finally get a call out it's to hear that the Care International offices, opposite her own, have been attacked and set on fire. A few minutes later her phone rings. It's not her driver, who has been caught on the other side of a police roadblock, but a driver she used to have, simply phoning up to check she's all right.

Reports of what happened have now become fairly clear. A US military convoy crashed into a number of cars, possibly accidentally, possibly due to some sort of mechanical failure. It's irrelevant. In this situation you're guilty, whatever the cause. Some of the total of 11 deaths are a direct consequence of the accident; others result from gunfire from the convoy personnel, the Afghan military or the police. That's hardly relevant either. Amusingly, an American embassy spokesman announces that everybody has been moved to a secure location within their heavily fortified building.

Round at the British embassy we're still sitting out in the garden.

Despite the events outside, my embassy contact still thinks there are reasons to be confident about Afghanistan's future. President Karzai has been successful at co-opting the warlords, weaning them away from their fiefdoms and installing them in some important-sounding (and possibly even actually important) roles in Kabul. Abdul Rashid Dostum has been lured away from Mazar and Ismail Khan from Herat. Could Khan possibly be persuaded to give up Herat for the title of Minister of Energy?

Turned out he could.

'People worry about simply ignoring the damage these guys did,' muses another of my fellow embassy captives, 'but they were successful warlords not only because they were ruthless, but also because they were good administrators. Afghanistan needs good administrators.'

Finally my phone rings and Mobin announces he's coming round to collect me. I've been trying to call him and Muqim regularly, but without success. I've been at the embassy for six hours.

Ten minutes later we're cruising through quiet although not deserted streets. There are plenty of police and Afghan military, but no coalition personnel, at every junction. We're turned back as we approach the guesthouse, but Mobin nonchalantly cruises down one-way Chicken Street in the wrong direction and we're soon home. Surprisingly, apart from one burnt-out car and a scattering of broken glass at a handful of shops and police boxes or their close brethren, the security boxes, which stand at the entrances to secured compounds, there's no sign of damage. Most shops are shuttered, but the Italian restaurant Popolano, just round the corner from the guesthouse, looks like it's planning to open for business this evening.

The next morning it's pretty clear that everything is unclear. I've watched the local TV (Tolo TV is all over town talking to people) and scanned the websites from CNN to BBC World, the *Guardian* in the UK to the *Age* back in Melbourne (where riots in Dili, East Timor, have so focused Australian media interest that there's no chance of Kabul, Afghanistan, scoring a column inch).

Mobin's morning report probably sums it up pretty well.

'It was a military convoy coming in to the city from the Shomali Valley', he reports. 'They were driving too fast [ah, just like the UN] and they had already hit a bus and another car before they arrived in the city. It was accident-accident-accident.'

This had a ring of truth to it. The *Guardian*'s website had talked of simmering anger due to aggressive driving tactics and the US defence that this style of driving is 'necessary for security'.

I could picture where the accident had happened. 'Was it coming down the hill into the city, where the dual highway ends at the big roundabout where we've fuelled up and where all the taxis and buses pick up passengers?' I ask.

'Right', confirmed Mobin. 'The truck ran right over a taxi [I'd seen the flattened vehicle on TV] and hit a whole line of cars. They killed four people and injured many others.'

Which is where the confusion starts. It's pretty clear on day one that seven or eight people were killed (the number later rose to 11), but was it one, or four, in the initial accident? And were the rest killed by panicked Americans (they only fired over the crowds, an American spokesman declared) or by panicked Afghans? As usual it's irrelevant. What's relevant is that the anger is out there and it's driven by all sorts of things – government corruption and government inefficiency, and the fact that plenty of international money sloshes around yet so much of it goes to the peacekeepers and NGOs and so little trickles down to the Afghan people.

The aggressive driving certainly doesn't improve things. 'And it would help a lot if they jumped out and provided medical assistance after an accident instead of pointing guns at people', suggests Rodney Cocks, an Australian UN worker I meet on the flight home.

• • • •

My enforced stay at the British embassy means I never get to the Kabul Museum and Mobin deems the lookout point we'd planned to climb to on our last morning at least temporarily unsafe.

Perhaps there is one little find I can make in my final hours in Kabul. I'll go looking for the Titanic. The movie *Titanic* – released in 1997, directed by James Cameron and starring Kate Winslet and Leonardo DiCaprio in a steamy romance among the icebergs – was a huge hit worldwide including in Afghanistan. The Taliban were in power and, of course, movies were banned, but nothing prevents videos reaching their audience and Titanic-the-movie soon morphed into Titanic-the-wedding-cake. Titanic after Titanic, impressive confections of cake and icing sugar, sailed out of Kabul bakeries into the dusty heat of the Afghan summer.

'People identified with the film', Mobin explained as we went in search of a Titanic bakery. 'They liked the story, the young couple searching for love, not directed by their parents. The people on the ship were facing disaster, just like Afghanistan. They looked at the Titanic, but they thought of Afghanistan. They wanted a wedding cake that symbolised not only love, but also our country's problems. It made you realise that we were not the only people in the world who were unhappy.'

Fashions come and go and the *Titanic* has clearly sailed away. There are no Titanic cakes in sight.

'They are no longer popular,' explains one wedding cake baker, 'but there is a photograph of a Titanic cake in my photo album.' He pulls a dishevelled album out from under the counter, but there are no Titanics in sight.

'It must be in the other album', he explains, hauling an even more time-worn album from its hiding place.

Again there are no Titanics. How long before Afghanistan can shake off its Titanic status and sail into iceberg-free seas?

ALBANIA

I encountered my first bunker before we'd driven a kilometre from the Mother Teresa International Airport. Of course the airport itself was a pleasant curiosity – how many countries have an international airport named after a nun, even if she is the world's best-known nun as well as the most famous Albanian? Apart from a few postcards, I didn't encounter Mother Teresa again until my departure day, but Albania's bunker collection was an oddity that would follow me all around.

In the 1950s Albania was already well advanced on the single-minded path that would take it via Stalinism and Maoism to its final position as the most isolated and least-visited country in Europe. Even when the Berlin Wall crumbled and Communism collapsed in the rest of Eastern Europe, the party stumbled on, like a chicken with its head chopped off. Then in February 1991 an angry mob hauled down the gigantic bronze statue of Enver Hoxha from its plinth in Sheshi Skënderbej, the main square of the capital, Tirana, and 45 years of one of the world's weirdest governments came to an end.

The bunkers were the ultimate symbol of Hoxha's paranoia – a symbol not likely to disappear in a hurry. Unlike the Berlin Wall, Albania's obsessive dictator built things to last. The bunkers are also an indicator that Albania was a very inward-looking Bad Land, quite harmless to anyone else in the world, but utterly convinced that the outside world was a major threat to them.

You can imagine the scene in the early 1950s as Enver inspects the first of the 700,000 concrete mushrooms that will eventually dot the tiny country.

'You're sure it's strong enough to withstand a tank attack?' Hoxha queries the prototype bunker's creator.

'Absolutely', declares the bunker designer, who is quickly shoved inside as Hoxha signals for a tank to trundle forward and blast the shelter with its gun. The shaken engineer eventually emerges, relatively unscathed, physically at least, and Hoxha orders the country's concrete makers to step up production. By the time Hoxha died in 1985, Albania had a bunker for every fourth person in the country. They dotted every strategic point from mountain passes to remote beaches, harbour entrances to airport approaches, consuming three times as much concrete as the French used in the construction of their equally useless pre–World War II Maginot Line.

The Maginot Line didn't hold up the German invasion of France, but Hoxha's bunkers never had to withstand an attack. After all, why would anyone want to invade Albania? Today the bunkers stand in virtually undiminished numbers. They are not easy to demolish and the Albanians have to live with them. It's hard to find a new use for the squat little domes. Many were tiny affairs, barely big enough for a couple of cramped people and pretty useless for anything today other than an extraordinarily solid dog kennel. Farmers have turned some into animal shelters. Beach bunkers are often filling up with drifting sand, but probably the most common bunker use is as a handy place for quick trysts. Albanian virginity is lost in a Hoxha bunker as often as American virginity was once lost in the back seats of cars.

• • • •

An hour later, after leaving the airport, I'm standing with pretty much the same viewpoint as Hoxha's statue used to have, except my eyes are 15 metres closer to ground level. To my left the National Museum of History is fronted by a huge mosaic mural owing some debt to the art of the Cultural Revolution in China. I can almost picture Mao front and centre, leading the workers, soldiers, revolutionaries and assorted historic figures towards some bright Marxist-Leninist future. In fact it's a woman, rifle held aloft, who leads the charge, although the Albanian flag flying behind her has been reworked to remove the Communist Party star.

Across the square to my right is the statue of national hero Skanderbeg astride his horse, and beyond his statue are the Et'hem Bey Mosque and the Clock Tower, both lucky survivors from Hoxha's 1967 campaign to convert Albania to an atheist state by destroying all of its mosques, churches and monasteries. Directly in front of me is the Palace of Culture, but the most interesting sight is directly at my feet. If the Hoxha statue were still around, it would be gazing down at a fine indication of the total victory of capitalism in Albania. Lined up around the pedestrian area is a varied collection of electric and petrol-driven toy cars, motorcycles and other child-size devices with happy children at the wheel zooming dangerously back and forth across their little playground. It's a fine preview for Albania's even more dangerous roads.

The most prominent Hoxha relic is a stone's throw from my hotel. The 'pyramid' is just that – a tattily built, white-tiled pyramid that started life as a museum to the long-term dictator. Opened in 1988, three years after his death, it was designed by his architect daughter, Pranvera Hoxha. I'd encounter another Pranvera Hoxha homage to an Albanian hero right at the end of my visit. In the spate of Hoxha deletions that followed the end

49.

of Communist rule, a Hoxha museum was clearly unwanted. The giant marble statue of the seated Hoxha was chopped up and the museum's contents ('more or less everything he ever touched or used', according to the Blue Guide) were removed. Today the pyramid is officially known as the International Centre of Culture, but it's also had a spell as a discotheque and kids find it makes a very usable playground slide.

The word 'pyramid' has a special resonance in modern Albania. The capitalism-run-wild period that followed the fall of Communism ended with a dramatic nationwide pyramid-banking scheme. It's estimated that 70 per cent of the population lost all their savings as, inevitably, the scam ground to a halt in an orgy of rioting and violence that nearly slid the country into civil war. Remarkably it marked the bottom of the slide and the economy has been steadily improving since 2002. After bankruptcy the only way is up, the cynics might say, and it's going to be a while before Albania is invited to join the EU.

That evening I bar-hop through the city's Blloku area, which, until 1991, was shut off to the general Albanian proletariat. This was where Hoxha and the other high-ups of the Albanian nomenklatura hung out. Hoxha's home may have been the best Albania could muster, but compared with the residences of some other Bad Land leaders it's a conservative suburban villa. Today Blloku has become Tirana's bar, restaurant and café centre. If Hoxha were still alive, he could pop straight across the road for a cocktail in the Buda Bar. I continue on down the road to Effendi, a restaurant where the 'Ottoman cuisine' reflects the long Turkish influence from when Albania was one of the furthest outreaches of the Ottoman Empire.

One of my dinner companions is Nevila Popa, who works for EDEM, the USAID-supported Enterprise Development and Export Market organisation. A few weeks previously I'd been wandering Washington, DC with Scott Wayne, an American tourism consultant and former Lonely Planet guidebook writer. Scott's Lonely Planet assignments had even included several visits to Sudan, a country fully deserving Bad Land status today. I'd told Scott that I was planning to visit Albania and he'd put me in touch with EDEM, one of his consultancy clients.

Nevila had worked at a hotel in Grand Rapids, Michigan, and she's the first example of what I soon decide is an Albanian norm – people who have gone abroad for a spell and returned with enthusiasm, skills and excellent English. My other dinner companions include Kliton Gërxhani and Armand Ferra, two young men who've done their time abroad and come back to set up websites, book hotels, dispense advice and organise tours in the new Albania.

Tirana has been a much brighter, livelier and more orderly town than I'd expected. The potholes in the streets haven't been as big as I'd been looking forward to and on the walk back to my hotel even the street lighting is better than it would be if Albania was still a Bad Land disaster zone. I've also been surprised not just that so many people speak English, but that they speak it so fluently.

'We are a small country', Kliton (or Tony as he told me to call him) explained. 'We have to be able to speak other languages.'

'And we have an aptitude for them', Armand confirmed.

Well, Albanian is not a language that trips off the tongue. Even the name of the country comes out as Shqipëria.

•   •   •   •

Just as Gaddafi never saw a revolution he didn't want to support, Hoxha never found a branch of Communism he didn't eventually fall out with. Euro-Communism, despite that French style (good enough as a finishing school for Pol Pot and Ho Chi Minh), was quickly discarded. Yugo-Communism got the boot equally as fast. Tito may have been good at whipping fractious Balkan states into line, but his brand of Communism quickly faded from bright Marxist-Leninist red to a wishy-washy revisionist shade of pink.

Joseph Stalin was much more to Hoxha's liking and under Uncle Joe's guidance Albania settled in for a long spell as the leading exponent of hard-left Stalinism. That was until Khrushchev and his pinko revisionism came along and Hoxha was forced – forced, mind you – to abandon the Soviet Union for the stricter rules of Maoism, as best expounded during the Cultural Revolution. And then, unhappy day, the Chairman took the really long march and before you knew it the Chinese had embarked on revisionism as well.

In *Two Friendly People*, a handy collection of Hoxha's speeches on Albanian-Greek relations, the Albanian leader sets the world straight on that one.

'It is not true', he declared, 'that we "broke away" from China. No. It was the Chinese revisionist and capitalist leaders who undertook anti-Albanian actions and unilaterally breached the agreements on economic co-operation with our country and they did this because we tried to convince them that they were applying a counter-revolutionary foreign policy and sliding ever more deeply into reprehensible actions and alliances with American imperialism.'

Well, what could you expect? Poor Albania had been through this all before, Hoxha continued, when 'we denounced the treacherous actions of the Khrushchevite revisionists'.

It was a tough world out there and it had been left to tiny Albania to stay true to the essentials of Marxism-Leninism. 'We thought that the Yugoslavs and the Soviets, and later the Chinese, were our friends', Hoxha sighed.

And what did they do? Why, they 'behaved like betrayers, revisionists of Marxism-Leninism, and sabotaged and damaged our economy'.

The USSR and China had been warned that they were going astray. What more could poor little Albania do? The only choice was to abandon the misguided great powers to their fate and stay on course by itself. So with the Chairman dead, embalmed and on display in Tiananmen

Square, and Joe ditto in Red Square, Hoxha set out to lead Albania down its solitary path. North Korea and Cuba were also staying true to real Communism, but neither was in a position to lend a little impoverished European a hand. Ties with China were cut in 1978 and for the remaining seven years of Hoxha's life Albania became more isolated. And poorer. Hoxha retreated into his Tirana villa and rationing became steadily stricter.

'My father needed to drink milk for his stomach condition,' Nevila explained, 'so we had to get up at 3.30am to be near the front of the queue at 6am when they started to dole out milk.'

Hoxha died in 1985. Ramiz Alia took over and moved an infinitesimal step to the right, but essentially nothing changed. Until in 1989 everything changed. The Berlin Wall came down, the Iron Curtain rusted away, the Soviet Union went into retreat and, finally, but not until two years later, Albania kicked over the bad old days as well. On 20 February 1991 the unbelievable happened. An angry mob hauled down Hoxha's statue in the centre of Tirana and dragged it away to be cut up and melted down. Within a remarkably short period not a statue, image or inscription of the dictator remained anywhere. Not even his grave survived. He was exhumed from his place watched over by the statue of Mother Albania in the Martyrs' Cemetery and whisked off to somewhere much more common.

In fact, I'm told by an anonymous source at the museum, there are Hoxha statues left and one day, when the anger has subsided, one will be hauled out to be put on display as a reminder of that crazy, but terrible, era.

• • • •

With Artur Haxhi at the wheel, Nevila and I travel south to Berati, whose definition as a 'museum city' protected the town's churches and mosques from Hoxha's atheistic destructive urges. They're perched on a fortified hilltop looking down at the newer (though still Ottoman-era) town below. The walls of the 14th-century citadel stand on foundations that date back to the 4th century BC. Inside the citadel, winding cobbled streets lead to old stones houses and churches.

The Onufri Museum, housed in the Church of the Dormition of St Mary, is the citadel's main attraction. Dormition is the Orthodox equivalent to the Catholic Church's 'assumption', the Virgin Mary's direct transfer to heaven. Onufri was a local master of the art of painting religious icons, and the old church is stuffed full of his icons along with works by other painters and a host of other religious art. Thank God, you might say, that Hoxha restrained himself from trashing this little collection, because it's terrific. The church itself is a wonder – ancient choir stalls, a gilded golden glow to everything and some ostrich-egg hanging lamps to add a nicely exotic touch to the whole ensemble.

We've met with Martin Heusinger, a German Albania enthusiast who has set up a travel company with his Albanian wife, Enkeleda Olldashi, to promote Berati. Together with an American resident who has joined us we wander the winding streets past the remains of the dozen or so churches and couple of mosques that survive, clamber up on to the citadel walls to gaze down at the Chapel of St Michael clinging to the hillside below, and then head down to the Mangalem quarter for lunch.

At the Bujari Restaurant I extravagantly grab the bill for our party of six. I've already had too many cups of coffee, snacks and meals paid for by my Albanian companions and I definitely feel it's my turn to pick up the tab. We've had hearty bowls of soup, plates of robust bread, bowls of the usual fresher-than-fresh salad, side plates of almonds and cheese, more plates of lasagne, a collection of bottles of Tepelena mineral water, followed by bowls of early-season cherries and slices of honeyed cake. The bill for the six of us comes to 1000 lek – let's call it US$11 with a tip.

After lunch we clamber up the narrow streets below the citadel. The fine old houses gave Berati the name 'the town of a thousand windows'.

A threesome – grandmother, daughter, grandson – emerge from one
of the houses to check us out. They're bemused by Martin, clearly a
foreigner, speaking Albanian when they ask us where we're from.

'Albanians are wonderful people, they have so many unique qualities',
announces the cheerful old lady.

'So if we're so wonderful, why are we behind everywhere else in the
world?' asks Nevila.

'Well, there were 50 years of Communism', is the reply – an
explanation I'm already realising is a catch-all for Albania's problems.

'And why does nobody like us?' asks Enkeleda.

The poor Albanians do seem to have got themselves on the wrong side
of everybody, blamed for everything that goes on in the neighbourhood,
but I'm beginning to feel that's ancient history, or 10 years out of date at
least.

We wander across the seven-arched stone bridge to the Gorica quarter,
but the threatening clouds deliver a downpour and Martin ferries us back
to the hotel where I take an afternoon nap. When I emerge an hour or so
later, the view from the rooftop is amazing. The sky has cleared to reveal
a superb backdrop of snow-capped mountains rising up behind Berati's
minaret-studded skyline.

Nevila, Artur and I stroll through the Mangalem quarter to join the
evening *xhiro*, the Balkan custom of walking, as in Italy, a *passeggiata*, a
circuit of the town centre en masse, but the weather must have curtailed
the stroll this evening. I'm pleased the custom continues. I remember
seeing walkers performing a similar ritual in Yugoslavia back in the
early 1970s. As we walk back to the hotel for dinner, I'm amused to note
that the Leaden Mosque (for its lead-coated dome) shares its compound
with the Misisipi Bar, close to where the *furgons*, intertown minibuses,
congregate.

• • • •

Heading south from Berati we pass a huge Chinese-built steel foundry. A Turkish steel-maker tried to revive it, but today it's near derelict. Further down the road there's Albania's biggest oil refinery from the Communist period. Naturally it's guarded by an assortment of bunkers.

For a country that faced serious hunger in the early 1980s after it disowned its Chinese benefactors when they turned soft on Communism, Albania today has an absolute overload of bars, cafés and restaurants. You cannot walk down the main street of any decent-size town without tripping over them, and along the highways and byways they pop up every few kilometres – almost as often as the roadside memorials to traffic deaths. They're often attractive places – clean, neat, tidy and, in the case of the roadside places, often with umbrellas (provided by Biria Stela, I jot in my notes) and shady trees. The food is generally straightforward, hearty, well prepared and fresh.

'Of course, our food is all organic,' Nevila explains, 'because our farmers can't afford chemicals and fertilisers.'

Even the toilets are usually clean (even if they are often squat-style) and for English speakers they may be conveniently labelled B and G, although the letters stand for Burra and Gra not, as I first thought, though with equal accuracy, Boys and Girls.

We've stopped because Nevila has just had a phone call (Albania's mobile phone coverage now is phenomenal as opposed to the Communist years when only the elite had access to telephones) from Auron Tare who, it turns out, is only 10 minutes behind us and also heading south to Gjirokastra and Butrint. When he turns up, it's quickly clear he's as big a character as his Wikipedia entry, which launches its description by announcing that he's an 'Albanian journalist, historian, and adventure traveller'. It goes on to reveal that 'he is the head of the Albanian National Trust Foundation' and then talks of his work as the founder of the Butrint National Park, his recovery of artwork stolen in the post-Communist chaos, his spell as a journalist with the British ITN television team during the Kosovo crisis, and his Indonesian post-tsunami efforts. And that's only the serious stuff. He also played for the Albanian national basketball team.

I abandon Nevila and our cautious and careful driver to ride with Auron in his Land Rover. Auron drives with much more appropriately Albanian verve. I've already noticed that any worthwhile corner will have at least one memorial, if not a cluster, to those who died when their Mercedes collided with the guard rail, shot over the precipice and plunged into the river, or simply rammed head-on into an oncoming vehicle. There are so many that it's probable a certain percentage of the victims met their end by colliding with the memorial to the preceding fatal accident. On some corners the memorials are lined up so densely a guardrail is clearly unnecessary.

Albanians have not had long-term driving experience. If you weren't in the government or a friend of Hoxha you needed a special permit to own a car during the Communist years and the permits were not dispensed in great numbers. In the whole 45-year Communist period precisely two were issued. Once the doors opened, the cars quickly flooded in and Albanians have clearly been crashing them like a Project Gotham Racing video game. To have filled up so many wreckers yards in just a decade and a half is clearly an achievement. The number of cars bearing the word *autoshkolle* (driving school) indicates that many more Albanians plan to take to these dodgy highways.

A quite ridiculous percentage of the vehicles are Mercedes and it was widely suggested in the first years after Albanian independence that they were being stolen to order from all over Europe. It's an idea that Auron indignantly pooh-poohs.

'How would they get them here?' he queries. 'If there was a procession of stolen Mercedes coming down through Italy to be shipped to Albania, wouldn't the shipping companies be looking out for them?'

The stolen-Mercedes affront may annoy Albanians, but that's nothing compared to how they feel about British author Robert Carver and his mid-1990s travel book *The Accursed Mountains*. Carver travels around the country convinced that every other person he meets is eyeing him with cheating, stealing, robbery or murder on their minds. The US$30 he's charged, or rather overcharged to his eyes, for dinner (a 'fish dinner' readers are frequently reminded) for three puts him in a sour mood that pervades the whole book.

'Albania wasn't like that when he was here and it certainly isn't like that today', Auron avows. 'When he wanders around Gjirokastra he imagines people are following him intending to rape him. It's ridiculous.'

I check the book's Gjirokastra chapter and Carver announces in the opening line that 'the first attempt to murder and rob me' took place in the castle. He then slinks back to the place he's staying to shave his beard off to look less like a foreigner. Despite people constantly edging towards him, knives drawn and hands ready to pickpocket, it never happens. Nobody else meets Carver's standards either. When he gets to the Greek site at Butrint, where I'm heading the next day, British archaeologists have ruined 'the delicate atmosphere by erecting large, ugly and quite unnecessary signboards' and the view is further despoiled by a party of 'waddling, elderly American Midwesterners, each wrapped in characteristic brightly coloured flannel baby-clothes'.

We zoom through Tepelena, birthplace of Ali Pasha. Depending on whom you trust, Pasha was either an Albanian national hero or a 'cruel and bloodthirsty tyrant' (Wikipedia again). There's a roadside memorial here to the son of Albania's president Alfred Moisiu. His four-wheel drive skidded off the road and into the river in 2004. I have a bottle of Tepelena mineral water in my daypack, bearing the useful commendation that it is 'The Water of the Albanian National Football Team' – *Uji i Skuadres Kombetare Shqiptare te Futbollit* if you want it in Albanian. A further line of type reveals that the water 'suffled how it gush from the source of the woods of Tepelena'. It's the appropriate brand to be carrying since Auron's brother is Igli Tare, an Albanian football star who plays in one of the world's top football leagues for the Rome Serie A team SS Lazio.

• • • •

I take an instant liking to Gjirokastra with its corkscrewing, roller-coaster laneways and its dark, brooding stone buildings. The whole town is overlooked by an even darker and more brooding castle. Down below the old town is the modern Communist-era town. We don't bother going to see it.

Unfortunately many of the fine stone buildings in the old town are crumbling with age and neglect. We have a look around a particularly magnificent Ottoman-period example. The owners live in a nondescript modern house fronting it and it's easy to see why they're not using the old place. It's huge, draughty and leaky, and would undoubtedly cost a small fortune to light, heat and maintain. Gjirokastra needs some wealthy Western mansion restorer and would-be writer to move here, do up one of these stately homes and write *My Year in Gjirokastra* or *Under the Gjirokastra Sun* about the experience.

Gjirokastra is the hometown for Ismail Kadare, far and away Albania's best-known author and the winner of the inaugural international Booker prize in 2005. It's not so proud of its other famous citizen – Enver Hoxha. His birthplace is now a museum, but an ethnographic one. There's no mention of the Hoxha connection and indeed the house was burnt down in 1916 when the future dictator was eight years old.

Despite enjoying a long, boozy lunch before we explored Gjirokastra, there's still room for another serious dinner after our explorations, where Nevila talks of the absurdities of life in Hoxha's Albania.

'I wanted to study economics at university,' she explains, 'but I was told I had to do physics. A year later my younger sister, who had no interest in economics, was told that was what she had to study.'

'The thing was,' she went on, 'we knew nothing about the outside world; we simply accepted our lives. Looking back it seems absurd what we put up with.'

Albania had its own equivalent of the USSR's KGB or East Germany's Stasi. Every third Albanian citizen had either been interrogated by the Sigurimi or actually served time in one of Hoxha's prison camps. A large section of the National Museum of History in Tirana is dedicated to the horrors of life under Hoxha's thumb, including a labour camp prison-cell you can try out for size. Sigurimi informers were known as '80 lek men' for the monthly 80-lek pay bonus they received for spying on their neighbours.

The next day we drop down to the coast at Saranda and turn south to Butrint. Auron Tare is justifiably proud of these Roman ruins in their own little national park. The site is topped by a small fortress housing a brand new museum. Saranda is one of Albania's most popular beach resorts, helped by its proximity to Corfu. In the Communist era, holidaymakers on the Greek island would sit in beach cafés at night sipping their ouzo, look across the Ionian sea at the searchlights scouring the beaches of Albania and wonder what dark deeds were being performed there. Today day-trippers from Corfu are Albania's biggest international tourist contingent.

The town is a curious mix of Ottoman, Italian and Communist-era influences and, unhappily, it's now being overrun by lots of cheap and nasty developments. Illegal development is a big problem for Albania. During the capitalist free-for-all interlude, all sorts of buildings were put up without any permit or permission; remarkably some of the owners are now being forced to demolish them. A Tirana restaurant, known as 'Taiwan' because it's like a little island, is in the middle of a park that was once covered by illegal buildings.

Saranda even features a town-centre archaeological site with the foundations of a basilica, which at one stage functioned as a synagogue.

Even this site was threatened by illegal developments, but they've been held at bay.

The coast road north actually hangs back from the coast for many kilometres – slow kilometres because Artur proceeds with exaggerated and painstaking care. I was happy with that on the open road from Tirana through Berati and Gjirokastra, but on this stretch it gets exasperating proceeding at 15 to 20 kilometres per hour as if we were in something with no suspension and minimal ground clearance, not in a big, husky four-wheel drive. A month later I'll be on a road in Afghanistan where a similar speed feels much more appropriate to the road conditions.

Eventually we stop for the night at Himarë. My guidebook notes that, with fine beaches and a couple of Greek tavernas, Himarë has 'tremendous potential as a holiday spot', but warns that 'strolling past rusting car wrecks and a tidal line of plastic may not be quite what you'd expected in a beach'. The Albanians have come late to plastic packaging and the detritus of Western consumerism, but they've adapted to it with considerable enthusiasm. So much so that many Albanians spend a lot of time apologising for what a mess their country has become. Unhappily I can console them that I've seen far worse. Libya, for one, is way ahead of them.

Before we retire to a restaurant for another fine and filling Albanian repast, we continue along the coast to Himarë's decaying castle, overlooking the old part of town and the coastal headland just south of the modern port. We continue further north and well off the road, which by this time has climbed into the hills, to visit Jal Beach, a beautiful little arc of white sand spoilt, once again, by some hideously ugly half-built developments. Claims that Albania has the last undeveloped stretch of coast along the Mediterranean may soon be history. There are a couple of very picturesquely sited bunkers guarding the bay and Himarë has a fine collection along its beach, all filling up with windblown sand.

Sitting on my toilet in the Himarë guesthouse, I could see this bathroom had clearly been designed by a plumber rather than an architect. You could use the shower to simultaneously flush the toilet and rinse out the sink that my chin was resting on. Architecture is clearly not a topic of great interest to Albanians. There are some beautiful buildings – the stone houses of Gjirokastra, for example – but they're old. There's one word that fits almost everything built under Hoxha and, even more so, after the great leader: ugly. In fact, 99 per cent of the buildings seem to have come off precisely the same dreary drawing-board. There's one slab floor plonked on top of another until the builder ran out of energy or money, but the steel reinforcing rods are left sticking out the top just in case he finds more energy (or money) and decides to add an extra floor or two.

• • • •

The road climbs away from the coast, zigzagging up to the Llogaraja Pass – the coast falling away below, while snow appears on the peaks above. Down the other side we soon return to sea level and drive through Fieri to reach Apollonia and the country's other notable Roman ruins. Apollonia has clearly not had the attention that Butrint has enjoyed. In particular, it's crying out for some rubbish bins and someone with a large stick to whack anybody who decides to throw plastic wrappers, soft-drink cans and empty Tepelena mineral-water bottles on the grass around the Agora.

The ruins climb up a hillside and there are fine views of the surrounding countryside, which, for some reason, is dotted with yet more of Hoxha's bunkers. Perhaps they'd simply run out of strategic sites to protect and decided that keeping invaders away from the ruins was a good idea!

Heading north, we're following the old Via Egnatia, the great Roman highway that led from Durrës on the coast across the Balkans to Thessaloniki in Greece and on to Constantinople. Hungering for lunch, we pull off the road to climb up to Ardenica, a hill popping up from the flat plains. There's a restaurant with great views right at the top of the hill, but there's also the Ardenica Monastery, which doesn't appear in any of the tourist material I've read but definitely should. Like the museum-church at Berati, the monastery's church is a gilded treasure box. It survived the regime's 1967 war on religion solely because the bishop at the time managed to persuade the demolition crew, who sounded remarkably like the student vandals of China's Cultural Revolution, that the monastery's historic importance required its protection. A Skanderbeg connection helped – the 15th-century national hero might have been crowned or even married here. Even the Communists revered Skanderbeg, something that would be underlined for me the next day.

Durrës, the final stop before we return to Tirana, is Albania's old capital, major port and second city after the capital. It also has the best bunker reuse I'll encounter on my short visit. At the beachside Bunkeri Restaurant you don't dine in a bunker – even a big bunker isn't really restaurant size – but it does make a cosy little bar for a pre-dinner drink, so long as you don't stand up too quickly and crack your head on that tank-proof concrete ceiling.

The town also has a very fine archaeological museum, a stretch of Byzantine-era city walls and a crumbling though impressively large Roman amphitheatre. There's also a well-kept Martyrs' Monument to members of the Albanian resistance who died in the struggle against the Germans in World War II. We have to squeeze through a gap in the fence to get in to look at it. There's no chance of getting in to check King Zog's former palace, now occupied by the military.

Love him or hate him, King Zog was quite a character; with a name like that you'd have to be. He started life as Ahmed Zogilli, changed his family name to Zogu (Albanian for 'hawk') and became prime minister and then president before deciding that being king was more to his taste. Crowned King Zog in 1928, he spent the next 10 years modernising Albania, admittedly from a fairly basic starting point.

Reflecting his early warlord status, he also made plenty of enemies: he survived 55 assassination attempts. They became so predictable that there were occasions he even drew his own gun and shot back at the would-be killers. The National Rifle Association would have loved him.

Unfortunately his modernisation projects were often funded by Italy, and Albania soon became so indebted to Mussolini's fascist state that it became a de facto Italian colony. In April 1939 Mussolini decided to completely take over and King Zog fled to Britain, the start of an exile that would last the remaining 22 years of his life. He took with him his bride of just 388 days, Queen Geraldine, and most of the gold from Albania's treasury (it paid for a floor of London's Ritz Hotel for a spell). The daughter of a Hungarian aristocrat and his American diplomat wife, Queen Geraldine was only 22 years old when she married King Zog. Her family was so penniless, she'd been selling postcards in Budapest's National Museum before King Zog, scouring Europe for a suitable bride, spotted her photograph (taken when she was 17 at a Hungarian society ball) and summoned her to Tirana. Ten days later they were engaged. Their glittering wedding featured presents from all over Europe, including a bright red supercharged Mercedes from Adolf Hitler.

Queen Geraldine stuck with King Zog through his long exile in Britain, Egypt and finally France (where he died), then lived in Spain and South Africa before finally returning to Albania shortly before her death in 2002 at the age of 87. Their son Leka Zog, only three days old when King Zog fled the country in 1939, has attempted to restart the Albanian monarchy, but without success.

• • • •

64. From Tirana the road hairpins up into the mountains to Kruja, a popular day trip from the capital and my last stop in Albania. In the town's old castle stands the Skanderbeg Museum, probably the best-kept building in all of Albania and a potent Hoxha reminder, since it was designed by his daughter and her husband. Albania's national hero, Skanderberg soon becomes a familiar sight, particularly in his horse-riding mode as in his square in the centre of Tirana.

Back in the 15th century, Kastrioti, the son of an Albanian prince, was held hostage by the Ottoman Turks, converted to Islam and took the name Iskander, from Alexander the Great. When he rose to the rank of bey, or governor, under the Ottomans, he tagged that on to his adopted name to become Skanderbeg. In 1443 the Turks suffered a defeat by a Hungarian force and Skanderbeg read this as a signal to abandon the Ottoman Empire (and Islam), return to Albania and kick out the occupying force.

From his stronghold at Kruja he defied the Ottoman powers until his death, withstanding sieges in 1450, 1466 and 1467. Albanian resistance weakened after his death in 1468 and 10 years later another siege was successful and the country once more fell to Ottoman control. It would remain that way until the final collapse of the empire after World War I. The Albanians take Skanderbeg very seriously and the museum is full of paintings and dioramas of his struggles with Turkey and reminders of how often his name pops up on statues and squares around Europe.

The traffic crawling back in to Tirana after the Kruja excursion is appalling. The city's a melange of roadworks and bridges, much of it lagging far behind the growth in traffic. That evening I wander the bars and restaurants of Blokku one more time before retiring to the revolving Skytower Bar to watch all of Tirana spin beneath me in a leisurely 40 minutes. It's not a bad view and not a bad carafe of red wine for less than US$3. Not a bad country either – I've enjoyed my short circuit of a Bad Land that only gained that status by resolutely cutting itself off from the outside world, and is now frantically trying to get itself back on the same wavelength.

BURMA
(MYANMAR)

'We'll call an election', commanded the military dictator.

'We'll have to give the Tatmadaw [Burma's army] a political party name. I think State Law & Order Reform Council sounds good', he continued, not realising that in English its acronym, SLORC, didn't sound so good at all.

'Then, when we get elected, I'll be president and everything will be under control again.'

It was a neat plan. Twenty-five years of military rule would end with the army still firmly on top. The thousands of students who had died in pro-democracy protests would, General Saw Maung concluded, be quickly forgotten. The economy? Well, democracy might do something good for the economy. Certainly nothing the Tatmadaw had done for the economy had resulted in much good. From being the rice basket of Asia, Burma (Myanmar) had spiralled steadily downwards to its present position as the basket case of Asia. Meanwhile arch-rival Thailand had sprinted equally as steadily ahead until the average Thai's per-capita income was 10 times the average Burmese's. And for every tourist who came to Burma, there were probably a hundred in Thailand.

Nevertheless, it was inconceivable that the army wouldn't win. After all, every issue of the *New Light of Myanmar* (formerly the *Working People's Daily*), the government-controlled daily English-language newspaper, carried stirring stories of how much the people of Burma loved the Tatmadaw and how much good the Tatmadaw did for the country and the people. All of it illustrated with photographs of one army general or another announcing a new project, cutting the ribbon to open a new road, being welcomed with rapturous applause by school children or listening intently as some new scientific wonder was explained to him. The Tatmadaw loved the people, the people loved the Tatmadaw – apart from a few thousand students and they were all dead now. Who else could win the election?

Well, there was Aung San Suu Kyi and her ragtag National League for Democracy (NLD) Party, but for a start she wasn't eligible to run for office. Her own father, the heroic Bogyoke Aung San, had thoughtfully written a clause into the constitution banning anybody married to a foreigner from politically powerful positions. Aung San Suu Kyi, quite apart from having spent most of her life overseas, was married to an English academic.

Anyway, in situations like these the opposition was always fragmented while the Tatmadaw was nothing if not unified, as well as having control of all the media. The election result was a sure thing.

Such a sure thing that it appears General Saw Maung, the SLORC and the Tatmadaw didn't even bother rigging the election in 1990 by double-counting votes or intimidating voters if they looked like casting their ballots incorrectly. Zimbabwe's Mugabe could have shown these hapless losers a thing or three about how to run an effective election. In fact Burma's first election in 25 years was, it appears, a remarkably fair fight. So fair that the end result was the NLD as a knockout winner, the SLORC an abysmal loser. No less than 392 of the 485 parliamentary seats went to the NLD.

'Let me clarify what I meant when I said we'll have an election', General Saw Maung quickly announced. 'Now the election is over, we first have to rewrite the constitution, then we'll decide if whoever won the election gets to take over.'

Nothing moves fast in Burma and it took close to 30 years of daily struggle to write a new constitution and put it to a referendum in 2008. Fortunately for the military, however, having an election did have a very important side-benefit. It clearly identified the traitorous individuals who did not love their country and its wonderful army. There were at the very least 392 of them – the 392 newly elected NLD members, for whom a spell in prison was clearly a very good idea.

That's where Burma, or Myanmar as the military rulers have renamed it, still stands. Most NLD members have been released from their period of re-education – some of them only after they signed agreements not to engage in any further political activity – but some still languish behind bars. Aung San Suu Kyi has been in and out of house arrest (and worse) ever since the elections, and although for many Burmese the economic story is far better – the once-empty shops are now full of consumer goods and the country is once again a rice exporter – Burma is certainly no Asian tiger.

• • • •

From Rangoon's (Rangoon is now called Yangon) ramshackle airport a Singapore taxi whisks us into town. The modern cars that now clog Rangoon's roads were one clear indicator of change. In the 1970s, when I'd first visited the reclusive country, there was hardly a traffic jam's worth of cars in the whole city and most were rusting, rattling relics of the British era. Today's taxi fleet certainly isn't showroom new – their signposting indicates they've all enjoyed a previous incarnation on the streets of Tokyo, Bangkok or Singapore – but one thing hasn't changed. They all have their steering wheels on the wrong side.

It's all Ne Win's fault. Most things in Burma are Ne Win's fault.

During World War II, when he was known as Shu Maung, he was one of the 'Thirty Comrades', the group of idealistic young nationalists led by Aung San Suu Kyi's dad, Aung San, who had slipped away to Japan, looking for help to unseat the British colonialists. With Japan's entry into the war they'd marched triumphantly back into Rangoon where the Japanese had announced that colonialism was over, the evil British were defeated and that Burma was now an independent country. Aung San and Shu Maung were now the leaders of the Burmese army – the name went from the Burmese Independence Army (BIA) to the Burma Defence Army (BDA) before settling on the Burma National Army (BNA). The army wasn't the only one to have a name change. Shu Maung had renamed himself Ne Win, 'Brilliant like the Sun'.

Despite being whisked back to Japan to be presented with the Order of the Rising Sun, Aung San soon began to doubt the wisdom of siding with the Japanese. If the British had treated the Burmese like bullocks, he concluded, under the Japanese 'we are treated like dogs'. It would be an improvement 'even to get back to the bullock stage'.

Furthermore, the war wasn't turning out to be such a foregone conclusion after all. The British and their Indian troops had been pushed right out of the country by the victorious Japanese, but then they'd turned round and started to march back towards Rangoon. They'd mounted an imaginative 'behind enemy lines' campaign, air-dropping small groups of guerrilla forces known as Chindits. Not everybody in Burma had welcomed the Japanese with open arms either. The Burmese-speaking people of the central plains, the Bamar, had, at first, gone along with the Japanese occupiers, but Burma wasn't a simple homogenous country. There were the Muslim Rakhaing people of the far west, along the border with what is today Bangladesh. To the south there were the Mons, who had at various times been a buffer state between Burma and Thailand, or even struggled with the Burmese for control of the great kingdom of Bagan.

To the east and northeast, in the hills that rose up towards the borders with Thailand, Laos and China were a host of hill tribes, many of them closely related to the hill peoples of Thailand and Indo-China. They included groups like the Karen, predominantly Buddhist like the majority of Burmese, but with an influential Christian minority. Wary of the Burmese's loyalty, the British had never incorporated them into their army – unlike the Indians in India – but they had trusted the Karen and now many former Karen soldiers cooperated with the British guerrilla forces. Soon, Aung San, Ne Win and their Burmese comrades found themselves fighting a proxy war for the Japanese. Their battles with the groups in Burma who had not willingly accepted Japanese rule stirred up a bitterness that would cripple Burma for many decades after the Japanese left.

As the British and their Indian allies marched ever closer to Rangoon, Aung San and the BNA hastily switched sides.

'Go on, Aung San. You only came to us because you see we are winning', joked Lieutenant-General William Slim, commander of the British forces.

'It wouldn't be much good coming to you if you weren't, would it?' countered Aung San.

So when the bombs fell on Hiroshima and Nagasaki and the war came to a rapid conclusion, Aung San and his companions were once more in the driver's seat to lead an independent Burma. The rush to Burmese independence concluded at the auspicious time of 4.20am on 4 January 1948. To this day nothing gets done in Burma without calling in the astrologers and fortune-tellers. That middle-of-the-night hour may have been the right time for independence, but it was too late for Aung San. In July of the previous year he'd been assassinated by a political rival. He'd left behind three children. His daughter, Aung San Suu Kyi, had just turned two.

Independent Burma was not so much a unified nation as a buzzing hornet's nest and at times the government's powers barely extended beyond the Rangoon city boundary. Certainly there were elections, but Burmese democracy never reached far and in 1958, not long after the 10th anniversary of independence, the economy was on the floor, the political situation was up against the wall, and the prime minister, U Nu, called 'time out'. In marched Ne Win, still at the head of the Burmese army, to establish a caretaker military government, which managed to restore law and order and if not completely halt, at least partially curtail, the uprisings devastating the country.

In 1960 the military returned to the barracks and new elections were held. Once more U Nu was elected prime minister and once more the country tumbled into chaos. This time when Ne Win marched back into power in 1962 it was for keeps. U Nu was slung into prison and Ne Win announced that the country would now embark on the 'Burmese Road to Socialism'. Perhaps he was trying to outflank the Communist Party of Burma, one of the principal rebel groups and strongly supported by the Maoist Chinese, but the Burmese Road proved to be a strictly downhill path.

Soon the economy, which had never really recovered from the destruction of World War II, was all but comatose. The Chinese and Indian traders, who controlled much of Burma's retail trade, were kicked out of the country and large banknotes were 'demonetised' on the theory that if you were rich enough to have them you were too rich for the country's good. The doors were firmly slammed shut to any would-be foreign visitors and before long the only way you could find anything was on the black market.

Which is why our airport taxi was, like nearly every vehicle stuck in the traffic jam around us, on the wrong side of the road relative to its steering wheel. Until 1970 the Burmese drove on the left, like the UK and like Burma's neighbours to the west (India and Bangladesh) and to the east (Thailand and Laos). Then the rules were suddenly changed and the Burmese took to driving on the right. It made no sense at all, firstly because the country was completely isolated, so it made no difference which side the Burmese drove on; secondly because if the government ever did open the land borders to Thailand (the most likely place), the two countries would be driving on opposite sides; and thirdly because almost all the cars in the country came from drive-on-the-left nations. They were either left behind by the British or imported from Japan.

So why had this utterly pointless change taken place? It was back to Ne Win and his faith in astrology and fortune-tellers. When his favourite astrologer was asked what he should do to improve Burma's collapsing economy, the soothsayer, who clearly had a much better grasp of economics than the dictator, struggled to find a polite way to tell him that his crazy economic strategies were bankrupting the country and that easing up on his leftist policies was the only answer.

'Move to the right', suggested the medium, thinking politically.

Ne Win immediately ordered Burmese drivers to switch sides.

• • • •

I am sipping a cold Mandalay Beer beside the swimming pool at the Pansea Hotel (now the Governor's Residence Hotel). It's hard to believe this is an all but bankrupt country run by an evil military dictatorship. The stylish hotel, built in a colonial-era teak mansion, once housed the employees of a British timber firm when they were in the city on business. It is certainly very unlike the places I'd stayed at on my first few visits to the country decades earlier.

On those occasions I'd been an idealistic young backpacker, kicking around the region with my wife, Maureen. In 1978 we'd arrived in

Rangoon and taken a backfiring old Humber taxi to the YMCA.
Halfway into town we encountered a traffic light. There certainly hadn't
been any traffic jams to slow us down prior to that point. In fact the
streets were almost empty with just the occasional old, overcrowded
World War II–era bus with dozens of Burmese hanging precariously
from the sides. Male or female, they were elegantly dressed in sarong-like
longyi and that, at least, hasn't changed. Jeans have still made no inroads
into the Burmese dress code.

When those late-1970s traffic lights shifted to green, a horrible
graunching noise indicated that the ancient 'Britmobile' was not
slipping smoothly into gear and the reason for our push-start at the
airport became clear – our battered banger was clutch-less. Our driver
had hoped for a smooth, stop-less passage all the way from terminal to
terminus, but the traffic light had thrown a spanner in the works. We
disembarked to help him push, but this time it wouldn't start and we
eventually abandoned the hiccupping Humber for an Austin almost as
ancient.

The YMCA was nearly as decrepit as our taxi and we spent a sleepless
night squashing mosquitoes that had zoomed in through the gaping holes
in the wire-mesh window-screens and hoping that our antimalarials were
effective. Our seven-day visas were a distinct improvement on the 24-
hour visas that were all that was on offer only a few years previously, so
six days later we were back in Rangoon and this time we abandoned the Y
for the greater comforts of the Strand Hotel. Built in 1901 the Strand was
one of the three great Asian hotels established by the Armenian Sarkies
brothers and in the late 1970s all three hotels were run down and overdue
for major renovations. Run down in Rangoon was on a wholly different
plane from what run down meant in Singapore at the Raffles or Penang at
the E&O.

In the early 1990s the Strand enjoyed a comprehensive overhaul,
courtesy of the Dutch-Indonesian hotel wizard Adrian Zecha, creator

of the Aman chain of super-luxury resorts, but in the 1970s it was a picture of decaying splendour. Outside was a line up of elderly Chevies, crumbling but still in far better shape than their English equivalents. One of these lead sleds could, with the underhand application of a handful of US dollars, convey you all the way to Pegu, 80 kilometres northeast of Rangoon. Any further than that was likely to lead to trouble with the authorities. Inside the hotel the reception area sported a glass-fronted lost-and-found cabinet containing never-to-be-claimed items, such as greying ladies' gloves, a single Cinderella-like high-heeled shoe, and a mildewed top hat, clearly abandoned at some British officer's formal affair a half-century earlier.

Our second-floor room was blissfully mosquito free, but the water pressure didn't seem to have enough 'oomph' to get that far above sea level and late that evening the Strand's lobby proved to be just as rat-infested as most other areas of the city. We'd been sitting around discussing Burma, travel and other important topics with a young Dutchman, a Mexican couple (20 years would pass before I encountered any other Mexicans travelling anywhere outside of Mexico) and a few other assorted travellers. The bar had shut down at 10pm. When it was open it dispensed nothing better than Mandalay Beer and a curious clear spirit called *tinle*, which you could mix with other ingredients to make a *tinle* and tonic or a *tinle* and Coke, if there had been such a thing as Coke in Burma, of course.

The bar's closure was not a problem – the front desk still had an icebox full of cold bottles of Mandalay Beer, stashed away for exactly such late-night gatherings. What was a problem was that at 10pm not only did the bar shut, but also the rats came out to play. Soon they were bounding across the lobby, leaping from sofa to table to chair. Occasionally they'd short-cut right across your lap, which reduced our Dutch friend to crouching on top of his chair with his feet drawn up, uttering unhappy squeaks.

A quarter of a century later the Strand was clearly not the same place. The lost-and-found cabinet was gone, replaced by a jewellery shop – American Express, Diners Club and Visa happily accepted – with the better pieces easily marching into the four-figures (in US dollars) range. The bar was now open for as many hours as any guests were willing to stay up and as for the rats… well, they could still be found on the streets of Rangoon, but in the Strand? Not a chance.

• • • •

The elderly Chevies had disappeared from the front of the Strand as well. So had the city's old Humbers, Hillmans, Austins and Morrises, replaced by much newer, and more reliable, Toyotas, Nissans and Mazdas. They'd go much further than Pegu as well.

Getting fuel when travelling 'up country' could still be a problem, but with application of the requisite number of US dollars, which no longer had to be handed across surreptitiously, you could drive pretty well anywhere in the country. Well, pretty well anywhere in the country controlled by the central government and not by some random rebel group.

Our driver, U Zaw Naing Oo, had worked for the construction division of the Korean *jaebeol* (business conglomerate) Hyundai when they built a major dam project. Like every Burmese I was to meet he was polite (he spoke excellent English), competent (he certainly knew all the short-cuts and all the best roadside noodle stops) and very communicative. Not far out of Rangoon we paused at the Taukkyan Commonwealth War Cemetery. Endless rows of small memorials in the beautifully maintained cemetery mark the last resting place for over 6000 British and Indian troops who had pushed the Japanese out in the longest, and probably least-known, land campaign in the war against Japan.

Nowhere else did Allied troops slug it out with the Japanese in such a protracted fashion. Much of the Pacific War was conducted from 30,000 feet by endless formations of US Air Force bombers raining thousands of tonnes of explosives down on Japanese cities until two atomic bombs brought everything to a rapid conclusion. Other clashes on land were often short and sharp, if brutally hard fought. The US troops at Guadalcanal, in the Solomon Islands, took six months to dispatch the Japanese forces, but the painful assault on Okinawa lasted just 82 days. From when the Japanese took Rangoon in March 1942, it was over three years before they abruptly withdrew in April 1945.

Further north, in the small town of Shwedaung, a sign indicated, in outdated English, that the Shwemyetman Paya was just one furlong off the road. The 220-yard side-trip took us to the 'Paya of the Golden Spectacles'. Buddhism, for all its noble truths and eightfold paths, often seems to be strongly based on Buddha-image one-upmanship. There are numerous claims to the biggest, longest, tallest or most heavily gold-plated Buddha, but no tape measure was required to check this huge seated image's claim to fame. Perched on the smiling Buddha's nose was a giant pair of gold-rimmed spectacles. Originally, so the paya's helpful brochure informed us, the image was 'devoid of spectacles' and it's a little unclear when they made their first appearance. What's more certain is that in 1886 they were stolen. King Thibaw, the last Burmese king to rule from Mandalay, had just been overthrown and shipped off to India by the British, and disrespectful activities, like stealing a Buddha image's glasses, were not uncommon.

The current pair of glasses was popped on during the colonial period when an English officer stationed in Prome (Pyay) donated them in the hope of fixing his wife's eye troubles. Naturally she was cured. The quite stylish, and very large, circular-lensed glasses are removed once a fortnight for a quick polish and clean – an operation that requires nine monks. A spare pair sits at the ready in a glass showcase, just in case the originals are dropped.

We overnighted in Prome on our way north. Prome had been totally off limits on my first few visits to Burma, but when I was there in 1983 there were rumours that you could rent a vehicle in Rangoon and get to some of these forbidden places, even though the seven-day visa limits were still in force. On that occasion, on my first night in Rangoon I tossed up between taking the train to Mandalay early the next morning or trying to find someone with a pick-up to rent. I wandered over to the tourist office in the centre of town to see what time it opened in the morning and before you could say 'Psst, wanna rent my Toyota Hilux?' I'd been approached by a Burmese gentleman hanging around in a nearby doorway and we were negotiating a one-week rental.

We set off before dawn the next morning with my original English-speaking contact as a guide, plus the driver and his assistant. In the back of the pick-up truck was a stack of five-gallon fuel containers, since you needed a special permit to buy petrol outside of your area of residence. The other important piece of equipment in the back was a large tarpaulin. When we passed checkpoints I would lie down in the back of the truck with the tarpaulin spread over me. On that first visit to Prome, I entered and departed the town hidden under the cover, but once inside it was easy to wander around the Shwesandaw Paya and gaze across to the gigantic Buddha image, gazing back at us across the trees at eye level with the hilltop pagoda.

This time staying in Prome was no problem, although visitors were clearly few and far between. We ventured beyond the town to the ruins of the ancient city of Thayekhittaya. Burma has so many of these forgotten sites that only the really big ones, like Bagan or Mrauk U, attract more than the most enthusiastic of visitors. We strolled around the crumbling ruins and through the villages that dot the site. By the time we got back to the car park beside the site museum, the sun was about to set. As we drove back towards the main road we passed a long line of men and boys marching out of the village with long poles slung over their shoulders and lamps swinging from the end of the poles.

'What are they doing, where are they going?' we asked our driver.

'Killing rats', he said. 'The rice fields are full of rats. They'll set up their lamps in the fields to attract the rats and when the rats come out they'll kill them. They'll be in the fields all night.'

The next morning we found another Westerner breakfasting on the roof of the hotel. Richard Forrest was an Australian tour leader who had led adventure travel groups around the country until the Burma boycotters persuaded his company to shut down their Burma operations.

'Actually, I'm doing exactly the same thing as before they withdrew', he explained. 'People come to me independently rather than through the company. There probably aren't as many of them, but it's exactly the same sort of people. Funnily enough back in Australia the vote on whether to withdraw or not depended completely on whether people had been here or not. If they had visited Burma and made friends here, they certainly didn't want to abandon them. If they'd never been here, then it was easy to say no.

'I'm carrying on partly because I think it will open up', Richard continued. 'There are lots more places opening up so I'm spending some of my time checking out the new areas. I've just been on a trek through the Shan states.'

We carried on north. The roads were narrow, but neither as potholed or as overcrowded as I'd become used to in India or other developing countries. Our lunchtime noodle halt was in a busy little truck-stop village where I wandered into a covered market beside the road and admired the heaped piles of vegetables and fruit. If the Burmese economy was on its last legs, the farmers still seemed to be doing their jobs. In comparison the markets in Cuba were miserable affairs and if we'd seen a market in North Korea, we probably wouldn't have believed it.

79.

Our northbound trip took us via Inle Lake to Mandalay from where
we would catch a converted old Irrawaddy ferryboat down to Bagan. Inle
Lake is outrageously picturesque and famed for its leg-rowers, who stand
at the back of their flat-bottomed boats, looking much like an English
Oxbridge punter, but then propel the boat forward by twisting a leg
around a single oar and leg-rowing it along. On my first trip to Inle Lake
the government was only reluctantly opening up to private enterprise and
although visitors were emphatically steered towards the government-
owned hotel at Taunggyi, 25 kilometres from the lake, I managed to stay
at U Ohn Maung's pioneering guesthouse at Nyaungshwe, right by the
water.

'We were still operating without a licence', he explained. 'If
government officials dropped by we would herd our guests over to one
side of the courtyard and hang *longyis* from a clothesline so they weren't
seen.'

Over a quarter of a century later U Ohn Maung had been elected to
parliament in 1990 on Aung San Suu Kyi's NLD ticket, been bundled
off to jail by the military government as a result, and emerged from
imprisonment to put more effort not only into lake tourism, but also
into a roll call of projects to improve life in the villages around the lake.
Nyaungshwe is now packed with guesthouses, restaurants, travel and tour
agencies and, inevitably, internet cafés. The action has also moved out
to the lake and U Ohn Maung's luxurious lakeside Inle Princess Resort
is right at the top of the price scale. The dining room and bar, with a
dramatically soaring ceiling, are modelled on a wooden monastery at
Kengtung.

We make a series of excursions across the lake, winding up the river to
Indein, on the west side, with its mouldering old complex of shrines and
dropping in to Nga Hpe Chaung, the famous Jumping Cat Monastery.
Clearly there's only so much meditating any monk can stand. Between
times they've devoted themselves to training the monastery's 13 resident

felines to leap through hoops. I note that the reward is a handful of Whiskas and not just any Whiskas – it's the French variety. These are clearly choosy jumping cats.

Right down at the southern end, the village of Kyauk Taung is entirely devoted to pottery making. Everywhere are lines, heaps and piles of pots in every size from tiny flowerpots to giant water-storage pots. The big pots are so beautiful and the whole village is so picturesque it's almost sad to contemplate that one day reticulated water, plumbing and taps will arrive. Water will no longer be stored in big ceramic pots and the world will move on.

Many of the houses around the lake are actually built out over the lake, on stilts. On our last visit to Inle Lake we were shown plans for a long bridge to connect the 'floating village' of Maing Thauk with its 'land village'. The bridge would let children walk to school and old people get to the village health centre without waiting for someone to transport them by boat. It was another of U Ohn Maung's pet projects and Maureen and I agreed to finance the building materials. This time we got to walk along our 300-metre bridge. It had even had its first birth when a woman didn't get to the health centre quite fast enough.

U Ohn Maung takes us by another of his projects, a village orphanage, and past the site where he wants to build a real hospital. The village has a forest monastery and the faint remains of the British Fort Steadman and an old British cemetery.

It's a harrowing drive north to Mandalay. The traffic has become much worse over the years, although the road is also somewhat better. Soon after my last visit the Moustache Brothers had been reunited and I'm keen to touch base with them. The two brothers and a cousin are *a-nyeint pwe* performers, a traditional Burmese blend of dances, music, jokes and slapstick. Back in 1996 the jokes got them into serious trouble. Burma's military rulers are nothing to joke about and when the brothers poked fun at them, U Par Par Lay and U Lu Zaw, brother and cousin, received seven

81.

years of hard labour. U Lu Maw kept the family going, performing with his wife mainly for foreign visitors.

'We're no longer allowed to perform', says U Lu Maw, resignedly. 'So we just give "demonstrations"', he laughs, painting large apostrophes around the word.

'This was Mandalay's Broadway', U Lu Maw continues, pointing down 39th Street. It may look less than Broadway-like, but for visitors it's certainly one of the city's big attractions.

The next day we're forging down the Ayeyarwady River at a stately eight knots in the RV *Pandaw*, a teak-and-brass Raj-era fantasy. In 1920 the Irrawaddy Flotilla Company (IFC), the Scottish-owned 'fabulous flotilla', was the largest privately owned ship fleet in the world. In 1942, with Japanese troops flooding into Burma, all 650 ships were scuttled. In the late 1990s another Scot, Paul Strachan, revived the IFC name and took over the RV *Pandaw*.

The 46-metre vessel was built in Glasgow in 1947 to the same steam-powered, stern-paddlewheel design as the pre-war flotilla ships. She was actually sailed out to Burma from Scotland. Although her sides were boarded up for the voyage to make her more seaworthy, it would have been an amazing feat to sail a vessel with just a metre draft across the open seas. For nearly half a century the *Pandaw* plied the rivers of Burma carrying passengers and cargo.

The Irrawaddy Flotilla Company's old Siam Class steamers carried 4200 deck-class passengers and 40 more in staterooms. They were 100 metres long and only relatively recently have present-day government boats managed downriver speeds faster than those monsters travelled upriver! The captains of these mighty riverboats were so important that a Mandalay shop once had a sign announcing they were 'Silk Mercers to the Kings and Queens of Burma and the Captains of the Steamers'.

The new operators stripped the old *Pandaw* down and rebuilt it with modern luxuries – the 16 cabins all have attached bathrooms and air-conditioners – but with a decidedly old-fashioned feel. The ancient steam engine and paddlewheel had already been replaced with modern diesels driving outboard propellers. Lounging outside your room in a cane armchair or sipping a gin and tonic in the bar, it's hard to avoid humming that old Kipling ditty:

> *Come ye back to Mandalay*
> *where the old Flotilla lay*
> *Can't you 'ear their paddles*
> *chunkin' from Rangoon to Mandalay*

We enjoyed lunch as the stately ship passed the old capital of Sagaing and sailed under the Ava Bridge, just south of Mandalay. That evening it was sundowners on the upper deck as the sun sank below the horizon, and dinner after we moored for the night near the town of Myinmu.

The next morning the *Pandaw* is on its way before dawn and by breakfast time moors beside the village of Yandabo. It was under a tree on the riverbank at Yandabo that the treaty was signed ending the first Anglo-Burmese War (1824–26) when the Burmese ceded Arakan, Assam, Manipur and Tenasserim to the British and allowed a British resident to set up at Ava. The village is not connected to the road network so its contact with the outside world is principally by river. Almost everyone in the village is engaged in making pottery and during the dry season there are thousands of pots lined up at various stages of manufacture. The pots are traded up and down the river and even exported. The IFC has sponsored the rebuilding and operation of the village school.

There's a steady flow of traffic up, down and across the river. Sometimes approaching ships carry a couple of bowmen, sounding the river depth with long red-and-white striped poles. There is always a pilot on board the *Pandaw*, each of whom knows his own stretch of river with its constantly shifting shallows and sandbanks. Periodically the riverboat pulls in at some small settlement to drop off one pilot and pick up another.

Late that afternoon, the *Pandaw* moors at Pakokku, a busy little provincial town only 25 kilometres north of Bagan. A fleet of chartered trishaws takes us to the town's colourful little market, to a blanket-weaving workshop and to a cheroot manufacturer, all the while pursued by a cheerful posse of bicycling women intent on selling blankets and other crafts.

I manage to drop in to the Mya Yatanar Inn, which for many years has been a favourite overnight halt for backpackers making their way to Bagan on local ferry boats. 'It's an old place run by old people', explain the owners, U Tint San and Daw Mya Mya. The fact that the facilities are rough and ready doesn't seem to worry the guests who have filled a collection of notebooks with effusive praise.

•   •   •   •

That night the *Pandaw* moors only a few kilometres south of the town and by the time breakfast is over the next morning she's in Bagan. My first two visits to Bagan bracketed the devastating July 1975 earthquake. There had been a great deal of repairs over the next five to 10 years, but in the mid-1990s a frenzy of renovation and rebuilding kicked off, much of it to the great displeasure of archaeologists who had been involved in far more painstaking work. The new-century restorations, in contrast, were 'anything goes'. Every stupa acquired a new gold-leafed finale and, just as *Jurassic Park* dinosaurs could be cloned from a single cell, so were towering temples being recreated from a brick height or two of foundations.

We floated over this gigantic construction project in a hot-air balloon. Balloons over Bagan was run by Khin Omar Win and her Australian husband. Just as with Aung San Suu Kyi, it was an ailing matriarch who had brought Khin Omar back to Burma. In Khin Omar's case it was her grandmother, but just as Aung San Suu Kyi stayed on after her mother's death so Khin Omar stayed on after her grandmother died.

Khin Omar left Burma in 1975 at the age of five, not long after I made my first visit to the country. At that time her father was a medical student. In 1974 U Thant, the Burmese UN secretary-general, had died and Ne Win reluctantly allowed his body to be returned to Burma for burial, setting off a tragic series of events that in other circumstances might have been almost comic. For some reason Ne Win decided that the much-revered Burmese elder statesman should be put to rest quietly and obscurely. Offended, an alliance of students and monks seized the coffin, performed their own funeral ceremony and buried him on the politically charged site of the university's Students' Union building. During Ne Win's violent takeover in 1962 the building had been blown up, along with the students inside at the time. Once more, troops marched in to the university campus, snatched the coffin and poor U Thant – his dead body playing a much bigger political part than his live one ever did – was buried yet again. In the subsequent rioting, between 16 (the official figure) and hundreds (probably much closer to reality) of people died and Khin Omar's family departed for Britain.

From her new home she had maintained contacts with her homeland, returning several times to visit family members. At the age of 18, she went to see her ailing grandmother and stayed in the country for six months before going back to England where she went to university and became involved in Burma activist activities. After finishing university she again returned to Burma, but this time she decided to stay, meeting and marrying an Australian, Brett Melzer, who worked for Premier Oil.

'Oh, so you married the forces of evil', I say.

'Yes', is, of course, the only possible reply.

Together they set up their hot-air ballooning business. Effectively she'd switched sides from the 'boycott Burma' activists' stance to her own pro-tourism activities.

'Sure I could stay away, live in the West, get a comfortable job,' she explained, 'but I decided to stay here and work for a better Burma from within.'

Establishing the operation took some time and required facing questions like, 'Are women allowed to be higher than the highest pagodas?' 'Well, they're already flying over them in aircraft coming in to Bagan airport' was the obvious response. That question of Buddhist religious protocol was particularly important for several seasons when the balloon pilot was a woman.

'And what about shoes? Should they be removed when you fly above a pagoda?' When an important monk was taken for a demo flight his feet were watched closely and his sandals stayed on.

The sparkle of gold stupa spires seen when floating across the ancient city was clear evidence of the sweeping rebuilding, and no stupa had enjoyed more lavish treatment than the Dhammayazika Paya. The extravagant restoration clearly bore little relation to the original.

'It's not surprising', said U Tun Naing Shwe, the guide showing us around the site later in the day. 'The Dhammayazika was a Khin Nyunt project when he was Secretary One.

'Now that Than Shwe [the army's top general] has kicked him out, it's unlikely to get such careful attention', he laughed. 'They acquire merit by rebuilding or refurbishing pagodas and they have acquired so much bad karma they need lots of merit', U Tun Naing Shwe explained. That was why all the pagodas were being tarted up in Bagan.

'It's a real waste of money', he went on. 'The archaeologists hate what they're doing. So many of the pagodas and temples are being rebuilt from bare foundations when they have no idea what the original construction was like. Or there are renovations like this one – crazy lavish gold-gilding jobs – that bear little relation to the original.'

It was hardly surprising that this particular pagoda had enjoyed such profligate spending. When Secretary One decided to slap on the gold leaf and lay out the marble flagstones, all sorts of local dignitaries felt obliged to climb on board and make their own contributions as well.

'Soldiers and pagodas are all we ever see in the papers', complained U Tun Naing Shwe.

It was certainly true. Every issue of *The Rising Light of Myanmar* devoted half of the front page to a story about some general opening another pagoda (or hospital, school, technology institute or rice mill), illustrated with photos of him inspecting rows of assembled monks (or nurses, school children, engineers or farmers). If a second-level general was elevated to page one, the first-ranking one would drop back to page two. By the time all the other generals and all their other appearances had been covered, you were generally halfway through the paper. The stories always included neat little summaries of the people's enthusiasm, the Tatmadaw's kind concerns and the overriding importance of working against enemies of the state – that is, anyone who didn't agree with military rule and the lousy job they had been doing for so many years.

There were clearly much better ways of donating money and time and much more pressing needs than restoring and rebuilding yet another ancient temple. We'd seen plenty of construction projects from our balloon ride, but the passengers included three German plastic surgeons and the leader of their Interplast team. This group of volunteer doctors and nurses made annual visits to the country, setting up surgery workshops. Many of their operations were for cleft palates, a problem easily fixed at an early age in the West, but devastating in the developing world.

'These children are locked away, hidden from the outside world', explained U Aung Nyunt, the Bagan restaurant owner who hosted the medical group on their visit. 'After their operation they can come out, join the other children, become part of the world. It's astounding how their lives change.'

Treating young burn victims was another common operation for the visiting surgeons. In Burma, as in much of the developing world, many children have disastrous encounters with cooking fires and the disfiguring burns not only make their lives incredibly difficult, but also far too often simply cut them off from the outside world. The surgery workshops can change all that.

'So why don't they donate money to something like that?' U Tun Naing Shwe queried. He had his own answer: 'Because a gold-capped stupa is much more visible than a child with a repaired mouth.'

• • • •

Our visit to Bagan featured one of those curious coincidental reconnections that can happen with travel. We'd been very impressed with U Hlau Maung, the driver-guide showing us around the ruins. Realising we were already familiar with all the main sites he proved to be an expert at leading us to unusual lesser-known temples and always seemed to know who would have the keys to unlock them.

'How did you get into this business?' I asked him towards the end of the afternoon.

' My family were very poor,' he said, 'so they sent me to a monastery because there I would get some education and I would be fed. But I hated life in the monastery and as soon as I could I left and got a job as a pony cart driver. I started to take tourists around the ruins and I began to learn English from them.

'The Israelis always asked so many questions. They were a big help with my English simply because they made me work so hard at it. The strange thing was that talking to the tourists I began to get interested in all the questions about Buddhism that I was not interested in when I was a monk. So I started going back to the monastery to learn more.

'Then a guidebook recommended me', he continued, reaching in to the minibus glove-box to pull out a timeworn copy of my *Burma* guidebook! There was mutual amazement – mine to see his name in the book, his to see mine.

'After my name appeared in the book,' U Hlau Maung went on, 'people began to ask for me to guide them. Eventually I went to Rangoon to study to be an official guide.'

Today his cart had become an air-conditioned minibus, but he was still very clearly a guide who knew his stuff and enjoyed imparting his wisdom. He was equally keen to see other young people make good. Outside our hotel the next morning he explained that his rise from the ranks was known and admired by other young pony cart drivers who in turn were working on their English and hoping to become tourist guides. People like U Hlau Maung are going to make it no matter what, but our book gave him that little extra boost, a small helping hand that he was very aware of and very grateful for. Later that day he introduced us to U Maung Maung, another pony cart guide made good, whose path to an education and later success also came from his contacts with young travellers. Today he owns four lacquerware workshops, employs 70 people and exports to Europe and North America.

•   •   •   •

It's impossible to exaggerate just how big a mess Burma has been almost continuously since World War II. Describing it as a repressive military government, oppressing a calm and resilient people with a handful of quarrelsome border regions thrown in, is a gross oversimplification. So I'll compare it with another utterly confusing modern chaos-nation.

In the late 1990s, I made a brief visit to Lebanon, a country recently emerged from a brutal 17-year civil war. Before I arrived in Beirut I thought I had a fairly good couple-of-sentences synopsis of what

happened: the delicate balance between Christians and Muslims fell apart
when Palestinians flooded in from Jordan after the Israelis took the West
Bank. The end result was an endless civil war, which only ground to a halt
through utter exhaustion.

A week later I understood far less about Lebanon. My simple outline
had completely fallen apart. In fact the Lebanese situation was never just
Christians versus Muslims. There were dozens of Christian and Muslim
militias as well as the Christian Lebanese Army. Then there was the
Palestine Liberation Organization and assorted other Muslim groups,
including Hamas and the Iranian-backed Hezbollah, along with the Syrian
army and the Israelis together with their surrogate Lebanese forces – even
some American marines for a spell.

It certainly wasn't just one side against the other.

Edgar O'Ballance's *Civil War in Lebanon, 1975–92*, a fascinating year-
by-year account of what happened during that period, reported that 'at
one time or other… each one of the dozen or so major armed groups
fought against each other'. In between punching it out with the Muslims,
every Christian militia took potshots at every other Christian militia,
every Muslim group fell out with every other Muslim group and nobody
got on with the Israelis.

On one occasion a fragile ceasefire fell apart when 'Lebanese Forces'
militia clashed with elements of the Lebanese army. Shooting broke out
because of 'a scuffle over queue-jumping on the ski slopes'. Both groups
of military skiers 'called for armed assistance', and before long the rocket-
propelled grenades were arcing over the Green Line again. Central
American countries may have soccer wars, but has anybody else ever had a
ski-lift shoot-out?

Take out the chairlift and extend the timeline from 17 years to more
than 50 and the Burmese story has just as many unlikely twists and turns.
The country was falling apart even before the British handed it back.
No sooner had the new government taken over (withdrawing from the

British Commonwealth was almost their first action) before everything collapsed. For a spell it was dubbed the 'Six-Mile Rangoon government', for that was as far from the capital that its control extended.

There were not one but two Communist insurrections, the Red Flag and White Flag sections of the CPB, or Communist Party of Burma. There was the PVO (People's Volunteer Organisation), Aung San's private army, which, after his death, decided it would make its own pitch for power rather than support the central government, plus all the regional minority groups from the Buddhist Mons to the Muslim Rohingya. For a time the Karen, or Kayin, the biggest non-Burmese ethnic group, supported the central government, but even that soon went wrong. When Karen troops successfully stormed through CPB-controlled areas, it simply stirred up old resentment from the Burmese – even the Burmese who had been trying to put down the CPB insurrection.

As if a variety of Burmese groups and a kaleidoscope of minority ethnic groups were not enough confusion, the Chinese KMT (Kuomintang) appeared on the scene in late 1949. Pushed out of China by the steady advance of Mao's Communists, remnants of the KMT set up shop in the northern Shan and Kachin region. Heavily armed, by the CIA no less, the KMT soon proved even harsher than the Japanese had been less than 10 years earlier. However, the arrival of Burmese troops to shoot it out with the KMT proved even less popular and soon there was a Shan rebellion under way as well.

This confusion has seesawed back and forth from the end of World War II right up to the present day. Brutal campaigns like the 'Four Cuts' programme of the 1970s, closely modelled on the British 'New Villages' strategy during the Malaya Emergency in the 1950s and the American 'Strategic Hamlets' policy in Vietnam, brought more of the country under central control, but only for a short time. Inevitably something else would come along and shift things into reverse.

Remarkably, the Burmese Way to Socialism not only pushed the country to the brink of bankruptcy, it also financed the border regions' struggle against the central government. Ne Win's ill-conceived economic policy backfired twice. As the economy went down the drain, and the Indian and Chinese traders were chased out of the country, everything from rice to soap to medicine to car parts disappeared off the shelves. Soon the black market controlled everything, paid for by a steady stream of smuggled rubies, teak and opium, most of which passed out of the country through the rebel-held border regions, paying taxes and tolls on the way. As the black-market goods flooded back in the opposite direction, the rebels charged more taxes and tolls and this new wealth helped to finance the ongoing battle with the central government.

By the time of the democracy protests in 1988, the Burmese had endured 25 years of Ne Win's quixotic route to socialism and were completely fed up. Socialism had become synonymous with government corruption and economic idiocy. Democracy might have been a rallying call for the protests, but it was the military government's economic ineptitude that really drove people onto the streets. The demonstrations were put down with typical ferocity and brutality and the subsequent elections were completely ignored, but economically there has been progress.

'Life is hard,' said one hotel owner, 'but it was much worse during the socialist times.'

My driver-guide U Ba Maw concurred.

'Don't think it was all rosy before Ne Win took over', he warned me. 'Before 1962 it was complete chaos. That was why Ne Win was able to take over.'

I was well aware of that. The Burma activist groups in the West painted a picture of an energetic, orderly, democratic nation from independence right through until Ne Win's grab for power in 1962.

92.

Burmese socialism has been consigned to the trash bin even more comprehensively than Communism in post-Mao China. Simply dumping the wilder excesses of economic mismanagement, however, hasn't solved all the problems. Ignoring the 1990 election results, continuing to engage in the use of forced labour and generally not being very nice to the assorted border region and minority groupings have made Burma a pariah state. Its military dictatorship has been charged by the UN with a 'crime against humanity', for its systematic abuses of human rights, and Western campaign groups have tried to increase economic pressure on the regime by discouraging investment and tourism.

Any Western company that invested in Burma was likely to find protesters turning out at AGMs or bombarding them with 'please explain' emails. As a result, investment dried up and even the line-up for foreign aid was likely to find Burma pushed to the bottom of the list. There'd been some ups, but it was mostly downs and the late 1990s Asian financial meltdown certainly hadn't helped.

The mere fact that U Ba Maw was so open about failings past and present was another indicator that what I'd heard from the activist groups – that people would be afraid to talk – wasn't necessarily the whole truth. I found it never took more than a little prompting to get Burmese to open up about the government and how much they hated it. Sometimes it took no prompting at all for people like U Myint Swe, who had barely slid the minivan door closed before he launched his attack. The government hotels were hopeless, he reported, the staff were bored and disinterested and he tried to avoid taking tourists to any government-run establishments.

'It's not surprising', he explained. 'They are paid so little, so very little, and even then the government cheats them. For example if a tourist pays in dollars and the service charge is 10 per cent, the government converts it into kyats at the pathetic official rate before passing it on to the staff.'

He was equally pessimistic about the hope for change.

'They are criminals. They have committed crimes, a long list of crimes. They are afraid that if a new government comes in they will be convicted and made to pay for their crimes.'

I'd heard the same analysis from many other people: 'The generals look at what has happened to Soeharto and his family and they are afraid, very afraid. When Milosevic was arrested and sent for trial that really scared them', a visitor at our hotel explained. 'If he can be tried for his crimes, why shouldn't the generals in this country?'

• • • •

Having two currencies running simultaneously is always confusing, but many of the Bad Lands seem to like the idea. Of course, people in many countries, good countries as well as bad ones, may find it convenient to have a second currency to hand. When your own currency is falling through the floor, putting any ready cash into something more stable can be a very good idea. There are many countries whose citizens are inclined to keep the bare minimum of their own currency, certainly have no intention of depositing money in the bank, and wherever possible stash it under the mattress in the form of greenbacks. And never mind what their government may say about the Great Satan. The Great Satan may be the devil incarnate, but the Great Satan's money is always just fine.

The Deutschmark used to perform much the same function for many Turks, who would take plenty of marks back home after spells of working in the Fatherland. It was a big question mark in the introduction of the euro whether Turkish mattress-marks would be converted into dollars or euros when the mark disappeared. In other places gold may be the reserve currency. Indian women's love of gold jewellery is in large part simply a convenient way of keeping cash at hand in a more trustworthy medium than the rupee. For many years Dubai earned a large slice of its income as a smuggling centre from where gold blocks were carried by dhow to the subcontinent.

Even in countries where the currency is strong and trustworthy another currency may often be readily accepted. Throughout the world today's exchange rate from the local currency, whatever it may be, to the US dollar is often common knowledge. For a spell Burma took the two-currency game one step further: Burma had three currencies. As soon as you arrived, right after immigration, and before you headed over to the baggage carousel, you were intercepted at a bank counter and required to change US$200 into 200 things that looked remarkably like Monopoly money (perhaps they used the same printer) and were known as FECs – Foreign Exchange Certificates. Advocates for a tourism boycott claimed that this compulsory transaction was just the first way a foolish tourist kept the nasty government afloat, by paying US$200 simply to enter the country. Really the stupid FEC was only a way station enroute to real money, the kyat (pronounced chat). You could quickly convert your FECs into kyats at pretty much the same exchange rate as the US dollar.

So why introduce this extra complication if it didn't really signify anything? Beats me. Like a lot of other strange things about Burma, the useless FEC was a mystery and eventually it was dumped.

• • • •

'They didn't have to change Rangoon', explained U Tin Maung Oo, a metallurgy student I'd bumped into in Pathein (formerly Bassein). 'Rangoon was quite all right. They didn't need to change it to Yangon. It was because of the engineering students.'

In most places in the world, engineering students are famed for being resolutely apolitical. When their fellow students are propping up the barricades, engineers are more likely to be found propping up the bar. Not in Rangoon, where the engineers were reputed to be especially fiery and always ready to appear at the front line of every protest. Furthermore, their college, the Rangoon Institute Of Technology, had a most unfortunate acronym.

'Change Rangoon', ordered the general-in-charge-of-name-changes.

'I don't care what you change it to, but I don't want to hear anything more about the students from RIOT rioting.'

Switching Rangoon to Yangon, and turning RIOT into YIOT may have pleased the generals, but all around Burma, now officially known as Myanmar, I'd been perplexed by the name changes. Mandalay had stayed Mandalay, thank God, but everywhere else had acquired a new name, starting with the country itself. Interestingly, that name change was one of the very few military moves that enjoyed some general approval.

'Calling the country Burma would be rather like calling Britain England', Tin Maung Oo went on. 'Certainly England is a very large part of Britain, just like Burma is a very large part of Myanmar, but nobody from Scotland or Wales wants to be called English. We may call people from Myanmar Burmese, but the real Burmese are the people from the central plains who speak Burmese. We call them the Bamar. The country of Myanmar includes lots of people who aren't Bamar, people like the Shan, the Karen, the Mon or the Rakhaing.'

The name Myanmar may have been accepted in the country itself, but that certainly isn't the case beyond its borders. I don't expect the Burma Action Group is ever going to become the Myanmar Action Group and, from their perspective, using the term Myanmar is likely to label you as a supporter of the regime.

Myanmar I could live with, and I was glad Mandalay had stayed that way, but most of the other changes had lost a certain flavour. To my ears Prome sounded much better than Pyay, Pegu than Bago, Pagan than Bagan. On my 1970s visit, a trip up to Maymyo (effectively 'May-town' after the British Colonel May) to stay in the time-warped old Raj-era relic Candacraig had been a real highlight. A town called Pyin U Lwin certainly didn't have the same ring, although it was simply reverting to its pre-colonial name tag. And as for renaming the mighty Irrawaddy River the Ayeyarwady...

•   •   •   •

It was our final night in Burma and we sipped cold beers and G&Ts on the lawn running down to the Inya Lake from the lakeside house. Our host worked for a Swiss engineering firm and their sundowner guests included Bill Keats, an English architect who was making a useful living out of being virtually the only resident Western architect in the country. Hotels, embassies and offices were all part of his portfolio, but it was houses he really specialised in – houses for generals and drug lords.

'English colonial is what they like', he explained. 'They're not concerned that they're castigated in the English media. And I'm not concerned about taking their money either. The SLORC-itect, that's what I am.'

'This is a great location', our host expounded, gazing across the lake to the setting sun. 'Everybody who's anybody in Rangoon lives around the lake. There's the Inya Lake Hotel', he said, pointing at the huge Russian-financed, Israeli-constructed hotel, which when it was first built was something of a Southeast Asian joke, but after recent renovations had reached a rather higher standard.

'Down there is Khun Sa', he went on, indicating the home of the Shan state drug-lord who had swapped his heroin-trading fortune for a peaceful retirement, despite the CIA million-dollar price on his head.

'Over there's the Ne Win mansion', he continued, pointing towards the secluded mansion of the late military dictator, failed economist, astrological fanatic and all-round bad guy.

'And, down there,' he concluded, pointing towards the south end of the lake, 'is Aung San Suu Kyi's home.' His gaze ran down the lake, towards 54 University Avenue, the home and detention centre of the Nobel Peace Prize winner.

CUBA

Florida Keys (US)

STRAITS OF FLORIDA

BAHAMAS

GREAT BAHAMA BANK

HAVANA

Varadero

Santa Clara

Trinidad

Playa María
la Gorda

Camagüey

Guardalavaca

Holguín

Baracoa

CARIBBEAN SEA

Guantánamo

Santiago
de Cuba

JAMAICA

So why do the Americans have it in so bad for poor old Fidel and the Cubans?

Look what he's done for the place. Kicked out a vicious dictator (nobody has a good word to say for his predecessor, Batista), established a secure government (none of those continual revolutions that have plagued so much of Latin America), ploughed money into education and health (Cuba's infant mortality and literacy figures are not just way ahead of anywhere else in Latin America, they're right up there with the USA) and certainly not made himself rich. If Fidel were ever to get the boot, he wouldn't be retiring to a mansion overlooking the Costa del Sol. Sounds like a thoroughly good guy. So how come he's so unpopular in the USA? Or in Miami at least?

Or conversely how come so many Cubans are so dependent on Miami?

'If you don't have relatives in Miami, you're fucked', said a Cuba-expert friend I bumped into in London just before I flew to Havana. 'The place is like Warsaw in the 1980s, back in the Solidarity days, but transported to the tropics.'

He was only half-right I thought, as I walked along a typically schizophrenic Cuban city street.

The shelves were full.

The shelves were empty.

All of the full shops could easily have been 7-Elevens anywhere in the world, well stocked with soft drinks, confectionery, instant foods, tissues, shampoos, toothpaste and more. There was an entry ticket to these shops – convertible pesos – Cuba's hard currency. Common Cuban pesos aren't good enough.

The empty shops were strictly for the locals and it was hard to tell what the handful of goods on display even were. There were never more than a half-dozen different items spread thinly across the shelves. Some mysterious liquid in a plastic bottle, some strange substance wrapped in shiny paper, not much choice, not much of anything and nothing likely to coax the pesos out of your pockets.

Outside, women would ask, politely, for soap. Always soap. There was plenty of it in the hard-currency shops and lots of those familiar miniature hotel soap-bars in the hard-currency hotels and resorts. It was the same everywhere in Cuba – one world and another, the world of plenty and the world of shortages.

I have never seen a country so devoid of street food. There are no food stalls, no street markets, no vending machines. Walking through the back streets of the beautifully preserved colonial town of Trinidad one day, I was surprised to see a couple of boxes of tomatoes sitting on the sidewalk. Already this sight of food – food simply sitting there in the street – was so astonishing I stopped walking and reflexively reached for my camera before realising that this was nothing special, just a box of tomatoes.

. . . .

'There are more tourists in Cuba right now than at any time since the revolution', said Jonathan Wordsworth, an American architectural writer Maureen and I bumped into in the lobby of the Hotel Riviera.

'And the architecture is wonderful. It's not just the old Spanish colonial stuff that everybody knows about. It's also places like this', he indicated with a sweep of his hand taking in the vast lobby.

'This place is pure late-1950s Las Vegas. It was built by Meyer Lansky, the Jewish Mafia guy, in 1957, just before the revolution and since then it's been virtually untouched. Have you seen the executive floor? Wow, it's pink, totally pink, the carpets, the walls, everything. We don't make them like that anymore.'

Jonathan could visit Cuba legally. Government business, study tours or journalism are official reasons for Americans to visit Castro's kingdom. Or, more correctly, to spend dollars there. Despite sanctions, the trade embargo and the strange diplomatic relations between the US and its tiny neighbour, it's quite OK for Americans to visit Cuba. Of course, they can't fly there directly. To make the 250-kilometre trip between Miami and Havana means, for most American visitors, a long detour north to Canada or a circuitous trip via Mexico. There's also a more direct, but underhand, flight via Nassau in the Bahamas. Ostensibly you're just flying to Nassau, but after a short stop the plane continues straight on to Havana, on a totally separate ticket, of course. You can play much the same 'fool the American government' game via Jamaica.

The legal twist for American Joe Tourist comes after he's made his way to the Caribbean Bad Land: he can't spend money. If somebody looks after him, pays for his room, food and transport, then that's fine, but if Joe Tourist spends his hard-earned US dollars in the enemy state, then he's broken the law and can be fined when he returns to the land of the free.

Now how does Uncle Sam know you've spent greenbacks in Castroland? Well, he doesn't, of course. Joe and Jane Tourist have flown to Toronto and two weeks later come back, perhaps with a rather better suntan than you'd normally expect to pick up in Ontario midwinter, but there's no law against that. Of course, if Joe and Jane went via Cancun – the Mexican mega-resort is a popular gateway to Cuba with flights several times a day – even the suntan wouldn't be suspicious.

Official US figures are that 160,000 US citizens legally visited Cuba in 2002 – the US seems to take an awfully long time to process their Cuban tourism statistics. Although the US government has been working to reduce that figure, and claims that visitor numbers have dropped, you can be certain a lot of Americans drop in on Havana unofficially and probably spend some dollars while they are there. Theoretically that terrible crime could result in a fine of a quarter of a million dollars and 10 years in jail. Of course, nobody has ever been put behind bars for flying to Havana and buying a Coke (Coke and other familiar American soft drinks come to Cuba via their Mexican subsidiaries), but in recent years the number of Americans fined for being bad tourists has been steadily climbing. One estimate, and everything to do with the US and Cuba seems to be either an estimate or a guess, is that the slap-on-the-wrist rate for visiting Cuba quadrupled during the Bush administration.

How do you get caught? Well, not by the FBI checking your credit-card records. Visa and MasterCard credit cards issued by American banks cannot be used in Cuba and American Express cards cannot be used at all, no matter where they're issued. Which is not to say Visa and MasterCard are not happily accepted in Cuba – an Australian, British, French, German, Canadian or Mexican version will do just fine – but there will be no incriminating credit-card slips to catch out unwary Americans unless they also have an overseas bank account.

A wad of Cuban hotel bills and restaurant receipts will do the trick, however. So will a nice boxful of those Cuban cigars, which, so it's said, JFK was careful to stock up on before he slammed the embargo doors shut. Or simply not having a ready answer when the immigration officer asks exactly where did you go and stay during that little Canadian vacation. And how come you managed to get such a good tan when it has been overcast and snowing for the past 10 days?

Americans who do get caught are likely to get an official letter demanding to know how many of those oh-so-pure greenbacks were spent for Fidel's benefit, followed by a second letter with a fine of, typically, about US$7500. Equally typically the fine can be bargained down to something between US$700 and US$2500. There are regular murmurs from Congress about repealing these crazy restrictions. Opponents of the sanctions insist that they're unconstitutional but, if anything, President Bush had an even harder-line stance on Cuba. After all, it was Florida that squeaked him in to the presidency on the first occasion.

So if you are planning a holiday in Cuba, have some answers ready. Of course you didn't leave Canada for somewhere warmer. There are no stamps in your passport (the Cubans are very understanding that way) so who's saying you've been strolling down the Malecón in Havana? The fact that you have no credit-card slips or paperwork from Canadian hotels or restaurants is easily explained: you stayed the whole time with your good Canadian friends, the couple you met in Spain a couple of years ago and always promised you'd visit.

In fact, for Cuban Americans and Americans on official business, you can fly directly from Miami to Cuba. American Airlines operates several flights a week between Miami and Havana or Santiago de Cuba. Of course, the flights depart anonymously from Miami International Airport. The flight won't appear on the departure monitors, there'll be no announcements about its imminent take-off and no flight number and destination will be posted at the boarding gate.

At the other end, however, everything will be totally normal. The American Airlines flight number will appear on the arrivals screens, the flight will be shown at the arrivals gateway, there may even be posters suggesting you 'Fly American' posted around the airport.

Technically, foreigners could get into expensive trouble by flying to

Cuba. There's no way you could buy a London–Miami–Havana–London ticket without the US government's blessing, but what's to stop you getting a London–Miami–Cancun–Havana–London ticket? You're not flying between the US and Cuba so what's the problem? Well, the US government doesn't like Cuba and the USA appearing on the same ticket. Get a ticket written that way and they could confiscate it when you showed up in the US.

Even those officially permitted American visitors have all sorts of restrictions imposed on them that would seem totally ridiculous anywhere else in the world. Just because they're allowed to spend dollars in Fidel-land doesn't mean they can spend too many of them. There's a daily limit of US$167 plus phone calls. Journalists do have an out, however. They can spend more so long as it's expenditure 'incidental to journalist activities'. That's US$167 in Havana, incidentally. Drop in on Guantánamo Bay and your per diem drops to US$78. The orange-clad Gitmo residents stay for free, although for longer than they might wish.

• • • •

What really fascinated me about the Hotel Riviera is what happened to it between 1959 and now. It opened on 10 December 1957, so it must have had just 12 months in operation before the revolution. Was it just put on ice, locked away for the next 40 years? Or did comrades from Eastern Europe and the Soviet Union enjoy this American decadence through the 1960s, 1970s and 1980s? Through that period tourists in Cuba were predominantly from the eastern side of the old Iron Curtain. For many years it was all but impossible for Westerners to get a visa, but gradually carefully selected tourist groups, many of them from Canada, started to slip in. Then the Berlin Wall fell, the Soviet Union collapsed and the Eastern European tourists simply dried up. There was a painful hiatus, the worst years of the 'special period', the *período especial,* before Western

Europeans started to flood in – attracted by sun, sand (in some cases sex) and low, low prices.

Gangster-chic is not the only architecture of note in Havana. As well as the classic American resort buildings of the 1950s, there's also wonderful colonial architecture from the 19th-century Spanish period. Elsewhere in the world much of it might have disappeared, demolished to make way for newer buildings, but in Havana everything was frozen in time from 1959 onwards. For decades it rotted away, but in recent years there has been a huge effort to restore and renovate the old parts of central Havana. Much of it is already beautifully restored, but every year it simply gets better and better.

In complete contrast there's also an enlightening selection of 'people's architecture' – grey and crumbling apartment blocks that could just as easily be East Berlin or Warsaw leftovers, and brutalist Soviet-style heroic monuments, particularly in the Plaza de la Revolución.

Then there are the cars. Cuban cars come in three eras. Right now glossy new Peugeots and economical new Hyundais dominate the streets. Rent a car in Cuba and that's what you'll get. Prior to that there's a 20-year hiatus to the Russian Lada era from the 1970s and 1980s, all of them looking a bit battered and bruised from the dings and narrows of outrageous traffic. And then it's 20 years back again to the American cars of the 1950s, only a few of them newer than 1958. Clearly there was a big buying binge in the last two years before the Americans lowered the boom. Havana's streets rock and roll with 1957 Plymouth Furies, 1956 Oldsmobile Rocket 88s and 1958 Chevy Bel Airs.

Isn't it weird that the world's true enthusiasts for American automobiles – the people who would drive their 'Chevy to the levy' any time – are the Syrians and the Cubans? Why would two countries so high up on America's Bad Land list love those icons of American culture so wholeheartedly?

Havana may have plenty of Detroit iron still circulating, but the number of lead sleds is not excessive. Part of the city's charm is that you can stroll across any street at any time without glancing twice for oncoming traffic and if you're driving there's always a free parking space.

Cuban music, on the other hand, fills every available space. The Buena Vista Social Club has a lot to answer for. Nowhere can you pause for two minutes without another band materialising out of thin air, setting up shop and launching into another shoulder-shaking number. This is definitely shoulder music. The rest of the body can stay absolutely stationary, but the shoulders show the beat. At Café Lambada one night there's not only an eight-piece band, but also a dancing couple to go with it. His beard and beret seem to say he fought the revolution with Che, Raul and Fidel, but the business card Wilki Arencibia drops on our table announces he's a 'maestro de Salsa'.

· · · ·

I pick up a rent-a-car, a new and well-kept Hyundai, in Havana, and Maureen and I drive clear to the western end of the island then U-turn and drive all the way back to the eastern end. Driving around Cuba is no problem, in daylight at least. Driving at night is an entirely different story, as I would soon discover. The roads are generally in pretty good shape. There's even a real divided-lane freeway, or *autopista*, running about half the length of the long, skinny island. The traffic is generally light and generally well behaved. For foreigners, getting fuel is no problem. In most towns there's at least one clean modern petrol station selling fuel for convertible pesos. The Cuban peso stations, for Cubans only, are grubbier and quite likely to be sold out.

Of course there are a few problems. You'd be disappointed if there wasn't something to make driving worth talking about. Overtaking trucks or buses can be a little nerve-wracking due to the low-quality diesel fuel they use. Most of them seem to belch out enough black smoke to hide an Allied World War II ship convoy from a fleet of pursuing U-boats. As a result, overtaking can be entertaining.

The big problem throughout Cuba, however, is signposting. There isn't any. Once they'd used up the annual paint budget for the obligatory 'Socialism or Death' billboards, there was nothing left for anything else. Living without the Western advertising onslaught is one thing. Not knowing whether to turn left, right or go straight on every time you come to a junction is quite another.

Leaving Havana we soon cross what has to be the Pinar del Rio Autopista, but can't work out how to get on to it. Eventually we bump down what feels like a farm laneway and find our way on to the road.

Most of the time, we soon discover, the lack of signposting is no problem. For at least three-quarters of the distance we cover there's a hitchhiker or two in the back and they always ensure we take the correct turn at every junction. For the average Cuban, hitchhiking is how you get from one place to another. You certainly can't afford your own car and there definitely aren't enough buses for everybody. So you stand by the roadside and stick out your thumb. There are even official hitchhiking points complete with platforms and stairs to make getting into trucks easier. We pick up engineers, architects and lawyers, young men and old ladies, couples and mothers with their children. The back seat is rarely empty.

• • • •

One day we end up in Varadero, partly out of interest, mostly because we can't get any further that night. Driving from the western end of the island we'd intended to skirt around Havana and then head off further east, but the Cuban disdain for direction signs catches us out and we end up on a very nice looking freeway – but the wrong very nice looking freeway. Fortunately we soon pick up a friendly young couple, a pair of recently qualified lawyers, hitchhiking on the *autopista* slip road, and they explain where we went wrong, suggest we try Varadero for the night and get us off the freeway at the correct (unmarked) exit, pointing in the right direction for Cuba's mega-resort.

By this time it's getting dark and we soon find ourselves travelling very slowly and very cautiously. Few vehicles can afford the expense of having lights after dark and it's eminently possible to overtake a smoke-belching truck only to find a completely blacked-out bullock cart coming in the opposite direction. Even vehicles travelling in the right direction can be dangerous, we discover, when we suddenly find ourselves bearing down on a totally unlit old American car, its driver crawling along the edge of the highway, trying to see where he is going by the faint glimmer of moonlight. From behind not even a reflector hints at his location.

Eventually we emerge on the coast, on the busy, well-lit Via Blanca, which runs 140 kilometres from the capital to the Torremolinos, the Surfer's Paradise, the Miami Beach, the Cancun of Cuba. Varadero is the biggest resort in the Caribbean, the place where one out of every three foreign visitors to Cuba ends up. For a large slice of that visitor population Varadero is all they will ever see of Cuba.

The fact that there are tens of thousands of hotel rooms along Varadero's 20-kilometre stretch of beautiful beach hasn't prevented most establishments from hanging out their 'full' signs, and even getting in through the front door to ask at the reception desk is, we quickly discover, not easy. Each of the big hotels seems to have a small posse of bouncers at the front door, all paying exceptional interest to your wrists as you approach. It is not a keen interest in what the time is and how long before their shift ends. Every guest is equipped with a plastic wristband, rather like an elderly hospital inmate. The band proves they are a hotel guest and qualified to indulge in the hotel's all-inclusive offerings.

108.

Varadero is all-inclusive, prepaid, cash-unnecessary on a grand scale. Once the happy European (or Canadian) vacationer has paid for the trip, nothing else is needed. From the breakfast buffet to the beer at sundowner time to the midnight mojitos, everything is included. The only time the Varadero visitor is likely to venture out of this carefully corralled little paradise is to make a day trip to Havana, where they are easily distinguished from other Varaderian groups on day-release by their different-coloured plastic wristbands.

For the Cuban government this is tourism in its most perfect form. The visitors are neatly sequestered in one little enclave where their only contact with everyday Cubans is with a carefully vetted squad of workers, most of whom are bussed in at the beginning of their shifts and bussed out at the end. There is no chance that any entrepreneurial Cuban individuals will dirty their hands by making money out of the tourists either. The businesses are all owned by the government or by joint Cuban–foreign-owned enterprises. Many of the hotels are owned by the same Spanish tourist operators who have learnt their trade along the beaches of the Costa del Sol, Costa Brava and Costa Blanca.

In other, lower key tourist enclaves, a little private enterprise is grudgingly permitted so long as it is severely circumscribed. *Casas particulares*, small family-operated bed and breakfasts, or the restaurants known as *paladares*, are allowed to operate as long as they don't take away business from places owned by the government. To ensure that this doesn't happen there are rules restricting how big a sign can be displayed, how many seats a *paladar* can provide (no more than 12), and even what dishes can be served. In a seaside restaurant, lobster and shrimp can only feature on the menus of the government establishments, and ditto for beef, since the government owns all the cows. Most importantly, employment has to be strictly limited to family members – in Castro-land you certainly don't want one comrade having to work for another. If after surmounting all these hurdles a hard-working comrade should contrive to make an unseemly profit, the taxes, charges and licence fees can be quickly jacked up to bring things back into perspective.

109.

None of these gentle relaxations of the rules apply in Varadero. In Cuba's mega-resort, business is strictly a government prerogative. There are no *casas particulares* or *paladares* in Varadero. It is quite OK for the Spanish Sol Meliá group to turn a profit from its hotels on the beach, but heaven forbid that a native Cuban should do the same thing. Let capitalism dirty the Spanish, not the locals. Sol Meliá is the biggest foreign hotel-operator in Cuba. In 1996, when the US Helms-Burton legislation was trying to bully foreign companies out of Cuba, the company decided to forget about the American market. They sold up their hotels in Miami and Orlando and concentrated on Cuba instead.

Economics isn't the only thing that grates at Varadero.

As we load up our trays at the lunch buffet, call for another all-included cocktail at the bar, open another bar of soap in the bathroom, we contemplate that none of this is available to the smiling waitress restocking the breakfast counters, the smiling barman mixing the mojitos, or the smiling maid tidying up the bathroom. At the end of their shifts they'll be paid in Cuban pesos, a currency that won't buy any of the goodies lavished upon the foreign visitors. They'll be bussed out of Varadero to their homes, well away from the international visitors, where the shelves in their peso shops will be bare.

• • • •

We had an educational window-shop down República, the main shopping street running from the railway station to the city centre in Camagüey, Cuba's third-largest city. The occasional glossy, well-lit shop aimed at foreigners punctuated a string of peso shops loaded with cheap tat, low-quality junk, horrible fashions and general rubbish.

My favourite – I was so intrigued by it that I walked past it a half-dozen times trying to gauge if there was a local reaction – was a miserable-looking window with a crumbling and bald dress dummy wearing what looked like something recycled from World War II. Next to this example of the wonders of the Cuban rag trade was a sign proclaiming the glories of all those years of socialism. Was this serious? Or was this window display simply a not-so-subtle comment on the failures rather than the glories of Cuban socialism?

Every other woman walking by was wearing the standard Cuban fashion statements: short, tight, low, high, stretched. Preferably in Lycra. That string of one-word diktats sums up Cuban fashions, and the more you've got to stuff into it the better. In Cuba no woman can be too big, too wide, too round for Lycra. 'Thrusting femininity' was the two-word definition of the Cuban approach to fashion, according to one visiting travel writer. Every Cuban woman has style and it's none of this 'white is this year's black' bullshit.

Actually Cuba is full of style. Even the Museo de la Revolución, essentially a museum to document what bastards Batista and his imperialist puppet masters the Americans were, and the contrasting heroism of the Cuban people, is full of style. Castro always looked stylish. Wasn't it Fidel who started the whole revolutionary combat fatigues thing? Didn't he always have a photographer on hand to record, in stylish-looking black and white, the whole revolution from start to glorious finish? Didn't he (and nearly every other Cuban revolutionary) remember to keep their boots (and shirts and trousers) from every stage of the struggle so they could be preserved in museums? A pair of Italian boots I'd bought on impulse from a Paris shoe shop a few years before, thinking they looked stylish, were clearly just the Fidel Mark 1 boots from the first stage of the struggle. If someone would tell me the shop to buy the Mark 3 boots, I'd pop out and buy a pair right now.

And Che... well, what can you say? A rock-star (Buddy Holly and dozens since), movie-star (James Dean), royalty-star (Princess Di) death. Do it while you still look perfect enough to launch a million T-shirts. Che is simply the Cuban souvenir – Che T-shirts outnumber five to one any other Cuban memento.

In fact Che, not Fidel, is the Cuban icon. El Jefe may be the undisputed leader, but visually Fidel is not often to be seen. There's no Fidel personality cult; it's Che's gigantic neon-lit portrait that gazes out heroically across the Plaza de la Revolución in Havana. Even Camilo Cienfuegos, the revolutionary hero who died in a plane crash in 1959, pops up more often than Fidel.

Nowhere is the Che cult displayed with more energy than in Santa Clara, where a gigantic statue of the superman towers over the museum dedicated to his life. Che was captured in Bolivia in 1967 and murdered at the CIA's behest. His remains were returned to Cuba in 1997 and interred here. The museum shows another side of Che's life: his comfortable Argentinean childhood and his adventures as a young medical student when he explored South America by motorcycle and encountered the grinding poverty that was to propel him into his life as a revolutionary. In 1954 Che was in Guatemala and witnessed the CIA-backed invasion that toppled the elected government and installed the repressive military regime that was to blight Guatemala for nearly 50 years.

It was Che Guevara's capture of Santa Clara on 29 December 1958 that spelt the end for Batista's despotic regime. Using a cobbled-together bulldozer, Che's rebels cut the railway line into the city, derailing an armoured train sent to reinforce Batista's troops. Despite being overwhelmingly outnumbered, Che's guerrillas soon defeated the 3000-strong garrison and, late on 31 December, Batista realised that Santiago de Cuba, the second-largest city in Cuba, was about to fall. In the early hours of 1 January 1959, Batista fled to the Dominican Republic, taking US$40 million with him to finance his comfortable retirement in Franco's Spain. He died in 1973.

· · · ·

Our travels around Cuba have been a curious blend of organised (you can't get more organised than staying in a resort filled with European package tourists) and disorganised (our visit to the scuba-diving haven of Playa María la Gorda, right at the western end of the island, was short-circuited by a serious room shortage – we could only stay for one night). We've stayed in dull, ordinary hotels and fancy old colonial-era hotels and in *casas particulares*, one of which reminded me of a particularly old-fashioned English bed and breakfast. We've been completely lost once or twice due to the serious lack of signposting and on one occasion stopped some foreign cyclists to ask where the hell we were. Sometimes we've found it very difficult to find food and then felt guilty knowing we were eating in places where effectively Cubans are not welcome.

In Guardalavaca, where I try Cuban scuba diving again, Maureen and I have one of those ludicrous over-dinner arguments, the reasons and causes for which disappear as soon as you stop shouting at each other.

'Maybe we're both in a bad mood because neither of us is really enjoying Cuba', I suggested.

'Well, Havana was great', Maureen disagreed. 'It looks wonderful. There's all the music, the revolution and so on.'

'Sure,' I allowed, 'the revolution is certainly interesting historically, but after you've seen a half-dozen revolutionary museums (was any revolution ever so well documented, so well photographed? God, they even kept the boat Fidel arrived on in 1957!) they begin to pall. After a thousand kilometres you begin to feel that a bit less energy into "Socialism or Death" billboards and a bit more into some other things could make a difference.'

'And nothing else does it for me', I continued. 'The other towns are OK, but essentially dull. So far the best has been Trinidad, but it's just a watered-down version of Antigua in Guatemala. Not as well kept, not as colourful, not as interesting, not as anything.'

'Yeah, I guess so,' Maureen agreed, 'and in between there are beach resorts like Varadero that are the pits, all-inclusive resorts where the locals are totally shut out.'

Which was where I'd really had enough. In this 'glorious socialism, wonders of the revolution Alice-in-Wonderland', the workers are excluded by guards and by money.

'And I really hate those plastic wristbands they put on their guests'. Maureen concluded. 'You look as if you're an asylum inmate or somebody in a hospital.'

• • • •

There was a final sightseeing stop on our way to Santiago de Cuba – Guantánamo Bay, favourite US station for captured Taliban and Al-Qaeda members. How did this chunk of Cuba come to be in the possession of its arch enemy?

Well, in 1903 the USA grabbed it, fair and square.

After the Spanish-American war in 1898, the US decided not to hand control of Cuba over to the Cuban rebels who had been fighting for their independence from Spain for years. Instead they set up a US military occupation, which was withdrawn, reluctantly, in 1902, but only after saddling Cuba with the Platt Amendment, a law that gave the US the right to intervene militarily any time they didn't like what was going on. In 1903 the US decided they didn't like the way the Cubans were running Cuba and annexed 116 square kilometres at the mouth of Guantánamo Bay to use as a naval station from where they could keep a close eye on things.

In 1934 President Roosevelt deigned to change the control to a 99-year lease so Cuba could look forward to getting their land back in 2033, except that it requires both sides to agree for the lease to be terminated and for nearly 50 years the US has been extremely reluctant to agree to anything with Cuba.

Following the revolution in 1959, Fidel asked for Guantánamo Bay to be returned. The US refused, of course, and in turn Castro has subsequently refused to accept the annual rent, all of about US$4000 a year. For a time the base served a useful purpose protecting the approaches to the Panama Canal, but its principal use today – apart from its recent function as a more convenient prison than Afghanistan – is as an irritant to Castro. As well as being home to the 7000-odd US personnel and the current batch of prisoners from Central Asia, the base has also housed far larger numbers of refugees. In 1992 there were 11,000 Haitians holed up here after they attempted to escape from their country's collapsing economy. In late 1994 they were followed by over 30,000 Cubans, intercepted by the US Coast Guard en route from Cuba to the bright lights of Miami. Most of them eventually ended up in the US. Clearly there's no shortage of facilities to house unlimited numbers of Taliban and Al-Qaeda n'er-do-wells.

Of course, there's no way to visit Guantánamo Bay from the rest of Cuba, although a handful of now elderly Cubans have kept their jobs on the base since the 1950s and still cross the border every day. They'd better take care since the base is encircled by trenches, fences, watchtowers and the largest minefield in the Western Hemisphere. No less than 75,000 mines stand ready to deter any thoughts Castro might have about unilateral lease terminations. Afghan arrivals would probably feel quite at home, since their own country has the unfortunate distinction of being one of the most heavily mined in the world.

Although we couldn't drop in to check out the golf course, yacht club, supermarkets, cinemas and the only McDonalds in Cuba, the Cubans do make it possible for us to have a peek into their unwanted visitors' home. At a military checkpoint on the road we drop off our current hitchhikers, leave our passports in the checkpoint office and drive 15 kilometres to the Mirador de Malones, a 320-metre-high viewpoint looking down on the base. Fortunately our CUC$5 admission charge includes a cold drink because there is nothing to see, even with the 25-cents-in-the-slot telescope. The base shimmered in the heat far below us and it's hard to make out anything. Amnesty International can't check up on the holding conditions for Al-Qaeda terrorists from up here.

Then, Amnesty International doesn't need to check up on the conditions. No matter how bad they are, they can hardly make the US government's image any worse than it is already. So why did the Bush government decide to establish the USA's own gulag in Cuba?

Three reasons: US law doesn't apply here, international law doesn't apply here and it's impossible for independent observers to see what the hell's going on. Which hardly contributes to Cuba's Bad Land status. Guantánamo Bay may be in Cuba the island, but effectively it's in the USA, and not the regular holier-than-thou USA. It's in the Bad Land USA.

Back on the main road our hitchhikers are still waiting for a ride so we take them on board again for the final few kilometres to their destination.

• • • •

A rickety old twin-engine Antonov AN-26 rattles us back to Havana. From the departure lounge at the Santiago de Cuba airport I had spotted a nice new Aerocaribbean ATR-42 outside and concluded we'd be zipping back to Havana in comfort. Half an hour later that aircraft flies off to the Dominican Republic and all that's left is the old Russian rust bucket. It's after dark and we are well over an hour late before finally being ushered out to the aircraft. There are no reading lights and the general cabin lighting is too weak to read by, so there's nothing to distract you from the aircraft's strange vibrations and noises.

At least I have a seat and my seat has a safety belt. My last Antonov flight was way back in 1992 in Cambodia, when the national airline was still called Air Kampuchea. When we'd all crowded on board and grabbed a seat there were still two or three passengers standing, so cane chairs were provided for the extras. On that occasion my seat was provided with both ends of a seat belt, but unfortunately they were both the same end. In comparison this Antonov is virtually showroom-new, although the entire flight, with a short intermediate stop at Holguìn, seems to be a process of accelerating until a speed is reached where the whole aircraft starts to vibrate and rattle, then coasting back to a smoother velocity before speeding up to the vibration point again.

We spill out at the domestic terminal in Havana, grab our bags, emerge into the gloomy car park and pile into the capacious back seat of a fine-looking old Chevy. Fine looking, but not fine running. We are only halfway to the car park exit before terminal noises from up front announce some sort of major mechanical failure and we are transferred to a Russian vehicle, an elderly Moskvich in much worse shape than our superannuated Antonov. Compared with this rust bucket the aircraft was a paragon of modern engineering and fine maintenance. Most of the windows are broken, the window winders don't work, the floor and the roof are bare metal and heat pours in from various gaps to the engine compartment. Simply having us in the back seat clearly makes our driver and his sidekick very nervous. Only the glossy modern taxis in Cuba are licensed to convey foreigners. There wasn't one was at the domestic airport that night and it's pretty clear that having us on board is illegal and worrying.

To compound the difficulties our driver doesn't know where our hotel is, but fortunately by this time we know our way around Havana enough to point him in the right direction. He eventually drops us off round the corner from the hotel entrance, well out of view.

· · · ·

There's one final pilgrimage to make in Havana. The Hemingway pilgrimage. I've already been bumping into Ernesto all over town. I've sipped a mojito – rum, lemon juice, sugar, soda, a big sprig of mint leaves, ice cubes, stir – in La Bodeguita del Medio, irrespective of the fact that my guidebook author has clearly taken a major dislike to the place. I've actually developed such a taste for mojitos (they are delicious) that I've probably indulged in a few too many of them in La Bodeguita, among other Cuban hostelries.

Scrawled on the wall of La Bodeguita is a message from the great writer himself that this is the place for mojitos, but that he prefers to take his daiquiris at El Floridita. We dutifully continue on to the elegantly old-fashioned El Floridita for dinner. The décor may have been old world, but the bill, when it comes, is right up to date. After two weeks in Cuba we've learnt to check the prices carefully since there's clearly a policy in touristy places of marking things up from the menu. Here a CUC$17 bottle of wine gets elevated to CUC$27 and although I am inclined to let the little elevations go (I can live with the CUC$4 meals that became CUC$5) this is a bit too much.

We'd also looked in at the Hotel Ambos Mundos, where Hemingway usually stayed in room 511. With his second wife, Pauline Pfeiffer, he was here on and off for six years during the 1930s. Even though the plot for *For Whom the Bell Tolls* was mapped out in this Old Havana hotel, the holy grail is Finca la Vigía, the house he bought in 1939, just outside of town. The name means Watchtower Farm and a taxi driver whisks us out there, explaining on the way the complicated paperwork he had to fill in for each trip, a government policy to ensure he doesn't make too much money.

'You can't go inside' is the first thing I'm told after I've paid the entry price, but that, it turns out, is unimportant. The house is surprisingly small and has plenty of windows so it's easy to see inside. What's even more surprising is that it's packed full, as if Hemingway had just popped out for a few bottles of rum, planning to be back in five minutes. The bookshelves are chock-full, the magazine racks are bulging, his clothes still hang in the closet, his Royal typewriter (he typed standing up) still rests on the stand by the bed.

Outside, the swimming pool is empty, which makes it hard to imagine Ava Gardner doing a few naked laps. Hemingway's fishing boat, *El Pilar*, is also on display, just like *Granma*, the ship that Castro used to return to Cuba to launch the revolution. *Granma* stands in a glass-walled showroom right in the centre of downtown Havana, along with many other items of revolutionary armoury. Hemingway had remarkably little to say about the revolution and, although a famous photo shows the revolutionary and the writer shaking hands after Castro won the cup that Hemingway had awarded for an annual game fishing tournament, he left Cuba soon after, never to return. A year later in Idaho he put his shotgun barrel in his mouth and it was all over.

Ernest's and Fidel's boats are a reminder that boating deaths are not uncommon for Cubans. They drown when their leaky craft go down en route to Florida. And would-be escapees don't just die on the 150-kilometre boat trip from Cuba to Miami. On Christmas Eve in 2000 the body of a teenager was discovered in a field near London's Gatwick Airport. He had fallen there when the undercarriage of a British Airways Boeing 777 was lowered as the aircraft was on its final approach after flying from Havana. The young Cuban had been hiding out in the wheel compartment. It wasn't the fall that killed him – he'd died from the cold and lack of oxygen many hours before he tumbled into a British field.

Nor was he alone. On Christmas Day, as the same aircraft took off to fly back across the Atlantic to Cancun in Mexico, the body of another Cuban teenager spilled out on to the runway. Freezing to death certainly hadn't featured in the escape plans of Alberto Vazquez, aged 17, and Michael Fonseca, aged 16. In fact they hadn't even intended to stowaway to Europe. What they had planned to do was certainly very risky, but not necessarily fatal. They'd climbed over the airport fence and hidden in the long grass beside the runway waiting for the departure of the American Airlines flight to Miami. When the aircraft turned for the start of its takeoff run the two boys intended to run across and climb up

119.

into the undercarriage compartment. The short trip to Miami would only take half an hour and the aircraft would not climb to its normal cruising altitude. It would be uncomfortable, it would be very cold, it was certainly stupidly dangerous – they could easily be crushed by the retracting wheels or fall out when the undercarriage was lowered – but with luck they would have got away with it... if they hadn't made the fatal error of mistaking one Boeing jetliner for another.

Thirty minutes to Miami was survivable, nine hours to London certainly wasn't. Cruising 10,000 feet higher than the summit of Mt Everest there was almost no way they were going to survive the lack of oxygen and temperatures as low as –50°C. Stowaways do occasionally get away with such foolhardy escape attempts. In 1996 an Indian teenager fell from another British Airways aircraft as it approached Heathrow, but his brother survived the 10-hour trip from New Delhi. In 2000 a Tahitian stowaway managed to make it alive to Los Angeles in the undercarriage compartment of an Air France 747. Far more frequently, however, stowaways die en route and their bodies are found aligned with some airport runway. The deaths of the two Cuban teenagers were the third known case of Cubans dying en route to Europe in 12 months.

• • • •

I have one more encounter with Cuba. Given the way everything about the place picks you up or drops you down, I'm happy that this final meeting should be another example of the Cuban upside. In March 2006 Maureen and I are in Pakistan, checking the post-earthquake situation with an aid group. As we head back down to the capital, Islamabad, from the mountains, we pass a string of buses, packed full of Cubans.

They're Cuban doctors and medical staff, departing Kashmir after months of work treating post-earthquake injuries. The huge earthquake hit northeastern Pakistan on 8 October 2005, killing 73,000 people, damaging or destroying 80 per cent of the buildings in large parts of the earthquake zone and leaving three million people homeless. The first Cubans arrived less than a week later – there would eventually be 2300 of them at 44 hospitals, the largest international contingent to come to Pakistan's aid.

There's no question the Cubans did a terrific job under extraordinarily difficult working conditions and hardly surprisingly there were some culture clashes between the freewheeling Cubans and conservative Islam.

'The Kashmiris were a little shocked at the male-female handholding and bare flesh at first,' said Marc Preston of Australian Aid International, 'but the Cubans soon fitted in and the cold weather loaded the clothes on.'

'What was more relevant was how strict Muslim attitudes affected the delivery of healthcare,' Conner Gorry, an American Cuba expert who went to Pakistan with the Cuban team, told me. 'I witnessed many examples of husbands denying permission to their wives for surgical procedures (sometimes life-saving) or taking them from intensive care units against doctors' orders, emergency medical triage consisting of men first, followed by children and finally women regardless of the severity of injury, or of women lying to male translators about medical conditions because religious-cultural norms prohibited them from talking to men about personal matters.

'What was most amazing to me was that the Cuban doctors and surgeons, nearly half of whom were female (precisely because of the religious restriction regarding female patients seeing male caregivers), treated so many quake victims in spite of all the differences (and the cold!).'

Amusingly, Castro had offered to send this same Cuban medical team in to another huge natural disaster just a month earlier: Hurricane Katrina in New Orleans.

'No thanks', said Mr Bush.

• • • •

Overall I didn't warm to Cuba. Oh, sure, Havana was every bit as beautiful as promised, the music was terrific, the people were friendly, travel was easy. And there was so much to be admired about what had been achieved in Cuba since the revolution – higher literacy and lower infant mortality than just about anywhere else in Latin America for starters. The literacy and infant mortality figures are not just good for a developing country, they are right up at First World standard. Cuba's infant mortality figures compare more than favourably with the USA, but then there's no deprived underclass in Cuba. It's simply that nobody is very rich.

It's interesting to track the infant mortality figures over the years. It started to drop as soon as Batista got his marching orders and has fallen consistently ever since, except for a short rise when the Soviet Union collapsed and the Cuban economy went into free fall. There was probably some CIA operative watching those infant mortality figures rising and rubbing his or her hands with delight: 'See, the blockade is really working.'

On consecutive days in Baracoa and Santiago de Cuba our thoughts about the country were pulled in one direction then another.

'It's the 1950s American dream', we thought as we strolled Baracoa's streets one evening. Music, dancing, small groups talking animatedly in the central square, everything a long way from the counter-view of America as a place of schoolroom massacres, urban drug problems and drive-by shootings. Of course, everything was a little run-down and rough at the edges, but there's a price for anything.

I really liked Santiago de Cuba. We whiled away the evening listening to a band play in the bar of our elegant old hotel and even bought a CD of their music. Round the corner I got the cheapest haircut I've had in years. The next day two women, one a doctor and one an architect, brought the downside of the Cuba story home to us.

'There are shortages of everything', complained Ana Moreno.

122.

'And so often there's no real work, but you have to spend endless hours scrabbling for hard currency', continued Mireya Quiroz. 'You have to get dollars to make life liveable. And there's no fish because it's all sold to tourists.'

This was the division that I really disliked, that made me edgy about the whole Cuban experience. The Cubans in their miserable cafés lining up to pay pesos for miserable-looking food while next door our place is air-conditioned and brightly lit and, while the food we (and the richer Cubans) pay for with real money may not be brilliant, it's a hell of a lot better than they're getting.

The beaches? I'd rather not think about them. The 'us and them' nature of Cuban beach resorts really made me feel uncomfortable. Dollar-paying European and Canadian tourists on one side of the fence, Cubans resolutely kept on the other. At the end of the day that was the aspect of Cuba I most disliked. Bright lights, air-con and stacked shelves for those with dollars to spend; gloom and an Eastern Europe 1950s ambience for everybody else.

Who is to blame? Well, America could certainly shoulder some. It is the only country that really thinks of Cuba as a Bad Land. Sure, Cuba is Communist, but so is China, and America goes out of its way to be nice to China. So is Vietnam, and they'd won the war – but Vietnam is back in the good books. Certainly Cuba is a military dictatorship, but nobody ever said you have to be democratic to get the US seal of approval. It's hard to think of a less democratic nation than Saudi Arabia and there have been plenty of very nasty dictatorships in Latin America that have not just enjoyed American approval, but have also been installed or propped up with American dollars and American military might. Terrorism? Well, that's never been a Cuban policy and the days of Cuban troops acting as Soviet surrogates in Angola or Somalia are long gone.

In fact it's American policy that has kept Castro in power. The Cubans may have their doubts about their government, but they sure as hell don't want an American president telling them how to run the place. If the USA had ever made friends with Fidel, he'd probably have fallen over the following week.

All in all it's very hard to figure out exactly why the US government bears such a grudge against Cuba, but then just how effective is the US grudge in any case? There are plenty of European, Asian and Latin American companies ready and willing to do business with Cuba. Nobody misses Chevies and Fords when they can get Hyundais and Peugeots. There are plenty of Spanish hotel companies ready to build hotels along the Cuban beaches and no shortage of European and Canadian tourists ready to stretch out on the sun lounges. The Golden Arches may not have appeared in Havana, but if you want a Coca-Cola the Mexican bottling plant has had no trouble providing the pause that refreshes.

Perhaps you can blame 25 per cent of Cuba's plight on stupid American policies, but the other 75 per cent? That's all down to Fidel.

IRAN

The Paykan swerved to the side of the road and a portly gentleman levered himself out from the driver's seat and steamed across the pavement towards me, like the *Titanic* on a pressing engagement with an iceberg.

I was in Iran and I was about to be kidnapped.

'I am a guide. I speak English', announced Ahmad Pourseyedi as he grabbed my arm. 'Come, we will go to the Fin Gardens.'

There was no arguing. The fact that I had only arrived in Kashan half an hour earlier and was on my way out to dinner only allowed me to put off the inevitable for 12 hours. The next morning I belonged to Ahmad. In fact I had become part of Ahmad's family. At each of the beautiful traditional homes for which Kashan will, one day, be justifiably famous, the ticket seller was expected – no, commanded – to offer me the family discount.

It was a typically Iranian encounter. I cannot remember the last country I visited where there was such an overwhelming urge to make you feel welcome, to roll out the Persian carpet, to include you in the family gatherings. That night, in the Khan-e Tabatabei, a fine old house where the central courtyard became a restaurant for the evening, the family at the next table introduced themselves. 'You are by yourself – why don't you join us?'

Walking through the park beside the Zayandeh River in Esfahan a couple of days earlier an older woman had called out from her park bench: 'Do you speak English? Come talk with us.' In Yazd I was intercepted by three young men and ushered back, after I walked straight past the entrance to the Bagh-e Doulat Abad gardens. One of them was keen to practise his already excellent English and when I told them I lived in Melbourne I was reminded, yet again, that the best thing Australia ever did to foster better relations with the Islamic Republic was not to win a football match. In late 1997 Iran drew with Australia in a World Cup preliminary in Melbourne, thus ensuring a place for Iran in the 1998 World Cup. Repeatedly the mere mention of the word 'Melbourne' brings a smile to an Iranian face. That night three old women, comfortably seated feasting on a watermelon on the roadside in a narrow laneway in the old city of Yazd, offer me a slice as I pass by.

This is what life is like on the Axis of Evil.

•   •   •   •

Apart from Albania, all of my Bad Lands put you through hoops of some sort before you can get in the door. Even Cuba requires you to have a 'tourist card'. Why is it that I can just front up in the United States, Japan, France, Italy and many other countries that half the world would dearly like to call home, while countries from which half the population would simply like to escape, and where nobody is queuing up to find a way in, go to all this effort to restrict your entry?

128. On paper – or on my computer screen – Iran wasn't all that bad. You could even download their visa application form from the embassy website, and issuing a visa would only take five days. Or so the website claimed. Ten days later I phoned the embassy to ask what was happening.

'We have sent the application to Tehran', the helpful official explained. 'You must wait at least two weeks.'

'So much for five days', I thought as I asked to have my visa-less passport returned. I had to go to Japan at the weekend.

'I've got a British passport as well', I suggested. 'If I applied for a visa with that passport, you could be preparing it while I am in Japan next week.' Their website had indicated that British passport-holders needed to allow two weeks for their visa applications, as opposed to the fictional five days for Australians.

'Oh, you should not do that', the still-helpful official replied. 'We have a great deal of difficulty getting visas for British citizens. You will probably have to wait two months. But we will process your application while you are away. If you send your passport back when you return, we will only have to stick the visa in the passport.'

And they were as good as their word.

A couple of weeks later I board a shiny new Emirates Airbus from Dubai, zip across the Gulf and head almost directly north to Tehran, sipping a glass of wine, which I assume, wrongly, will be the last alcohol I'll see for a couple of weeks.

In Tehran I grab my bag off the carousel, my passport is stamped, I clear customs and I'm in Iran. I have made absolutely no plans, not even booked a hotel for the night. I'm just going to cruise into the city and see what happens.

The three young women at Tehran airport's tourist desk have their hair discreetly covered, but otherwise we could have been at Heathrow or JFK. Clearly tourists don't turn up every day, certainly not without even a hotel booking. They joke about not doing this too often, comment that they don't know the hotel I've pulled out of my guidebook, phone through to book me a room and finally wish me a pleasant stay in Iran. It's the first of many contacts I'll have with the opposite sex in Iran and a firm reminder that this is not the Arab world. The very idea that you might be asking a woman to book a hotel in Saudi Arabia is inconceivable.

I'm intercepted by a man at the terminal door. 'You need a taxi? Come, I will take you into Tehran', he announces in good English.

'OK, what's the fare?' I reply.

'The usual fare', he evades, trying to grab my bag to seal the deal.

'Ten thousand', he eventually allows, when pushed.

I've got a lot of ten thousands. Back in the baggage-claim area I'd changed US$100 into rials and quickly realised it was a good thing I'd not changed US$200. The biggest rial note is 10,000, worth a smidge more than one US dollar. So I had a pocketful of ten thousands – 84 of them to be precise.

'No, 10 like this', he admits, holding a finger over the final zero to indicate that he was performing the most standard Iranian 'confuse the foreigner' trick, quoting prices in *toman*. For some reason many prices in Iran are not in rials, but in a totally imaginary unit known as a *toman* or 10 rials. So prices can always be out by 10 and my would-be-driver's 'usual fare' of 10,000 is really 100,000 rial.

The next day, with my price sensitivity not yet keyed in, I'm amazed at how low the prices are in a fancy restaurant until I notice the T after each figure. Suddenly main courses are US$12 to $15, not $1.20 to $1.50. Even a week later I am still occasionally getting tripped up. 'That's remarkably cheap', I think, then rapidly conclude that at 10 times the cost it wasn't such a bargain.

'There's your driver', says the taxi-kiosk dispatcher, taking 35,000 rials from me and writing out a chit.

We sling my bag in the back of, disappointingly, a Peugeot rather than a Paykan, and head out into Tehran's terrible traffic. Nothing written about Tehran can avoid mentioning that this is a contender for any 'world's worst traffic' award, so let's get it out of the way. The traffic in Tehran is appalling. It's not just the volume, it's also the crazily exuberant driving style and the often-battered vehicles challenging for their space in the jam. It seemed bad on my first visit to Tehran, way back in 1972, but it's undeniably far worse now. Seoul, Bangkok (before it was cleaned up), Manila, Cairo, Riyadh, you name it – Tehran is always the winner.

I have a special affection for Iran's national car, the Paykan, or 'Arrow'. Thirty-five years ago, in what seems like a previous life, I was a young engineer with the Rootes Group car manufacturers in Coventry. I worked on the old Hillman Hunter, a project known in-house as Arrow. Rootes, taken over by Chrysler just before I joined them and bankrupted not long after I left, managed to sell not just the car but a whole car-manufacturing plant to the Iranians during the Shah's era and in a remarkably short time the sturdy Paykan flooded the Iranian market.

In Britain production of the old Hillmans and their assorted clones ground to a halt decades ago, but in Iran they just kept rolling off the assembly line. By the 1990s the old Paykan was years out of date – a clunky, polluting, unsafe menace and completely gutless compared with modern vehicles. Every year the government announced that Paykan production was about to end and a year later they were still going. Now it finally looks like the Paykan era is about to finish, but there are so many out there they will remain the most popular car for many years.

There's something else blended into the traffic maelstrom. Apart from the piss-weak Paykans, a mix of more modern cars, lumbering buses and weaving motorcycles, there are also suicidal pedestrians. There seems to be a simple trade-off agreed to between wheeled and foot traffic. The wheeled stuff will totally ignore pedestrian crossings and in return the pedestrians will totally ignore traffic lights. In fact pedestrians totally ignore traffic. They simply walk out onto the road, barely glancing at the cars, buses and motorcycles bearing down on them (often from both directions since one-way signs don't stop Tehrani drivers from proceeding in the wrong direction). Crossing the road is strictly dog-eat-dog. Even a stooped-over little old lady will be ignored – there's absolutely no compassion. Yet if you march out blindly, they'll stop.

Sometimes you'll see little informal groups gathering by the roadside, waiting for a critical mass to form before they surge collectively out into the turmoil. 'If there are enough of us, we're less likely to be mown down' seems to be the theory.

I have a hotel to head to. The last time I was in Tehran was way back in October 1978, in the tumultuous slow-motion months as the Shah tumbled in freeze-frame off his throne and the Ayatollah and his cohorts marched back in after a long vacation in neighbouring Iraq (although the actual return was from France). On that occasion my taxi dropped me outside the Amir Kabir Hotel, a long-term backpacker favourite, around midnight. The streets were eerily deserted (empty streets are always much more threatening than crowded ones) and the Amir Kabir was equally empty – shuttered, closed down, out of business.

I had wandered the streets and quickly found a slightly better substitute for the threadbare old Amir Kabir. This time I know what to expect. The Atlas Hotel is a comfortable midrange place, although the toilet in my quite modern bathroom is squat style.

· · · ·

The next morning I stroll a couple of blocks east from my hotel to the 'Den of US Espionage'. The former US embassy was seized by the revolutionary Iranians in 1979 and held for 444 days, substantially contributing to Jimmy Carter's re-election defeat. Today it's occupied by a hard-line militia group and the wall around the compound is decorated with anti-American slogans and murals including a painting of a skull-faced Statue of Liberty.

132.

The den of espionage moniker may sound like overheated Ayatollah rhetoric, but beneath the ex-embassy building is the basement bunker where, in 1953, CIA operatives, led by Kermit Roosevelt, grandson of Theodore 'big stick' Roosevelt, plotted to bring down the elected government of Mohammad Mossadegh and install the last Shah, Mohammed Reza. In 1951 Mossadegh had been *Time* magazine's Man of the Year for standing up to international oil companies to protect his people's rights. The 1953 coup attempt flopped and the Shah had to flee to Rome, but more money changed hands and three days later a second go ended democracy in Iran for the next quarter of a century. It was hardly the CIA at its most effective, but then we've become used to seeing the CIA at its least effective in recent years.

In subsequent years the CIA got better at overthrowing democratically elected leaders and installing somebody more in line with the US view of the world. Patrice Lumumba of the Congo went in 1960, Salvador Allende in 1973 and many people also blame the dismissal of Indonesia's Soekarno in 1966 on the CIA. Those attempting to whitewash the takeover of the US embassy insist the Iranians feared the embassy was plotting another coup to reinstall the hated Shah.

I have a contact at the British embassy (let's call him Graham) and after checking my emails at an internet café across the road I zigzag through the concrete barriers and enter the fortified embassy compound.

'We're the American embassy proxy', Graham explains.

'If there was an American embassy, they'd be stoning them and chanting "death to America" outside their walls. Unfortunately we stand in for them.

'Of course, the protests are all very well organised', he continues. 'The police could easily stop them completely and as it is they always move in before things get too heavy. Although we did have 80 windows broken last week.'

Despite which there is a long visa-applications queue.

'That's a bit of tit-for-tat', he explains. 'If we're fussier about the visas we issue, you can be certain they'll make it more difficult for Brits to get visas for Iran.'

As we cross the compound he points out the house where Roosevelt, Churchill and Stalin held their famous conference in November–December 1943, a meeting that began the process of dividing the world into competing spheres of influence through the Cold War years. It was Germany's invasion of Poland in 1939 that kicked off World War II, but in Tehran in 1943 Poland was abandoned to Stalin's tender mercies.

Over dinner one evening Stalin proposed that the German problem could be permanently resolved by simply executing 50,000 to 100,000 of the top-ranking German military once Germany was defeated. Roosevelt, not realising that Stalin's proposal was deadly serious, countered that perhaps 49,000 would be enough.

'The table they sat around for that discussion is still in the room where they met', says Graham.

I spend the rest of that first day and most of the second wandering the city, at times somewhat haphazardly, although I do manage to fit in the National Museum, the Islamic Museum, the Carpet Museum and the Contemporary Arts Gallery. Tehran is really not as bad as its reputation. Sure, the traffic is chaotic and the pollution can be throat-burning, but there's lots of green. The city has plenty of parks and almost every street seems to be lined with trees and the jube, the water channel that is a feature of so many Persian cities. Even in the July heat the mountains to the north of Tehran are still snow-capped.

After a couple of days in Tehran I'm also beginning to get a feel for the female fashion question.

On the one hand there are very definite rules about what women must wear. They not only stipulate the rules for chador design (nearly knee-length and baggy), the colour (black) and even the thickness (winter weight), but also the rules for shoes (black, clumpy) and socks (black, thick). We don't want to see any sexy ankles peeking out from below a chador.

In reality liberal interpretation of the rules seems very possible. Of course, there is safety in numbers. When there are lots of people (and there are certainly lots of people in Tehran), then an individual can get away with more. So, although black predominates, there are sudden splashes of colour. And as long as they wear something that covers them up, even a sweatshirt, these fashionistas seem to be OK.

There are many women in trousers and long, tight-fitting versions of the tunics known as manteaus. The headscarf solution is particularly interesting. I notice some women in caps, rather like the cap with a sun-protection back-flap that someone might wear in the West, and another with what looks like a bathing cap. This is a long way from Saudi Arabia!

One woman goes striding by in an orange coat, with matching orange scarf and orange shoes, looking very chic. If I'd seen her in New York or Paris, I might have thought 'Hey, an interesting look', certainly not 'Islamic dress code'.

It's funny. In France girls and women fight to be allowed to wear scarves. Here many women would like the right to discard them. Well, if Iran can force foreign women to wear a scarf covering their hair, why shouldn't France require schoolchildren not to wear them? It would be amusing if there was something silly for men to wear, a spiky, frilled collar perhaps, or if men were compelled to wear a winter overcoat all the time. Beards are definitely out, I've been told. Makes you look as if you're sucking up to the mullahs.

Before I arrived in Tehran I'd made an Iranian contact through a university course in Australia and I've been invited to a party this evening. It's in a classy area of Tehran and dress-wise, once we're indoors and the doors are closed, things are immediately very different. The men look the same, but the women, Iranians as well as foreigners, suddenly ditch the scarves and appear in jeans, T-shirts, singlets. Hair and bare arms, never seen on the street, suddenly appear.

This could easily be a party in the West. There's even a bar... and booze.

'Where does the beer come from?' I ask Mansoor.

'One of the religious militia groups', he explains. 'We have several different militia groups apart from the regular army. This one has the monopoly on beer imports from Turkey. They'll bring in a container of "arms", which is actually Efes beer', he continues, handing me another cold can.

It could easily be the same revolutionary guard militia group that shut down Tehran's new Imam Khomeini Airport 10 minutes after its long-delayed opening in 2004 because they didn't like the Turkish-Austrian consortium that was going to run the airport. They thought the consortium might have connections to Israel. It was a storm in a teacup remarkably like the American concern about a Dubai company running US container ports two years later.

I'm being so charmed in so many different directions by the people I've met in Tehran that it brings me up short when an Irish woman explains in colourful detail what a hassle the men can be and how she has put a great deal of effort into learning Farsi insults to hurl back at the men who come on to her.

'Telling them "Go fuck your mother, it's cheaper" works pretty well,' she explains, 'or "I'd rather sleep with your sister". If all else fails, there's always, "You've got a willy – I'd like a penis".'

None of this sounds like particularly good advice. Perhaps like me she's had a few too many cans of Efes tonight. It's 2am by the time the taxi drops me off at my hotel and I have trouble walking an absolutely straight line up the stairs to my room.

•   •   •   •

When Omar Khayyam wrote 'a loaf of bread, a jug of wine and thou', he was probably dreaming about a jug of Shiraz. Sadly, although Shiraz, that dark, peppery red, is popular worldwide (and particularly in Australia), you won't find any Shiraz in Shiraz. Or, openly at least, anywhere else in the strictly teetotal Islamic Republic of Iran. Fortunately

I did sample some Shiraz Shiraz way back on my first visit, sitting in the back of a VW Kombi at an Esfahan campsite.

Shiraz may be off the wine list, but Omar Khayyam was never the favourite poet in any case. His popularity in the West – all that 'moving finger moving on' verse – is in part due to Edward Fitzgerald, who put a lot of effort into translating and promoting him. In Iran Omar Khayyam's reputation rests on his mastery of maths rather than his prowess as a poet. Sa'di and Hafez, both of whom are buried in Shiraz, are the big names in a country where poetry is still important.

I start my short tour of Iran in a new Iran Air Airbus, which zips me south to Shiraz. The ticket for the London–Paris, San Francisco–Los Angeles or Sydney–Melbourne equivalent distance costs about US$30. It was a late night and an early start and I've got a fine hangover to go with it. Something I had not expected in the supposedly alcohol-free Islamic Republic.

Quite apart from the two poets' tombs, Shiraz has a fine old fort, some interesting mosques and mausoleums and the Bagh-e Eram or 'Garden of Paradise'. By lunchtime I've made my way to Hafez's tomb, which stands in a beautiful garden and features a popular teahouse where you can sit around, puff on a *qalyan* (water pipe), sip *chay* (tea) and quote the master. Sipping *chay* is definitely an important activity. Much of life takes place around a teapot. I trace my 30-year love affair with tea straight back to my first visit to Turkey and Iran in the 1970s. Tea was a stewed, milked, sugared affair until I discovered it could come in tiny glasses and, while sugar was on offer, it wasn't necessary.

I'm lunching on a healthy bowl of *abgusht* – ab means water and gusht means meat – and that's essentially what this utilitarian meal consists of: a clear broth with meat, potatoes, tomatoes and beans or lentils. *Abgusht* has a reputation as the poor person's meal, but it also provides the basis for the popular Iranian saying, 'Add more water to the *abgusht*', because if unexpected guests turn up you can always stretch the *abgusht* by diluting it. Like any popular dish, it has its subtle charms; correct seasoning and long, slow stewing are what makes a stand-out *abgusht*. It's also known as *dizi*, from the earthenware pot it's served in, and often, as here, it comes with a pestle-like device to mash up the ingredients.

That afternoon I visit the Bagh-e Eram gardens and then, with what seems like half the population of Shiraz, take a leisurely stroll out to the west of the city along Dr Chamran Boulevard. It's Friday night and it's a Shiraz ritual to picnic in one of the parks lining this long street.

Iran may not have many tourists – there were far more in the early 1970s when I made my first visit – but that hasn't stopped Iranians putting a great deal of effort and money into restoring old buildings as hotels and restaurants. I'll find more in Yazd and Kashan, but my first encounter in Shiraz is impressive. The Hammam-e Vaikal is an old bathhouse, or *hammam*, restored as a teahouse and restaurant. The beautiful octagonal room has a pool bubbling in the centre, and there's a musical trio playing a violin, a tabla-like drum and a strange stringed instrument to one side. The food is excellent, the setting is wonderful. Nor am I the only tourist. There's a cheerful group from Hong Kong, half energetic Hong Kong Chinese, and the rest an assortment of Western expats.

Shiraz is interesting enough, but the real attraction is 50 kilometres away where the ancient ruins of Persepolis perch on a plateau below a cliff face. Darius I (the Great) began construction of his showpiece city in 518 BC. Its glory days ended in 330 BC when Alexander the Great invaded Persia, sacked the city and for good measure burnt it down. Historians are uncertain if the destruction of Persepolis was the unfortunate result of a drunken party that got out of hand or deliberate revenge for Xerxes' destruction of Athens 150 years earlier.

Today things move faster. It took less than two years from the destruction of the Twin Towers to the trashing of Baghdad. Alexander may have been slower in exacting revenge, but he was also somewhat more organised than our modern-day Middle East invaders. He cleared

Persepolis out before it was burnt. Signs at the site note that emptying the Treasury took 3000 camels and mules to cart off '12,000 talents' of silver. I've no idea how much a talent is worth, but it certainly sounds impressive.

It's the bas-reliefs that really tell the Persepolis story and the impressive Apadana Stairway has the best of them. The 23 subject nations who turned up to show their respects march in line after bas-relief line, with gifts like a lioness and two cubs (from the Elamite delegation), two humped camels (from the Bactrians among others), a buffalo (from the Babylonians), a humped bull (from the Gandarians of the Kabul Valley, the Buddhist folk who carved out the Bamiyan Buddhas), two horse-chariots (from both the Lydians and Libyans), bags of gold (from the Indians of the Sindh – even then gold was important in India) and a small giraffe and elephant tusks (from the Ethiopians).

Apart from Persepolis, we also visit the ancient city site of Pasargadae and the impressive rock tombs of Naqsh-e Rostam and Naqsh-e Rajab with their beautiful bas-reliefs cut into the cliff faces. It's been a long day even before I take a taxi to the Yord Restaurant near a village outside of Shiraz that night. The restaurant is named after the traditional nomad tent set up to house it during the summer months. My hotel is uncertain it exists at all, then has trouble working out how I should get there, and my taxi driver has a great deal of difficulty finding it even with their written and verbal instructions.

The good food and traditional music performances make the effort worthwhile, but getting back is even worse. There are no taxis so I stumble along a path through the forest until I get to the village where there are also no taxis. I'm not even certain which direction it is to Shiraz, but as usual Iranian kindness kicks in. When I stick my thumb out to try to hitch a ride, a Paykan pulls over almost immediately and the driver takes me not just back to Shiraz, but right to my hotel door.

. . . .

I'd intended to take a bus for the 450-kilometre trip to Yazd, but Hassan, my Persepolis taxi driver, had been such a friendly guide I decide the US$70 splurge for air-con comfort and the opportunity to make some stops en route was justified in the 40°C heat. We cruise off with his Chris de Burgh tape providing the wholly inappropriate soundtrack and his nine-year-old daughter along for the ride.

Yazd features a Zoroastrian fire temple and Zoroastrian Towers of Silence where, once upon a time, vultures would pick over the dead bodies. A few days later in Esfahan I'll encounter another interesting reminder that there are other religions in the Islamic Republic.

Water features everywhere in Iran, flowing along street edges in the jube (open drains), cascading down channels in gardens and parks, sprinkling in fountains and appearing in pools in the open courtyards found in so many traditional old houses. It's also dispensed with remarkable civic generosity. In museums, parks, mosques – even along every length of street – there's usually a public refrigerated water dispenser, an Iranian version of a drinking fountain. In the big cities piped water is safe to drink (I certainly got through plenty of it in my summer visit to Iran) and a happy consequence of this ready availability of cold drinking water is that Iran is not afflicted with the litter of empty plastic water bottles that plagues so many developing countries.

Yazd is a centre for the underground irrigation channels known as *qanat* and there's even a Water Museum, which explains all about them and, of course, features a *qanat* running through a subterranean chamber.

The city's water channels may be hidden from view, but examples of its other traditional architectural feature are very evident. Any worthwhile old home is topped by what looks like a cross between a stylish chimney and a lookout tower. This is a *badgir*, a wind tower cunningly designed to catch a passing breeze and funnel it down over a pool of water in the house to provide a surprisingly effective form of natural air-conditioning. Standing under a *badgir*, you can feel the cool downward breeze and, at the appropriate spot, the upward return flow. They are found not only in this area of Iran, but also on the Arab side of the Gulf (they feature in some fine old houses in Dubai), in some villages in western Afghanistan and in the Sindh region of Pakistan. Every old house of note around the town is topped by a fine example, and a small reservoir, where the wind cools the water, is known as Shesh Badgir, from the six towers that ring the domed reservoir.

Restoring and reopening traditional old *badgir*-equipped houses as hotels and restaurants has become a local craze. I stay at the handsome Malek-o Tojjar, a fine example of one of these old houses. That afternoon, sipping tea in the courtyard café and reading *Reading Lolita in Tehran* (I had to use that repetition somehow), Azar Nafisi's novel about a reading group dipping into forbidden Western literature, I'm invited over to join a real reading group. The four Yazd university students, three of them female, are keen to practise their English and talk about the English language books they're studying.

This so clearly isn't Saudi Arabia. Young couples openly hold hands, women shake hands with you, talk to you and smile at you. In Saudi not only is there virtually no opportunity to talk to a Saudi woman, even if you did you'd see no more than her eyes, and possibly not even those.

Despite (or perhaps because of) their should-be-camouflaging attire, Iranian women are always eyeing you off. It's all shy smiles and seductive glances. While I was photographing the passing traffic in front of a mosque that evening, a woman, sitting behind her boyfriend on a motorcycle, tosses me a wink and a wave; later that evening three old ladies chorus 'hello' from their late-evening watermelon feast in an old city back alley.

Dinner tonight is at the Silk Road, another photogenic hotel in a renovated traditional old house, like the one I'm staying in. Once again the courtyard centres around a pool, the architecture is beautiful, the evening light glows, and the *badgir* rises up as a backdrop to one end.

Some of the guests and diners sit at tables, with some of the tables at knee height and others at a normal level. Others, like me, lounge back on wide, carpeted, sofa-like affairs, sitting cross-legged and sideways, leaning back against the armrest. When your meal is served it's arrayed in front of you, in the centre of the 'sofa'. If there are two of you, then you face each other. The sofa is wide enough to accommodate four.

I'm served some tea and sweets, but no food emerges from the kitchen until well after 9pm.

The Iranians clearly rival the Spanish when it comes to eating late. It's no problem because simply watching what's going on is a delight. There's a buzz of happy activity – families, individuals, a handful of tourists but mostly Iranians. Occasionally people climb upstairs for the view and we can see them silhouetted on the flat-topped roof. Lots of people smile over at me, stop to exchange a few words, enquire about my impressions of Iran or offer a 'welcome' if nothing more. These people are so energetic, so cheerful, so unlike what the media would have us believe about Iranians.

• • • •

I skipped the bus trip from Shiraz to Yazd, but I do opt for bus travel on the next leg to Esfahan. The bus is air-conditioned, comfortable (it even has an on-board toilet) and costs about US$3 for the 300-kilometre trip.

This single city alone could justify a trip to Iran, but it's hard to decide whether the prime attraction is the magnificent sweep of the Imam Square, with its perimeter of shopping arcades and its breathtaking blue-tiled mosques, or the gentle curve of the Zayandeh River with its multi-arched bridges and fringing parkland.

Five of the 11 bridges that span the river are elegant old affairs. One of my favourite photographs from the trip Maureen and I made across Asia in 1972 is of Maureen sitting on the river edge with the double-level Khaju Bridge in the background. She is in an outfit, quite respectable though it was, that would have got her instantly arrested by the Morality Police in 21st-century Iran.

I wander down one side of the river, pausing for tea in the middle-of-the-river teahouse built into the Chubi Bridge. Sipping tea and puffing a waterpipe in a teahouse is a favourite Esfahan activity. The Chubi Bridge teahouse is decorated with carpets, pictures and an eclectic collection of lamps and lights hanging from the arched ceiling. It's easy to see why it's reputed to be the most appealing in the city.

I sit in a window alcove where a tray of tea is instantly brought to me, equally quickly followed by the standard Q and As from the waiter.

'Where are you from?'

'Australia.'

'What is your name?'

'Tony.'

'My name is Mohammed. Do you like Iran?'

'Iran is wonderful, especially Esfahan.'

'Welcome.'

Mid-afternoon the teahouse is busy. The waiter quickly returns to my end of the bay with a waterpipe for the attractive young woman in the next alcove who, like me, is scribbling in a notebook.

An hour or so later, walking up the other side of the river, I make another tea stop in the island teahouse just downriver from the Si-o-Seh or Bridge of 33 Arches. The riverside parks are busy with people sitting on the grass and young couples strolling along the riverbank holding hands.

An old woman waves me over to the park bench where she is sitting with some friends. 'Do you speak English?' she asks. 'Come talk with us.'

Finally I walk back past my hotel to the main square for yet another pot of tea, this time in a teahouse perched beside the bazaar entrance gate at the north end of the square. A family asks me to pose with them in a photograph, standing on the teahouse balcony with the long sweep of the square as a backdrop.

As the sun drops lower and the temperature cools, the square is full of evening activity. Once again that Persian passion for spreading out a rug on any patch of grass and having a picnic comes into play. The French, with their equivalent passion for 'keep off the grass' signs, would totally disapprove.

The next day I start with the square, walking past the shops, dropping in to the Sheikh Lotfollah and Imam Mosques and exploring the Ali Qapu Palace. The 'square' is actually a long rectangle and cars are strictly restricted to the northern 20 per cent. The remainder is vehicle-free.

The Sheikh Lotfollah Mosque is a little jewel box, so intricate and detailed it's hard to believe it's a building, not something you can just pick up and carry away. There's the trademark Persian blue and turquoise tile-work, but it's also tiled in green-white-gold. In contrast the Imam Mosque is the whole damn Tiffany's. Big and slightly odd, the entrance forms the end of the square, facing straight down the plaza, but inside the building skews off to the right in order to face Mecca. The front is just a front.

On the balcony of the Ali Qapu Palace, with the square spread out below us, I meet a young Iranian-American couple. Hassan and Sanaz live in Los Angeles, a city with probably the biggest Iranian population in the USA. He left Iran when he was a child, before the revolution, and has never been back before. She left 18 years ago, after the revolution.

'I was expecting it to be much worse', Sanaz admits. 'I think it's actually improved since I left.'

'But everybody complains', Hassan adds. 'I was expecting some people to dislike the system, but everybody I speak to – taxi drivers, farmers, you name it – complains. In some ways they've just swapped a crown for a turban.

'Of course, people always want change. Last Thursday we went to Jaam-e Jam in North Tehran. It's a shopping centre, very popular with young people and on Thursday afternoon they come out to show off.'

I have this immediate vision of Yoyogi Park at Harajuku in the centre of Tokyo, where on Sundays the cos-play-zoku (the costume-play-tribe) appears.

'It's weird', ponders Hassan. 'Young guys with rings in their eyebrows and girls clearly pushing it as far as they can, with very tight and almost transparent manteaus, scarves falling off to show their hair, lots of make-up. I'd like to have taken some photographs, but they'd probably not want their sins recorded.'

I swap hotels, moving across the road from an economical backpacker place to the expensive, if not exactly luxurious, Abbasi Hotel, occupying an old caravanserai. Last time in Esfahan, over 30 years ago, the Abbasi was way out of my price range and I certainly wanted to try it this time.

After changing hotels I do a long walking tour from the Chehel Sotun Palace through to the Jameh Mosque, then back through the bazaar to the main square to make the requisite visit to some carpet shops, followed by a visit to the Hasht Behest Palace before jumping in a taxi to cross the river to visit the group of Armenian churches in the affluent Jolfa area with its elegant cafés and glossy shops. This quarter of the city is a reminder, like the Zoroastrian temples in Yazd, that the Islamic Republic is not exclusively Islamic. Once again it underlines how different Iran is from Saudi Arabia. Only the Mary Church in Jolfa is open so I'll have to come back tomorrow to visit the Vank Cathedral, but I stop in at a surprisingly edgy shopping centre with lots of hot fashions, make-up and music.

I've done so much running around I'm exhausted and it's heading towards sunset by the time I get back to the Imam Square. At the south end of the square the sun is down and the floodlit blue tiles of the huge Imam Mosque have an eye-catching glow. A carpet dealer intercepts me and after a short sales pitch switches to tour guide and suggests I should have another look at the mosque.

'If you have seen it in daylight, you will find it quite different now that night has fallen,' he suggests, 'and you can go in now for free. They don't charge tourists in the evening.'

Unfortunately a guard stops me entering.

'It's prayer time', he explains. 'You cannot go in.'

Instantly an animated discussion starts up among the men sitting around him. Within minutes he relents. 'They all say you must see the mosque by night', he explains. 'If you keep over to one side, you will not disturb anybody. Go ahead.'

They're right. The floodlit blaze of blue, turquoise, yellow and gold stands out with razor-cut clarity against the inky sky.

•   •   •   •

The next morning there's the shaking minarets to quake at, an amazing old pigeon-house sited in the middle of a traffic roundabout to see, and the extravagantly painted frescoes of the Vank Cathedral to admire before I head off to Kashan.

I have a car and driver again because there are some stops to make en route to Kashan. Today's major diversion is to Abyaneh. The old village's twisting lanes and mud architecture have brought it Unesco recognition, but not yet many tourists. If it was in some exotic corner of France or Spain, every other house would be a café or craft shop. Here the mosque is closed, there's one solitary little counter selling a handful of souvenirs, and there are no other shops, no place selling drinks, no restaurant.

Between the village and Kashan there's a brief encounter with that other Iran, the one that features in the press and TV much more often than beautiful hotels and friendly people.

146.

'It's a nuclear research centre', my driver explains as we pass anti-aircraft gun emplacements beside the road and half-buried buildings.

In Kashan the driver drops me off at my hotel, a mundane affair after my luxurious interlude in Esfahan and the beautiful old houses of Yazd, and I emerge to take a pre-dinner stroll. I only take a few steps before a Paykan swings in to the side of the road. A portly gentleman leaps – or would do, if his bulk hadn't prevented him – out of the car and grabs my arm. Ahmad Pourseyedi, my Kashan kidnapper, has me in his grip. Arguing is out of the question. I can put him off, but he is an irresistible object, impossible to simply reject.

'OK, we'll meet right here at 9am tomorrow', I finally agree. I am very reluctant to tell him which hotel I am at. 'If I don't turn up, then you know I can't make it,' I continue, 'but I'll definitely try to be here at 9am.'

My kidnapping postponed for 12 hours, I dine at the Delpazir Restaurant. It's become the restaurant in Kashan that all overseas visitors go to because it's run by Englishwoman Jane Modarresian and her Iranian partner. They still have the Persian restaurant they established in the London suburb of Mitcham, but they decided to move to Kashan because they thought it would be a better, safer environment for their three children, two boys and a girl. Sounds remarkable? Well, I heard precisely the same story from an American woman and her Iranian husband when I met them in Tehran.

When the American-Iranian couple's son, born in the USA and raised there for the first eight years of his life, returned to the States 10 years later, he travelled around the country, stayed with relations, worked in various odd jobs. And then returned to Iran, because he preferred it.

Coming out of my hotel in the morning, Ahmad's trusty Paykan is parked right outside. He'd clearly deduced I must have been staying close to where he'd found me the previous evening.

'Ahmad, you're right on time', I announce.

'Yes,' he agrees, 'but how do you know my name? I didn't tell you my name last night.'

'You're Ahmad Pourseyedi', I counter. 'Oh, I have ways of knowing these things.'

At our morning reunion I have managed to provide him with a puzzle that would intrigue him for our whole time together. Completely by accident I'd bumped into the 'charming old rogue' recommended in my guidebook as the town's best guide and for the next 24 hours he does charm me.

Everyone we meet is either Ahmad's friend or relation and all of them are expected to let me in at half price. Even the tollbooth operator at the end of a stretch of freeway is an acquaintance who can be persuaded to drop the price. By the end of the day I've even been round to his house, where his wife brings us lunch while we take a break during the midday heat. Lunch over, we stretch out on the Persian-carpeted floor for an afternoon nap before we recommence our sightseeing.

We start with the Tappeh-ye Seyalk archaeological site where, naturally, Ahmad is friends with the resident archaeologist Abbar Etemad Fini, busily reconstructing a pot, just as you'd expect an archaeologist to be doing at a site noted for its pottery finds. Further along the road is the Fin Garden with ponds, pools, springs and all the other attributes of the Persian view of paradise. This was also the place where the 19th-century Iranian hero Amir Kabir (the former chancellor of Persia and reformist; his name pops up all over the country) was treacherously murdered. He died in the garden's bathhouse, which has a waxworks-style recreation of the event. Allowed to choose how he would die, he opted to slash his wrists although the tableau seems to show him sitting back calmly while the villain is about to plunge the knife into his wrist.

Our circuit of the city stops by the remnants of the city walls and drops into a number of mosques, but it's Kashan's superb collection of old houses that deserves the most attention. Before and after photographs in a number of the houses illustrate just how much work has gone into the restorations. In one house I bump into a big extended family, several members of which speak excellent English.

'It must be very difficult to restore a place like this', suggests the daughter who is perhaps 12 years old, still sporting braces on her teeth. 'They have so little to work from, just some of these old pictures.'

Her father is more concerned about the outside world's view of Iran than Kashan's architectural restoration problems. If the Western world's media isn't fretting about the latest wild pronouncements from President Mahmoud Ahmadinejad, there's always a threatening bearded Ayatollah in the background and the underlying concern that all that research to peacefully produce electricity from nuclear power may really be just another step towards joining North Korea, Pakistan, Israel, India and all those countries with atomic Weapons of Mass Destruction.

'How can we give people a better view of Iran?' he asks. 'When people visit they realise this is not a bad place', he reflects. 'I can't understand why they have these ideas about us.'

Well, carrying on about 'death to America' and preserving all those paintings around the walls of the old American embassy building in Tehran doesn't help, but my impression is that so much of this is just play-acting. Wander through any park full of picnicking Persians, endure another barrage of 'welcomes' and accept another glass or two of tea, and you begin to realise that these are not the rabid extremists some segments of the Western media would have us believe.

As we're leaving the house the matriarch of the group asks if I'd like to join them on their tour of the town. There's space in one of their cars, but I explain that I already have a guide and car.

There's a final stop before Ahmad leaves me to my own devices for the evening. Wandering around the old bazaar he turns down a derelict alley and leads me through an anonymous door into a beautiful old caravanserai. It's neglected and dilapidated, but with its towering multi-domed ceiling over an octagonal pool (with real water!) and typical Persian tile work, it could be exquisite. I can see it as a restaurant, wonderfully revived with tables around the pool. My mind zips back to a poolside lunch (with rather nice white wine) in a Beverley Hills hotel a few months earlier.

There are more encounters with Iranian hospitality come dinnertime in Khan-e Tabatabei. Built in 1834 for a wealthy carpet merchant, it's one of the houses I visited earlier in the day. To get there I jump in a share taxi heading in more or less the right direction. A local would make sure it's going exactly where he wants, but I often just hop aboard anything heading the right way and if it's not going right there, well they're not expensive and I can easily take another one. This one stops part way towards the restaurant and lets all the other passengers out. The driver then ascertains exactly where I'm going and takes me straight there without any suggestions about increasing the standard 5000-rial (60-cent) fare.

• • • •

The next morning Ahmad is waiting outside the hotel to take me on one final excursion to some sites outside the city. Finally my Kashan kidnapper drops me off at the bus station, but only after checking exactly what time my bus will depart for Tehran. I've enjoyed cruising around Kashan in Ahmad's Paykan and he seems genuinely sorry to see me go. He's still scratching his head, wondering how on earth I knew his name.

'Lizard city', announces the young man sitting next to me as the bus rolls through Qom, Iran's religious centre.

The film *Marmoulak* (*The Lizard*, 2004) has been a controversial box-office hit and, almost inevitably, has ended up being banned. Reza Marmoulak is in jail for his exploits as a petty thief able to climb buildings with lizard-like agility. He escapes from a spell in hospital by stealing a mullah's robes and then ends up in a small village where he's mistaken as the village mosque's new mullah. He soon becomes a major hit with his off-the-top-of-his-head advice and Koranic interpretations. Of course, the mullahs began to get really pissed off when people began to refer to them as lizards, so it was almost inevitable that the film was proscribed.

'Mullahs are no good,' my seat companion insists, swirling his hand vertically round his head to indicate their turban and then his finger horizontally beside his head: 'they're nuts.'

Mullahs are famed for curious 'what the Koran would say' elucidations. Khomeini himself was once asked for a ruling on what should happen to a chicken if a man had sex with it. Could the chicken violator then barbecue the buggered bird? No, thundered Khomeini. Certainly not. Nor could his family. Or their neighbours.

How about somebody who lived two doors away? Well, that was OK. Fried fornicated fowl is all right further down the street. Ditto for poached poked poultry?

•　•　•　•

Back in Tehran the bus stops at the frenetic Southern Bus Station and I head out for another round with the city's madhouse traffic. On the bus I'd been talking to Paul and Carolyn, the first American travellers I've met who are not of Iranian descent. They've had no problems exploring Iran, although Carolyn has had to grapple with the dress question.

'I don't think a Western visitor is necessarily respected for going the whole [chador] way', she concludes. 'I think we probably get more kudos for being locally "correct", but stylish at the same time.' I've heard similar conclusions from other travellers, male and female, elsewhere in the region.

'In the back blocks of Afghanistan, wearing local clothing can help to fit in,' suggested one intrepid visitor I met in that country, 'but wearing exactly the same thing in Kabul can have precisely the opposite effect.

It either looks like you're trying too hard or suggests that you're an American spy. In Kabul I always wear inconspicuous Western attire.'

There's a curious artificiality about the dress question. Watching a TV soap in a hotel lobby a few days before, I'd pondered the living room scenes, the young wife chatting with her husband with her hair still discreetly covered by a scarf. Of course in real life – not Iranian TV soap-opera life – she'd have discarded the scarf the instant she stepped inside.

I emerge from the bus station, check my guidebook and work out that I need to cross to the other side of the road to hail a taxi heading in the right direction. Halfway across the highway I'm hit, not by a car, bus or motorcycle, but once again by the realisation that Iran can be a surprisingly sophisticated country, well aware of the outside world and how they connect to it.

'Hey, Lonely Planet!' yells the cop directing the traffic and simultaneously pointing at my open guidebook. 'Which way you going, man?'

· · · ·

'That was a golden era', Mohamad, a tourist guide I'd encountered in the stunningly attractive restaurant housed in the old Hammam-e Vakil in Shiraz, responded when I told him I'd driven through Iran so many years earlier, during the Shah's era. 'There were problems, but we had so much more freedom in those days.'

'Not quite', I thought, thinking of the dreaded Savak, the Shah's secret police, who were every bit as capable of exacting terrible revenge on the regime's opponents as the religious police are today.

'After every revolution there are winners and losers', muses Mansoor, back in Tehran. 'The Shah thought Iran ended at the boundaries of Tehran. He completely neglected the country and the villages. People outside Tehran are much better off than in the Shah's era.

'Look out on the street', he indicates, pointing at the traffic turmoil that boils all around us. As usual the mayhem would be a gold-medal contender in any 'world's worst traffic' Olympiad.

'You see plenty of women driving, don't you? That wouldn't have been true in the Shah's era.'

Not only do Iranian women drive, but in a country where bad driving is a given they sometimes seem to drive particularly badly. As if in confirmation, a woman clips the back of the car in front of us as she pushes in to the roundabout turmoil. Not looking in your mirrors is standard procedure in Iran, but how can you see what's going on when you have a scarf billowing around your face?

'Recent elections may have been a disaster for the progressives, but look what's happened since', Mansoor continues. 'Legislation either ended up in deadlock or if it got passed the clergy immediately vetoed it. Now the conservatives control the parliament, but things are actually happening. They're even letting through legislation that they would have barred if the progressives had passed it.

'And it's quite true they constantly shut down newspapers,' he says, as the traffic surges past a newsstand, 'but the staff walk out the door, move three buildings down the street and start another newspaper.'

It certainly seems credible. I'd counted 23 broadsheet newspapers, 14 tabloids and 12 sports papers at a newsstand that morning. At less than 20 cents each I'd usually buy all three English-language papers and it seemed to take the average Iranian newsstand browser half an hour just to decide which paper to buy. I'm still wondering what an Iranian page-three girl would look like in the local tabloids? Lifting a chador for a glimpse of ankle?

Omid, a friend of Mansoor's, arrives soon after we've sat down in Mansoor's apartment and produces a letter, which is handed around the room.

153.

'What do you think it means?' he asks.

It's pretty clear to me what it means and there are nods of agreement around the room when I give my interpretation.

'Well, it's written in the sort of confusing legalistic language you'd expect from any immigration department', I start. 'Essentially it seems to say that your immigration status is OK and will not be changed. You can stay as long as you like, but if you ever leave the country there is no guarantee that you will be let back in and they don't plan to change that.

'So you're stuck in the US,' I presume, 'which is where I get confused, because you're not in the US, you're here in Tehran.'

'Yeah, yeah, I know', Omid responds. 'I came back to İran eight years ago. I'm not even planning to go back to the US at the moment. I'd just like to be able to return if I change my mind.'

'Yet US immigration still thinks you're there?' I query.

'Of course', he agrees. 'I always write to them from my friend's address so they think I'm still living there.'

'Didn't they notice when you left?' I ask.

'Nah,' Omid concludes, 'I just crossed the border into Canada. Nobody noticed.'

• • • •

I've had a great time in Iran. I've had a lot of interesting encounters and met a lot of people quite apart from the amazing places I've seen. Repeatedly I've been reminded that Iran today stands with millennia of culture, education and sophistication as a background. There have been more translations of German philosopher Immanuel Kant into Persian than any other language in the last decade, according to the *New Republic*. Iranians are people with opinions and broad-minded attitudes, irrespective of what their fundamentalist religious leaders might insist.

'We're not like Pakistan' is a statement I've heard more than once from Iranians. So much of Iran is window-dressing and appearances, whether it's waving fists at America or even segregating the sexes. The religious rule-makers may insist on it and there's no denying that gender inequality is a big factor, but this is not Saudi Arabia.

On the flight out of Tehran I'm suddenly back in the worst of the Arab world. Across the aisle is a Saudi couple, their two young children sitting a row in front. The couple are both traditionally attired; she's in full-covered-face mode. So how do you eat when your head's in a bag? You take food in one hand, grab your face covering in the other to pull it above your mouth, pop the food in and pull the covering back down. Awkward and ridiculous looking? Absolutely.

IRAQ

TURKEY

Zakho○ ○Amadiya
Dohuk○
Nineveh○ ○Khorsabad
○Mosul
Nimrud○ ○Arbil
Kurdistan
Region
Kirkuk○ ○Sulaymaniyah
Halabja○○ Penjuen
(Penjwin)

SYRIA

IRAN

Fallujah○ ★ **BAGHDAD**

JORDAN

Babylon○

Ur○

Basra○

SAUDI
ARABIA

THE GULF

KUWAIT

We've spent over an hour wandering from office to office in the pouring rain. At one, Husni Tutug reluctantly slips a banknote into the pages of my passport before he hands it over the counter. It seems to work. The passport comes back within minutes with a stamp inside. I'm finally out of Turkey. We drive over the bridge and stop in a car park just beyond the sign announcing 'Welcome to Iraq'.

• • • •

I had several bites at Iraqi tourism before I finally crossed the border in 2006.

Way back in 1989 Iraq ghosted on to my guidebook radar screen. Getting into Iran or Iraq had been all but impossible when the two countries were slugging it out in what correctly could be defined as Gulf War I. The Kuwait Gulf War is really Gulf War II and the current get-rid-of-Saddam disaster is Gulf War III. When the eight-year Iraq-Iran slaughter, in many ways a reprise of the worst trench-warfare-stalemate years of World War I, finally ground to a halt, intrepid travellers started looking at these two fascinating countries again.

There were plenty of reasons to be interested. Iran had the great ancient city of Persepolis (built by Darius the Great from 518 BC and sacked by Alexander the Great in 330 BC) and the exquisite beauties of cities like Esfahan. Iraq had Babylon, Nineveh, Nimrud and Ur. Who wouldn't want to go to either country? Back in the 1970s getting into Iran was fairly straightforward. Iraq was much more difficult, but post–Gulf War I the doors to the Islamic Republic of Iran remained firmly shut. So intrepid travellers began to pay more attention to Iraq and for a brief spell at Lonely Planet we began to ponder the economics of an Iraq guidebook.

In 1989 we sent Rosemary Hall, an intrepid English travel writer, off to Iraq to investigate its tourism possibilities. Her research provided the Iraq chapter of our West Asia guidebook and we began to think about expanding it into a stand-alone Iraq guidebook. Then in 1990 Iraq invaded Kuwait, leading to Gulf War II in 1991, and all ideas of Iraq travel went into the freezer.

Meanwhile I had another Iraq tourism taster – many miles away from Iraq.

In October 1991 at the Frankfurt Book Fair, Jens Peters, Stefan Loose and Renate Loose had been regaling me with stories of life in Berlin when the Wall came down.

'We were just about to have dinner,' recalled Stefan, 'and Misha called out from the living room, "Mum! Dad! People are crossing the Wall".'

'We didn't believe him, even though there had been so much change in the East in recent weeks, but when we saw what was happening we immediately decided to hold dinner and go straight to the Wall.'

The Looses live in Kreuzberg, only a stone's throw from the Wall, and

East Berlin.

'We didn't get back home until the next day', continued Renate.

They went on to tell me of the passion with which they attacked the

Wall. 'For months you could not find a hammer or chisel in Berlin', Jens said. 'You could tell which way the Wall was by the constant chipping noise.'

'Amazing,' I said for the nth time. 'I really must visit Berlin one day.'

'No, not one day', they replied in unison. 'Right now. The Wall hasn't been down for two years yet. Today it's still east and west, but every day the differences are fading. If you want a taste of what East and West Berlin used to be like, you've got to come right now.'

So a week later I was sleeping on the couch in the Looses' Kreuzberg apartment and, like any serious East Berlin visitor, I made the pilgrimage to the Pergamon Museum where, like any Pergamon visitor, I was blown away by the Ishtar Gate, which had been spirited away from Babylon by German archaeologists.

• • • •

Yet I still didn't get to Iraq. A handful of strictly policed Iraq tours took place, but I was waiting for real travel, independent travel, to become possible. With the new century more Iraq comments and thoughts ghosted past. Looking out over the glittering lights of Dubai from the sky-high bar of the Emirates Towers Hotel one night in 2002, I found myself sitting next to a cheerful South African rugby enthusiast. He'd recently visited Iraq, partly on business, but much more, I thought, out of interest. And he'd found it fascinating. He raved about its attractions, the Biblical sites, the age-old history.

Only a few weeks later, talking with Eugene Mall, a German expat working in Japan and an inveterate traveller, we kicked around the concern that if we didn't get there soon there might not be an Iraq to visit.

'I really fear the Americans will invade Iraq,' he explained, 'and if they blunder in, everything could be destroyed. I've always wanted to see Iraq – perhaps I should go there right now, before it's too late.'

159.

In early 2002 the approaching war seemed inevitable even though it was still a year away. Somehow we couldn't believe Bush would be crazy enough and somehow it seemed he couldn't resist. In London I had dinner with Charlotte Hindle, Lonely Planet's UK manager for many years, Simon Calder, her husband who also happens to be the travel editor of the *Independent*, and Jonathan Glancey, a writer for the *Guardian*. Jonathan was convinced Bush and Blair would soon launch their war and was working overtime to get a visa to get into Iraq before it was wrecked.

A couple of months later Jonathan did get there and wrote of visiting the ancient Sumerian capital of Ur, near Nasiriyya, 375 kilometres southeast of Baghdad. A year later, when Iraq had been comprehensively shocked and awed, and before the conquerors had settled in for their own long-term period of being horrified and harried, Jonathan pointed out that air attacks on the unfortunate Iraqis were nothing new.

Like many countries in the region, Iraq was a fall-out from the collapse of the Ottoman Empire. The Ottomans had kicked off in the late 1200s, established themselves in Constantinople (today's Istanbul) in 1453, and reached their peak with Sultan Süleyman the Magnificent knocking at the gates of Vienna in 1529. By the time of his death in 1566 the Ottoman Empire incorporated most of the modern Middle East, the North African coast all the way to Morocco, the Balkans and a healthy slice of Eastern Europe.

From there it was steadily downhill, culminating with choosing the wrong side in World War I. Even the Turkish heartland of the old empire might have disappeared if Mustafa Kemal, aka Ataturk, had not rallied the disheartened Turks and thrown out the invading Greeks during the Turkish War of Independence from 1920 to 1922.

Other fragments of the Ottoman Empire either found their own independence or traded one colonising power for another. Which was precisely what happened to Iraq in 1920 when Britain grabbed its slice of the old empire, an area encompassing everything from the

AFGHANISTAN

(**1.**) → TONY IN FRONT OF THE MINARET OF JAM
(**2.**) → FEEDING THE FAMOUS WHITE PIGEONS AT THE SHRINE
OF HAZRAT ALI (**3.**) → THE EMPTY NICHE OF AN ANCIENT
BUDDHA AT BAMIYAN, DESTROYED BY THE TALIBAN IN 2001
(**4.**) → POSTERS FOR SALE, MANY OF NORTHERN ALLIANCE
HERO AHMAD SHAH MASSOUD

(**5.**) → AN UGLY ASSORTMENT OF LAND MINES
(**6.**) → THE JAMSHADY BROTHERS RUN A
TRAVEL AND TOURISM BUSINESS (**7.**) → ANOTHER
TANK ABANDONED BY THE ROADSIDE (**8.**) → TONY
AND THE ELDEST JAMSHADY, MOBIN, AT THE
SHRINE OF HAZRAT ALI

ALBANIA

(**1.**) → A STATUE OF NATIONAL HERO SKANDERBEG
STANDS IN THE CENTRE OF TIRANA (**2.**) → GREAT VIEWS
AT A RESTAURANT ON THE TOP OF ARDENICA HILL
(**3.**) → A BUNKER LOOKS OUT TO SEA AT JAL BEACH
(**4.**) → THE RUINED AGORA OF THE ANCIENT GREEK
AND ROMAN CITY OF APOLLONIA

(**5.**) → A DETAIL OF THE HUGE MOSAIC MURAL COVERING THE FAÇADE OF TIRANA'S NATIONAL MUSEUM OF HISTORY (**6.**) → KRUJA'S SKANDERBEG MUSEUM, BUILT IN THE TOWN'S 6TH-CENTURY CASTLE (**7.**) → A HOXHA BUNKER MAKES A COSY BAR IN THE SEASIDE BUNKERI RESTAURANT, DURRËS (**8.**) → THE FORMER ENVER HOXHA MUSEUM, AKA 'THE PYRAMID', IN TIRANA

BURMA (MYANMAR)

(**1.**) → MONKS PLAY VOLLEYBALL IN FRONT OF THE SHWE INN THAIN PAGODA, IN INDEIN AT INLE LAKE (**2.**) → THE MOUSTACHE BROTHERS, TRADITIONAL *A-NYEINT PWE* (A BLEND OF DANCES, MUSIC AND SLAPSTICK) PERFORMERS (**3.**) → THE STRAND HOTEL IN YANGON (**4.**) → THE SHWEMYETMAN PAYA'S BESPECTACLED BUDDHA

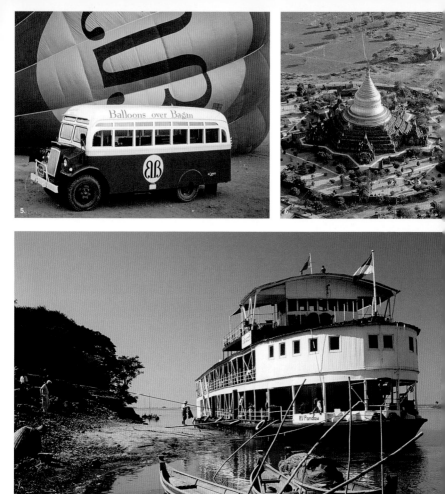

(**5.**) → THE 'BALLOONS OVER BAGAN' COMPANY'S BUS
(**6.**) → THE GILDED SPIRE OF THE DHAMMAYAZIKA
PAYA STUPA (**7.**) → THE RV *PANDAW*, MOORED ON
THE AYEYARWADY RIVER (**8.**) → THE BRIDGE TO
CONNECT THE 'FLOATING VILLAGE' OF MAING
THAUK WITH ITS 'LAND VILLAGE'

CUBA

(**1.**) → CHE SOUVENIRS OUTNUMBER EVERY OTHER
CUBAN MEMENTO (**2.**) → ONE OF THE MANY
'HOMELAND OR DEATH' BILLBOARDS ON THE *AUTOPISTA*
(**3.**) → AN AMERICAN CAR – *DE RIGUEUR* IN HAVANA
(**4.**) → AN ARTISTIC 'EXPLOSION' MARKS WHERE CHE'S
REBELS CUT THE TRAIN LINE INTO SANTA CLARA

IRAN

(**1.**) → TONY WITH HIS KASHAN TOUR GUIDE, AHMAD
POURSEYEDI (**2.**) → THE BEAUTIFUL COURTYARD RESTAURANT
AT THE SILK ROAD HOTEL (**3.**) → BAS-RELIEFS ON THE
APADANA STAIRWAY IN THE PALACE OF DARIUS, PERSEPOLIS
(**4.**) → THE 1972 PHOTO OF MAUREEN WHEELER IN FRONT OF
THE KHAJU BRIDGE

IRAQ

(**1.**) → TWO *PESHMERGA* SOLDIERS POSE FOR A PHOTO ON TONY'S ARRIVAL IN IRAQ (**2.**) → THE HISTORIC DELAL BRIDGE IN ZAKHO (**3.**) → SIPPING TEA BESIDE THE BOSPHORUS IN THE ANCIENT KADIKÖY DISTRICT, ISTANBUL (TURKEY) (**4.**) → THE ARBIL CITADEL'S HUGE IBN AL-MISTAWFI STATUE

(**5.**) → ONE OF DOHUK'S PLETHORA
OF APPEALING JUICE STANDS (**6.**) → A GENEROUS
LUNCH WITH DRIVER ADRIS ON THE WAY TO ARBIL
(**7.**) → SUPERSIZED BUSTS OF KURDISH HEROES
LINE THE PATHS IN A SULAYMANIYAH PARK (**8.**) → THE
CITADEL OF ARBIL TOWERS ABOVE THE TOWN CENTRE

LIBYA

(**1.**) → STORAGE CHAMBERS IN THE INTERIOR WALL OF KABAW'S *QASR* (FORTIFIED GRANARY) (**2.**) → A CAMEL RIDES IN THE BACK OF A PICK-UP TRUCK, EN ROUTE TO FEZZAN (**3.**) → A TYPICAL GADDAFI BILLBOARD (**4.**) → SCOPING OUT A ROUTE THROUGH THE UBARI SAND SEA, FEZZAN

(**5.**) → A BARBERSHOP ADVERTISES AFRICAN HAIRSTYLES IN TRIPOLI'S MEDINA (**6.**) → SCHOOLCHILDREN PUT ON AN IMPROMPTU PERFORMANCE AT LEPTIS MAGNA (**7.**) → A SUPERB PREHISTORIC ROCK CARVING OF A GIRAFFE, WADI METHKANDOUSH (**8.**) → TRAVELLERS ENJOY THE VIEW FROM THE BALCONY SEATS OF LEPTIS MAGNA'S AMPHITHEATRE

NORTH KOREA

(**1.**) → PYONGYANG-BOUND – TONY OUTSIDE A SLEEPER CARRIAGE (**2.**) → A GREAT BILLBOARD OF KIM IL-SUNG, WITH KIM JONG-IL AND TWO GRATEFUL FARMERS
(**3.**) → FROZEN LAKE CHON, IN THE CRATER OF MT PAEKDU, STRADDLES THE NORTH KOREA–CHINA BORDER (**4.**) → THE CHARMING AND TINY MISS LEE, OUR TOUR GUIDE AT THE PAEKDU SECRET CAMP

(**5.**) → THE IMPOSING DEMILITARIZED ZONE BUILDINGS
(**6.**) → A VISIT TO THE 20-METRE-HIGH MANSUDAE
STATUE OF KIM IL-SUNG IS OBLIGATORY
FOR VISITORS (**7.**) → THE DANCING ARMY PERFORM
DURING PYONGYANG'S ARIRANG MASS GAMES
(**8.**) → TONY'S NORTH KOREA TOUR GROUP STRIKE
A CHEERFUL POSE

SAUDI ARABIA

(**1.**) → FAISALIAH TOWER – DESIGNED BY UK ARCHITECT
SIR NORMAN FOSTER AND BUILT BY THE
BIN LADEN GROUP (**2.**) → THE RESTORED HEJAZ
RAILWAY AT MADAIN SALEH, SAUDI ARABIA'S PETRA
(**3.**) → THE *DIWAN* (MEETING ROOM) OF MADAIN SALEH
(**4.**) → TONY WITH SAEED JUMAAN, HIS NAJRAN GUIDE

(**5.**) → A DOOR IN MASMAK FORTRESS, WITH THE FAMOUS
BROKEN SPEARHEAD EMBEDDED IN IT (**6.**) → NAJRAN'S
FAIRYTALE CASTLE, IN THE MIDDLE OF THE *SOUQ* (MARKET)
(**7.**) → MASMAK FORTRESS, RIYADH, BUILT AROUND 1865
(**8.**) → THE NATIONAL MUSEUM OF RIYADH

old Mesopotamia – the Greek term meaning 'between two rivers' and defining the ancient Sumerian region between the Tigris and Euphrates Rivers – to the mountainous Kurdistan area of the north.

The Iraqis, a mishmash of Arabs, Kurds and Assyrians following both the Shiite and Sunni divisions of Islam, quickly revolted against British rule and as a result found themselves facing some aerial shock and awe, 80 years ahead of the repeat performance in 2003. Iraq became an aerial-bombardment testing ground for Arthur Harris, the RAF squadron leader who two decades later would oversee the destruction of the German cities of Hamburg and Dresden in massive raids, with death tolls sometimes said to rival Hiroshima or Nagasaki. In Iraq in the 1920s Harris reported that 'within 45 minutes a full-sized village can be practically wiped out, and a third of its inhabitants killed or injured, by four or five machines which offer them no real target, no opportunity for glory as warriors, no effective means of escape'.

While the RAF was getting Iraq under control from above, the British army was also showing how to do things at ground level. Saddam Hussein's famous gas attack on the Kurds at Halabja in 1988 was not a first. The British had tried out gas on Iraqi rebels in 1920 'with excellent moral effect'.

· · · ·

The US assumption seemed to be that the Iraq choice was black and white, black being Saddam of course, white being democracy. Preferably a democracy just like America's – that is, not the sort of democracy you find next door in Iran or the sort of democracy the Palestinians would opt for a few years later.

In fact this was never a coin toss with the odds heavily weighed in favour of heads (democracy) over tails (Saddam). It was much more like tossing a pack of cards up in the air then picking out the ones that landed face up and tossing again. There were clearly multiple alternative end-games to the pre-liberation situation, some of them even less pleasant than what was started with.

First, of course, there was straight back to the status quo, black followed by black. Until his death sentence actually resulted in Saddam dangling from the gallows we could have ended up with Saddam's Iraq Version 2. All we had to do was bust Saddam out of jail and the statue makers could be melting the metal for another round of heroic images. There's still the possibility of black followed by another shade of black – another Saddam-style dictator could end up at the top of the heap after all the shooting and voting finishes.

Or we could end up with an Iran-style theocracy, ranging all the way from something fairly democratic (but with Islamic state trimmings) to a real mullah-run operation that would, presumably, be not at all fond of the Great Satan and all it stands for.

Then there's the Arab tribal option, a country run by the biggest sheikh around (Saudi style) or with power shared between a bunch of them (like the United Arab Emirates). There's nothing particularly democratic about this option, but the end result could vary all the way from the Saudi end of the spectrum (greedy rulers who turn a blind eye to all sorts of things so long as they stay in control of the purse strings) through to UAE pragmatism.

Then there's the straightforward chaos option. Iraq could fragment into a Middle East Balkans with the Kurds hiving off their northern enclave, to the considerable displeasure of Turkey and Iran, neighbouring states with big Kurd minorities. Meanwhile the Shiites (backed by Iran) could be slugging it out with the Sunnis. Presumably part or all of a chaotic Iraq could be the new Afghanistan, home for whoever needs a nicely secluded base from which to operate.

Why was installing democracy in Iraq so important anyway? Lack of anything like democracy has never endangered Saudi Arabia's most favoured status. And back in 1953, when the Iranians looked like opting for the wrong sort of democracy, a democracy that would hurt Western oil interests, democracy was quickly given the boot and a friendly-to-Western-interests dictator, the Shah, installed on the throne.

• • • •

Once the shock and awe phase was over and George W made his 'Mission Accomplished' visit to an aircraft carrier off the California coast, dressed up military fashion so he looked like he'd done it all himself, people started to turn up in Baghdad. Virgin was talking about soon starting London–Baghdad flights and the Thorn Tree, Lonely Planet's travellers' chat area on the website, was full of discussions about how much a seat in a car should cost from Amman in Jordan to Baghdad and which hotel to go to in search of that Baghdad-bound taxi. Even 'Is it safe for solo women travellers?' was a topic of discussion for the next few months.

'Kirkuk and Mosul look quite good', reported Peshmarga, and 'Things are fine in most areas (be careful around Fallujah, Saddam City etc)', said Vaughn, both on 11 June 2003. The next day Scott Filtenborg was fretting about backpackers 'who couldn't tell the difference between Bangkok and Baghdad' and suggesting it would be better to 'wait till things settle' even if it was 'a year or more'. That same day ransome22 suggested that 'If you're a woman, I would just suggest covering your hair to make you look less Western.'

If you couldn't get to Iraq itself, where to track down traces of Iraq in other countries was another topic of conversation at that time. Of course, the Pergamon Museum's collection in Berlin topped most lists, followed by the Louvre's collection of Assyrian material from Khorsabad. Or there were the Nineveh and Nimrud collections in the British Museum and the sculptures from Ur at the University Museum in Philadelphia.

Very soon, however, Thorn Tree discussions of 'how to do Iraq' tapered off and dried up, because it was very clear nobody was going to be doing Iraq unless they had a death wish. Through 2004 the situation steadily

163.

worsened. In a December 2004 interview *Time* magazine's Baghdad bureau chief, Michael Ware, discussing the Fallujah attack, described Iraq as an 'absolute disaster' and underlined the obvious fact that far from containing terrorism the ill-thought-out invasion was creating brand new terrorists like an assembly line. If the Soviet invasion of Afghanistan had inspired one generation of Jihad, then this crazy misadventure was the follow up, he figured.

Recruits who last the distance go through four stages, said one book I read. In the first stage they think, 'The war is proceeding on a normal course.' If only there were more men, the problems could be solved. A few months later it's, 'Since we've already gotten ourselves in this jam, we should get the fighting over with as quickly as possible.' Which again means add more men. Then it's the realisation that 'Something is desperately wrong here. What a mess!' And finally: 'We'd be wise to get the hell out of here – and the sooner the better.'

Of course history repeats itself, or our leaders don't learn from it, for that neat little four-step analysis was not written about the Iraq debacle at all. Vietnam? No, not that one either. It's from *The Hidden War* by Russian journalist Artyom Borovik, an account of the Soviet Union's disastrous intervention in Afghanistan. Like Vietnam, the USSR's Afghanistan adventure ended up with ignominious withdrawal, which is how most unbiased observers believe the Iraq catastrophe will also conclude.

● ● ● ●

In early 2006 events in Iraq, already going steadily downhill, take a distinct turn for the worse. There's talk of the mess descending into all-out civil war with the USA standing to one side, unable to do anything. So I decide it's time to go there.

Not to central and southern Iraq – Nineveh, Nimrud, Babylon, Ur and all those other ancient centres are going to have to wait, as is Baghdad.

There is no way I am going to see Iraq properly in the foreseeable future, so I'll settle for seeing Iraq improperly – I'll just have a taste of the accessible part of Iraq. Most of the country may be a disaster, but there's one part of the country that is accessible and fairly safe: Kurdistan.

I'm going to a tourism conference in Washington, DC. If I make a nice little transit of northern Iraq, entering from Turkey and exiting to Iran, I can arrive in Washington direct from two of the three Axes of Evil. I fly to Istanbul from Singapore and Dubai early one morning and soon get into the swing of Turkey by taking a ferry across the Sea of Marmara at the mouth of the Bosphorus to Kadıköy, the commuter seaport on Istanbul's Asian side. My next flight doesn't leave from Istanbul's secondary airport, named after Sabina Gökçen, the Turkish air force's first female combat pilot, until mid-afternoon, so I have plenty of time to sip a leisurely glass of tea at a harbourside café and watch the world go by. I'm flying to Diyarbakir, in the heart of Turkey's Kurdish region and well over in the eastern part of the country.

Stepping out of Diyarbakir's modern little airport terminal late that afternoon, I'm greeted with a chorus from the waiting crowd of taxi drivers: 'Iraq, Iraq, you want to go to Iraq?' they ask in unison.

'Well, yes, but not tonight', I explain. All I want to do tonight is find a hotel and get some sleep.

'Don't mention Kurdistan', a Kurd I met in London had advised me. 'You want to go to Iraq. As far as the Turks are concerned there is no such place as Kurdistan.'

I dump my bag in the Balkar Otel and set off to explore the town, quickly deciding that Diyarbakir is not likely to hit my favourite towns list. The town has an impressive six-kilometre city wall dating from the Byzantine era, 1500 years ago, but the wall itself is dark and foreboding and everything about the city is either modern and tatty, like a run-down Communist-era Soviet centre, or old and decidedly decrepit. There's also a lot of broken glass around and some very attentive-looking

165.

military checkpoints.

Later I discover there were clashes between the local Kurdish population and the Turkish security forces just a few days previously.

By the time I've strolled across the old town to look at a hotel converted from an ancient caravanserai, the weather is shifting from overcast and threatening to drizzling and then to bucketing down. Of course, I'm also pretty jet-lagged after my overnight flight from Singapore, so I grab some food, duck into an internet café to get out of the rain, and then head back to the hotel. I've just got off to sleep when the front desk phones to ask me to come downstairs to talk with my driver. It turns out he's handed the job on to someone else, Husni Tutug.

Next morning Husni is there and ready to go at 7am. We travel via Mardin and Midyat (with an impressive collection of Syrian churches), and pause to look at the Morgabriel Monastery before stopping for lunch at Silopi, just before the border. For eight solid kilometres before Silopi a nose-to-tail line of trucks waits to cross the border into Iraq. There's some paperwork to complete in Silopi, which I wouldn't have known about, but I've been wondering why it's necessary to take a driver right across the border rather than just get dropped there. I'm about to find out.

Syria's directly across the river from the road for the next few kilometres, but the truck line-up continues for another 10 kilometres and now it's often two, three or even four trucks wide. There must be thousands of them. With most of them it's impossible to tell what they're transporting, but there are transporters full of new cars and pick-up trucks, and trucks laden with construction equipment, pipelines, reels of wire and bags of cement. Clearly there's a lot of building work going on across the border.

What I don't see – and I know I'm going to be asked about this – are endless rows of trucks carrying Australian wheat. It was a huge scandal in Australia when it was discovered that the AWB (the Australian Wheat Board) funnelled AU$300 million into Saddam's pockets to ensure Iraq bought its wheat from Australia rather than Canada, the USA or some other supplier. It was a king-size bribe and the politicians danced the 'didn't happen on my shift' tango overtime. It prompted a storm of cartoons and jokes in the Australian press and provided a neat explanation for why the Australian government was so easily convinced about those fictitious Weapons of Mass Destruction (WMDs): they thought they'd paid for them.

The border is a chaotic, muddy mess and it's raining solidly again. Husni seems to know exactly which door to head for, which window to bang on, which queue to barge to the front of and exactly whom to bribe. I spot him slipping a note into my passport before he hands it over to one official. Nevertheless it takes over an hour of zigzagging from one ramshackle building to another before we make the short drive across the bridge that conveys us into Iraq.

Arriving in Iraq is like a doorway to heaven. Suddenly I'm sitting in a clean, dry, mud-free waiting room being served glasses of tea while we wait for the passports to be processed – Husni's too. He has to exit Turkey, enter Iraq and then repeat the process in the opposite direction to get me through. The officials decide to put me through hoops, however, and I have to spend 20 minutes explaining why I want to visit Iraq and what I do for a living. Finally they relent, hand my passport over, and welcome me to Iraq. I've already been welcomed by half a dozen *peshmerga* soldiers, photographed with two of them and had a chat, in French, with one.

Husni drops me in a car park, over two hours after we arrived at the border, and I take a taxi to Zakho to look at the town's ancient bridge before continuing on to Dohuk for the night. This little trip is a foretaste of my next few days in Iraq: there's a certain amount of communication confusion. I can't get across to Adris, my driver, where I want to go; 'bridge' doesn't seem to appear in my Kurdistani phrase list, riffling through the handful of books in my daypack doesn't turn up a picture of a bridge and the quick sketches I make of bridges in my notebook don't produce a glimmer of recognition.

'Take me to a hotel', I finally request and, sure enough, there's

167.

somebody at the front desk who knows exactly what I'm looking for, even if he is a little disappointed that the first tourist for a while doesn't actually want a room.

Known as the Delal Bridge, Beautiful Bridge in Kurdish, Zakho's number-one tourist attraction is said to have been built by a local Abbasidian ruler, which dates it anywhere from AD 750 to AD 1258, although there are suggestions it might date back to Roman times. Whatever, it's an impressive multiple-arched bridge over a rocky river and clearly very old. Zakho is also said to have a stretch of old castle wall but nobody at the hotel knew about that so we press on to Dohuk.

It's not far, along a freeway dotted with advertising billboards, and as we drive in to the centre there are a surprising number of hotels. The Sulav Hotel might be one of the biggest (and most expensive) in town; my room costs US$36. I take an instant liking to Dohuk. It's bright, energetic and crowded and has lots of fruit-juice stands. I wander around the town, try out an internet café (it had such a tangle of wires leading in to the building, I concluded it had to be the centre of the World Wide Web), search inconclusively for Dohuk's bit of decaying castle wall, look in various shops in the bazaar, check out the money-changing quarter (there are no ATMs that work and credit cards don't function either) and take quite a few photographs. Everybody is very enthusiastic about being photographed, a sure sign that there aren't many tourists around.

The weather, however, is still miserable and after a very agreeable meal in a restaurant I repair to the hotel. It's still raining when I get up and, as I leave Dohuk, I've taken on Adris as a driver again, it starts to bucket down. The rain continues all the way north to Amadiya, which I am expecting to have hints of a Kurdish hill town but in the rain it looks like a miserable dump more than a mountain escape. Perhaps it all looks better when the sun's shining and, as I head south again, glimpses of snow-dusted peaks appear. Before long the sun is shining and everything does indeed look much better.

Travelling east towards Arbil requires lots of diversions, presumably to avoid approaching too close to Mosul. There's lots of security although it centres on a visual check of each vehicle's inhabitants. I expect Arab passengers get more than a cursory glance. Only once today (and once yesterday) do I have to produce my passport and explain what the hell I am doing in Iraq. Along the way we stop for a hearty roadside lunch (the Kurds like to eat well) and I take some photographs of the restaurant and staff, which delights everybody.

Arbil is a delight as well. I'd always thought that Damascus was the world's oldest continuously inhabited city but Arbil (or Erbil or, in Kurdish, Hawler or Hewler) disputes that claim. The modern city crowds around the ancient citadel, which surmounts a hill in the middle of the town, so as soon as I've found a hotel room I head towards that prominent landmark. A stairway ascends to the citadel entrance, guarded by a huge seated statue of Ibn Al-Mistawfi. Who was he? An important government official back in the 13th century, I later discover, and he wrote a book titled *History of Erbil*. It's a fine-looking statue, especially with kids clambering over it and sitting in the local hero's lap.

Just inside the citadel entrance should be three large 19th-century Kurdish houses, turned into museums according to my 15-year-old guidebook. Sadly it turns out Saddam trashed them. Back in 1991 in the Kuwait Gulf War, George Bush Senior had encouraged the Kurds to rise up against Saddam, but then failed to follow through, halting the allied advance well before it got to Baghdad. Saddam suppressed the uprising with customary brutality, sending huge numbers of Kurdish refugees fleeing into the Kurdish regions of neighbouring Iran and Turkey. The beautiful old houses were gutted.

Not finding the houses was a disappointment, but there's a surprising substitute. A sign announces the Kurdish Textile Museum. Recently opened and very well presented, the museum displays an eclectic collection of carpets, kilims, saddle bags, baby carriers and other local crafts along with well-presented displays and information about the Kurdish people and nomadic tribes. Lolan Mustefa, who established the museum, is a mine of information on Arbil and the surrounding region. I'm enormously impressed that he has put so much effort into creating an excellent tourist attraction, when Iraq today has so very few tourists.

From the museum I continue to the citadel's mosque, visit the *hammam* (or bathhouse) and enjoy the view over the city from the citadel walls on the other side. Back down below the citadel walls I explore the bazaars, inspect the kilim shops, joke with the shoeshine guys, check the selection of papers on sale at the newsstands, photograph the photographers waiting for customers outside the citadel, snack on a kebab and drop in to a fruit-juice stand for an orange juice. It seems ridiculous, but I'm really enjoying Iraq.

•   •   •   •

Funny how things always look darker at night. I wake up in the middle of the night worried about how the crossing to Iran might go and that unease colours the rest of the day. Before departing Arbil I waste some time tracking down the small, rather dusty and forgotten archaeological museum. Finding things that nobody seems to know about is never easy and having language difficulties to grapple with doesn't help.

Coming back into the Sheraton car park, halfway through my museum search, I encounter a couple of burly Western guys checking over their armoured Land Cruiser. One of them sports a T-shirt announcing that sleeping soundly in bed is only an option for some people (presumably his clients) because some other people (presumably wearing T-shirts like his) are ready to exact extreme violence upon some other unspecified people. It's a slightly enhanced version of the quote attributed to George Orwell that 'people sleep peaceably in their beds at night only because rough men stand ready to do violence on their behalf', but it fits the situation well.

I don't expect for a second they're going to know where the museum is (they don't), but I ask anyway and at least get some advice about safety.

'You haven't got a driver? Take care. This may be Kurdistan, but it's still Iraq. It's dangerous out there.'

Which I guess it would be with a T-shirt like that.

At the hotel desk, after some discussion, since most of the staff also aren't aware there is a museum, I'm given instructions: straight up the way I was going, but driving distance rather than walking. With Kurdish written instructions in hand I flag down a taxi, set off up the road, stop to ask bystanders, U-turn and eventually end up right back where I gave up in the first place. I was standing right outside the museum when I was directed back past the Sheraton and, remarkably, it's exactly where my ancient guidebook said it was, just past the Hamarawan Hotel.

I've arranged another car and driver and soon after we're heading south, with Arvan sporting his Beijing 2008 Olympics sweatshirt at the wheel. The road towards Sulaymaniyah is fast and fraught, a straight road with lots of traffic and lots of hairy overtaking manoeuvres. In northern Iraq driving is probably the most dangerous activity. Frustratingly none of the names on my Iraq map pop up and when there is a name it isn't on my map. I have a suspicion that cartographers working on maps like this simply put in the big places we all know about – Arbil, Kirkuk and Baghdad along this route – and then make up a bunch of names to scatter in between.

So between dodging oncoming trucks we're heading down the highway towards Kirkuk, although I'm expecting we'll turn off to the east sometime before we get there.

A few months earlier Geoff Hann, an Englishman who ran tours through Iraq back in the 1970s and was looking at the place again, had also set out from Arbil towards Kirkuk, 'despite being strongly warned against it'.

'What town is this?' I ask as buildings and a flyover appear ahead.

'Kirkuk', replies Arvan, in what sounds like an unhappy tone.

I thought we were going to skirt around Kirkuk, as we'd done with

171.

Mosul, and Arvan is instantly looking for a way out again. The first road we try deteriorates into a construction zone and then is blocked completely. We U-turn, and continue on our original route, presumably sticking to the Kurdish southern fringe of the city. Speeding through is not an option. The road is interrupted by a series of speed humps so big that we virtually come to a halt to tip over them without grounding.

I'm relieved to come through another comprehensive roadblock and we take a fast divided road heading straight east to Sulaymaniyah.

Like me, Geoff Hann also soon found himself hurrying east. 'As we entered the city and crossed the last checkpoint, still in the Kurdish part of town, my driver picked up bad vibes, deemed that wisdom was the better part of valour and we left rapidly, passing through the slums of Kurdish refugees towards Sulaymaniyah. It was not for me to argue given the latest round of killings there. You have to trust these people's instincts as much as your own.

'So I still have not visited the tomb of the Prophet Daniel', Geoff regretted.

•　•　•　•

The conclusion of the Kuwait Gulf War in 1991 and the proclamation of No Fly Zones shackled Saddam Hussein and allowed the Kurdistan region to effectively declare independence from Baghdad. Correction: regions rather than region, because northern Iraq promptly split into two statelets. Massoud Barzani and the Kurdistan Democratic Party ran northwest Kurdistan from Arbil, while Jalal Talabani and the Patriotic Union of Kurdistan ran southeast Kurdistan from Sulaymaniyah.

In 1998 an American peace deal stopped the two Kurdistan parties from actually shooting at each other, but it was not until mid-2006 that they finally unified the two halves of Kurdistan. Talabani is now the president of all of Iraq, while Barzani is the president of the Kurdistan region of the country.

Kurdistan's peacefulness and relative independence is a double-edged sword for the rest of Iraq. The positive viewpoint: if Kurdistan can be peaceful and stable, why can't the rest of Iraq? The negative one: if Kurdistan can cut itself off from the rest of Iraq, why can't the Shiites and Sunnis divide up the rest of the country? 'Doing a Slovenia' is an ongoing topic in Kurdistan. Slovenia managed to abandon the rest of Yugoslavia and cut itself free before the fighting in the Balkans really began. As a result Slovenia is one of the success stories of the old Eastern Europe and comfortably better off than Croatia, Serbia and the other pieces of the Yugoslavia jigsaw puzzle.

Iraq without its northern Kurdistan region might still be a viable state, but Iran and Turkey, both with substantial Kurdish minorities bordering the region, certainly don't want an independent Kurdistan inspiring their Kurds to demand greater autonomy or, far worse, independence. Nor would the rest of Iraq be a pretty sight if it split into independent Shiite and Sunni entities. Under Saddam the Sunni minority had the power, but not the oil. That's predominantly in the Shiite regions of the country. Split southern Iraq into the two Islamic divisions and the Sunnis would be left with nothing more than palm trees, sand and a big chip on their collective shoulders.

For Iran a divided Iraq might not be so bad. After all, they're Shiites and could be expected to get on well with a Shiite lesser-Iraq. Saudi Arabia might not find it so agreeable, since that country's Shiite minority has always been treated as second best by the Sunni majority, and where is Saudi Arabia's oil? In the northeast of the country where Saudi Shiites predominate.

My first task in Sulaymaniyah is to find the museum, which I have been told is much better than the one in Arbil. It's already closed for the day, but fortunately it's close to my hotel. I have no idea what else Sulaymaniyah has to offer, but wandering the park with its collection of busts of Kurdish heroes and the bazaar area, with its mosques and more Kurdish hero statuary and portraits, uses up the rest of the day very satisfactorily. I also look in to a couple of more modern shopping centres and check out (although I don't dine there) the town's MaDonal restaurant, an Iraqi-Kurdish interpretation of the Golden Arches. Finally I return to the Ashti Hotel, which is definitely not up to the high standards of Dohuk and Arbil.

There's not a lot to do in Sulaymaniyah at night. I hang around in the lobby for a while and drink more tea, but eventually I drift up to my dreary room, check the security guys at the rear entrance to the hotel from my window, flick through the TV channels (chancing upon the Lonely Planet TV programme on Sydney on the way), read a little, write up some notes, fall asleep.

I sleep badly. Again I wake up in the middle of the night running through the logistics of this trip. I have to get to Tabriz in Iran by tomorrow night in order to fly out the next morning to Istanbul and on to the USA. It looks like the drive from Arbil to the Iran border could take four or five hours. Add a similar time from the border to Tabriz and it's going to be a push to get it done in one day, especially if there are any delays at the border. And what if I can't get across the border at all? That's going to be a huge hassle.

Of course these sort of problems always seem bigger at 3am than they do in daylight but eventually I come to the decision not just to simply head back to Arbil in the morning, but to continue straight through and try to get across to Iran that day. Then I'll have all the following day to make my way to Tabriz.

In the morning I have a look around the museum. It doesn't open at 8.30am (according to the guard at the front entrance last night) or 9am (the guard at the rear entrance), but at 9.30am. While I'm waiting I chat with Jalal Kakeyi who works at the museum as a chemist, dating finds, he informs me. It's a surprisingly good museum and it certainly didn't get trashed in the post-invasion chaos, like the Baghdad museum.

The museum has a big collection of reliefs, statues, steles, pottery, jewellery and tools dating right back to the Palaeolithic and Mesolithic eras. There are small pottery figures from the Old Babylonian period, ivory plaques and small delicate pottery from the New Assyrian period, and glazed pottery and gold coins from the Abbasidian period. Even the comparatively recent Ottoman period is covered.

Museums seem to have hit hard times in quite a few cities around my Bad Lands wanderings. The destruction of the Baghdad Museum was a sorry tale, although not unexpected. After all, Saddam's men had done a thorough job of sacking the excellent Kuwait Museum as well as setting all the oil wells alight before they headed home in 1991 after the Kuwait invasion and Gulf War. Having carted away the contents of the museum they also smashed and burned the building for good measure. It's the one building in Kuwait that has been left unrestored.

The unfortunate Kabul Museum in Afghanistan, at one time probably the finest museum in the region, suffered multiple attacks. First, every mujaheddin mob that took Kabul took time out to loot the museum, so anything valuable and portable soon departed Afghanistan and today probably resides in the homes of affluent art collectors in more peaceful parts of the world. Then the Taliban turned up and after ignoring the collection for the first five years finally got around to trashing it in early 2001 – at the same time as they destroyed the great Buddhas of Bamiyan.

Remarkably it appears there were survivors from the Kabul's museum collection inspection by the Taliban. The museum's director had taken the precaution of hiding, even burying, some statues and as the museum reopens they are being returned to display.

Unfortunately it isn't just Muslim iconoclasm. In the first days of the Iraq invasion in 2003 it was Americans doing the looting and vandalising just as much as the Iraqis. Watching the Saddam statue fall in Firdos

Square – helped by a contingent of Marines who roped up the statue
to an armoured recovery vehicle – reminded me that the Hungarians
cannily kept dozens of their unwanted statues of Marx, Lenin and other
Communist-era heroes and collected them together in the Szobor Statue
Park just outside Budapest. The collection now attracts 40,000 visitors a
year who happily pay to see it.

Another piece of Saddam-era artwork that I'd quite looked forward
to seeing in some future museum also fell to American destructive
urges. On this occasion a group of soldiers demolished the famed mosaic
portrait of George Bush Senior that visitors to the Al-Rashid Hotel
walked over as they entered the lobby.

The entrance mosaic was created after a cruise missile damaged the
hotel and killed a receptionist and a guest from Jordan in January 1993.
Only a few months later 23 US cruise missiles hit the city in the early
hours of the morning of 27 June. One of the missiles killed Leila al-
Attar, who was staying at her sister Suad al-Attar's home because her
own home had already been destroyed by an earlier US attack. For one
woman to have two homes destroyed in bombing raids was too great a
coincidence, Iraqi conspiracy theorists decided. Leila al-Attar must have
been deliberately targeted because, as the director of Baghdad's Museum
of Fine Arts, she was responsible for the Bush mosaic.

A collection of Saddam statues and portraits of George Bush Senior
could have made a useful starting point for a museum of recent Iraqi
history, along with a big exhibit of the Weapons of Mass Destruction
(always capitalised) or at least pictures of what they were supposed to look
like. The museum souvenir shop would probably have done a good trade
in T-shirts bearing the smiling face of former Iraqi Information Minister
Mohamed Saeed al-Sahhaf with a voice balloon saying 'Tanks? I don't see
any tanks.'

• • • •

Arvan turns up and we head off to Arbil and then to the Iran border. My map seems to indicate that you could head directly north, cutting a lot of distance off the trip and avoiding dicey Kirkuk completely, but the map has been pretty much a work of fiction so I'm not at all surprised when this idea is aborted. After another fuel-bargaining session on the edge of Sulaymaniyah, we're soon speeding down that familiar freeway, skirting round far-too-familiar Kirkuk and then heading north on the Baghdad–Arbil road.

Arvan seems mildly surprised at my change in plans, but we skirt around Arbil and turn off east towards Iran. The road starts to climb almost immediately and soon we're high above the town on a surprisingly good road. Salahuddin is a good lunch stop and after a long northward stretch at the foot of an endless ridge we turn east again through the Rowanduz Gorge. This is the 'Hamilton Road', a fine piece of British colonial road building by Archibald Hamilton, a young New Zealand–born engineer, between 1928 and 1932. He wrote a book about it, *The Road Through Kurdistan*, which after nearly half a century out of print was reprinted recently and which I'm reading on this trip.

The road up through the gorge is quite spectacular with a number of bridges that I presume are Archibald Hamilton's handiwork, although I don't manage to match the actual bridges with the old black-and-white photographs in his book. There's a group of young people at the Gali Ali Beg waterfall, crowding together to be photographed at one of the prime attractions in the gorge.

Beyond the gorge the road continues to climb and I begin to get more concerned about the crossing. This is nothing like the busy road from the Turkish border. The traffic is getting lighter and lighter, the road is climbing and winding, and it's all taking much longer than I'd anticipated. It's clearly a very remote region surrounded by snow-covered peaks and little else. It's now late afternoon and if the border is closed for the evening, what am I going to do until morning? Stand in the rain?

Yes, the rain has started again.

Finally we arrive at the Kurdistan border control and my worst fears are realised. I'm not sure what it is that I'm told at great length, but the general message is that I'm not going to get into Iran. Perhaps the border is closed to anybody who is not Iraqi or Iranian? A week later I discover that this is actually no longer the northern border crossing between Iraq and Iran. There are still three crossings between the two countries, two further south in regions I definitely do not want to venture into, but the third crossing, the northern Kurdistan crossing, is now east of Sulaymaniyah at Bashmakh, crossing from Penjuen (or Penjwin) in Iraq to Marivan in Iran. If I'd known, I could have arrived there this morning!

What a drag. Here I am right at the border, about the same distance from Tabriz as Arbil, but that's where I'm heading back to. Still the sun breaks through to provide a nice clouds-over-the-snow sunset as we hurtle back downhill. It's a scary ride, a nine-hour Arbil–border–Arbil round trip by the time I arrive at my hotel. En route we've got lost twice. Once, I realise Arvan has gone wrong and tell him to U-turn, the second time my trusty GPS tells me that we're heading in the wrong direction.

There are flights out of Arbil – I'd checked that possibility before I left – but tomorrow the only option is to Beirut. It looks like my best bet is to retrace my steps to Diyarbakir in Turkey, where I started my Kurdistan foray, but are there flights tomorrow and can I get there in time to fly to Istanbul to pick up my flight to the USA the next morning? It's nearly 10pm when I dump my bag in the Arbil Tower Hotel and race to the internet café next door, where I'm told they close in five minutes. Which, it turns out, is plenty of time to get on to the Turkish Airlines website and check their flight schedules. Isn't the World Wide Web wonderful? Even in Iraq it works. If there's a seat available and if I can get across the border fairly quickly, I should make it.

• • • •

I grab a quick meal in the hotel's restaurant and even treat myself to a beer before heading for bed at midnight. Just before 5.30am I tiptoe into the lobby. Assorted staff are asleep on the sofas, but the security guy outside still seems to be awake although he doesn't notice my arrival. Arvan doesn't turn up at 5.30am, which is probably just as well as the first hint of dawn only shows after 6am, when he does arrive. He's brought his brother Alan along for the ride. Then there are thick patches of fog to slow us and we get lost once, just after I decide we are heading straight in to the Mosul no-go zone, and for a while we seem to be travelling in totally the wrong direction.

I'm relieved when something familiar pops up and pleased when we stop for a late breakfast–early lunch at exactly the same roadside restaurant I'd stopped at en route from Dohuk to Arbil a few days ago.

We arrive at the border just after 10am and I'm immediately pounced on by a gang of Turkish drivers keen to take me to somewhere, anywhere, in Turkey. I quickly negotiate a price with one dapper gentleman and it's less than half what I paid for the same trip heading to Iraq. Then it's the excruciating departure procedures, including a fine-tooth-comb search of the car for smuggled cigarettes. Some vehicles seem to spew cigarettes out of every cavity, but the three cartons my driver has are not found.

Altogether the paperwork, rubber stamps, racing from office to office, standing in line and car searching (out of Kurdistan as well as in to Turkey) consumes almost three hours. The line of trucks waiting to cross the border seems even longer than at the beginning of the week, well over 20 kilometres long.

Finally we're on the road and what a road it is. The sun is shining and the countryside looks beautiful. Later in the trip snow-capped mountains spread right across the frame. The town of Mardin looks like a postcard (wish I had time to stop for a day or two) and we even pause for an excellent lunch, which also includes a car wash and shoeshines for both of us.

We arrive at the airport at 4.45pm for the 5.45pm Turkish Airlines flight, but it's full. Diyarbakir's modern little airport (excellent wi-fi reception throughout) has one curious omission – there is no departure or arrival board anywhere so the only way you can find out if any of the four airlines represented (Pegasus, Sun Express and Onur Air as well as Turkish Airlines) have flights and when is to ask at each desk.

There are some no-shows, so I get the last seat on the flight, but there's one final amusement. Out on the tarmac we have to identify our bags before they're loaded on board and mine isn't there. Some more last-minute bags arrive, but mine still isn't there. Finally somebody looks at my baggage tag and boarding pass and points out that I'm standing beside the wrong aircraft. The Airbus over there – waiting for one final passenger and with a lonely blue travel pack sitting beside it – is where I should be.

• • • •

So was there an alternative to the shock and awe performance? Did we have to bomb the shit out of the place and then march in to knock the statues over and search for Saddam's hidey-hole? Well, two other places in this book – one right up on the Axis and one a clear contender for a position, until its leader shaped up – received very different treatment.

North Korea, that other evil axis podium placer, hasn't been shocked and awed, bombed, invaded or even really threatened. Isolated a bit perhaps, leaned on heavily, pilloried in the press, but certainly not comprehensively wrecked the way Iraq has been. If you compare the two countries on internal evil, external evil, WMDs and terrorist threats, it's clear that North Korea comes out well ahead. The North Korean government has been just as horrible to its own citizens as Saddam, falls behind Saddam's Iraq when it comes to belligerence to its neighbours, but pulls ahead when it comes to support for terrorism.

In the all-important WMD category, North Korea is a clear winner. Iraq didn't have any, North Korea most probably does, makes no secrets about it (especially with its nuclear tests), probably helped other countries (Pakistan, Libya) towards developing their own WMDs, and boasts missiles as a major export, along with fake dollar bills, drugs and drink, although they supplied Scuds not to Iraq, but to Iran. The 39 Scuds Iraq launched against Israel in 1991 were home-made, and essentially they were duds, wildly inaccurate and prone to breaking up in flight. Two Israelis were killed by the Scud barrage and, although the 50-odd Scuds launched against Saudi Arabia did more damage, it was more by luck than accuracy. They didn't need Patriot missiles to shoot them down. Just as well since the initial Kuwait Gulf War claim that Patriots brought down 80 per cent of Iraqi Scuds was later scaled back to 70, 40, 10 or perhaps even 0 per cent.

Nevertheless North Korea gets cold-shouldered rather than invaded. The Kim Il-sung/Jong-il combo are clearly Saddam Hussein competitors when it comes to undesirability, so how come they escaped?

There's a third alternative to invasion or isolation and that's the carrot and stick routine that has winkled Libya's Gaddafi out of his self-imposed seclusion. Gaddafi isn't up to Saddam's standards for rotten treatment of his own citizens, but he has thrown his weight around locally and been a keen promoter and actual instigator of terrorist attacks. Plus Libya definitely did work on WMDs, although the new, reformed Libya has washed its hand of those nasty activities.

That's all history. Libya gets pushed and pulled, North Korea gets isolated. Iraq gets invaded and occupied.

LIBYA

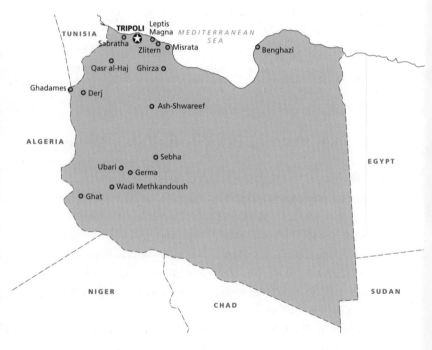

TUNISIA

TRIPOLI

Leptis
Magna

*MEDITERRANEAN
SEA*

Sabratha

Zlitern

Misrata

Benghazi

Qasr al-Haj

Ghirza

Ghadames

Derj

Ash-Shwareef

ALGERIA

Sebha

Ubari

Germa

Wadi Methkandoush

EGYPT

Ghat

NIGER

CHAD

SUDAN

In the mid-1990s Colonel Muammar Gaddafi suddenly decided the Great Socialist People's Libyan Arab Jamahiriya needed something other than the oil business and socialism to keep the population occupied. It wasn't like they needed the money – there was plenty of that, enough to both look after everybody and print as many copies of the Colonel's little Green Book as necessary while still leaving some spare cash in hand for fomenting international terrorism.

'What about tourism?' the Colonel mused, forgetting for a moment his government's unpleasant practice of blowing up French DC10s over the Sahara Desert in Niger, American 747s over Scotland and the odd discotheque in Berlin.

Nasty habits apart, it was not an unreasonable thought. There's no question that as a tourist destination Libya could be huge. Greek history, Roman history, the battlefields of World War II, the old camel caravan towns, the rock-art sites in the desert and the romance of the Sahara and its remote oases. Egypt, immediately to the east, and Tunisia, just to the west, are also desert countries and not unlike Libya in many respects.

Egypt had millions of tourists every year, despite the occasional tourist massacre. And while Egypt had all those Pharaonic ruins and some fine scuba-diving possibilities in the Red Sea, didn't Libya have Leptis Magna, the finest Roman ruins outside of Rome itself? And didn't Libya have beaches every bit as good as Tunisia's, where every year millions of European tourists flocked to Club Med resorts and other sun-sand-and-sex attractions? In contrast to the millions flocking to Egypt and Tunisia, Libya didn't even manage 100,000.

'Why shouldn't Libya have at least a measly little million of them?' Gaddafi reflected before dispatching a minion to London, not with instructions to snipe on London police from the safety of the Libyan embassy – another little slip-up from the bad old days – but with orders to contract a tourism research organisation.

A few months later I bumped into Rowan Sutherland at a tourism conference in Malaysia.

'He turned up at our door,' said Rowan, a researcher at a London-based tourism consultancy, 'and said that Gaddafi wanted to know what he needed to do to get Libyan tourism off the ground. We said that would be £20,000 please. He wrote the cheque and we're working on the project now.'

'First, however,' Rowan continued, 'we said we needed the answers to three basic questions. For starters, would there be any flights? Libya was still on the "most wanted" list. No self-respecting Western airline would fly there and not only was Libyan Arab Airlines very restricted in where they could fly, they also had difficulty even keeping their planes in the air due to trade sanctions. Not many Libya visitors were likely to arrive by land or sea.

'Secondly, would Libya issue visas for tourists? They'd always been notoriously tight-fisted with visas. It's very difficult to get anybody to come inside if you keep the front door locked and don't answer it when somebody knocks. We quickly found out that it was virtually impossible to get a visa for Libya if you weren't going on official business.

'Don't laugh', Rowan went on. 'There are lots of countries, like India, where the tourist department works hard at attracting visitors while the immigration department works even harder at keeping them out.'

'And the third question?' I asked.

'That was to do with booze', Rowan concluded. 'Libya is staunchly Islamic and alcohol is banned. Lots of those laze-on-the-beach visitors in Tunisia expect to get a cold beer at sundowner time. All those Club Med enthusiasts expect unlimited free wine with their meals. A dry beach holiday wasn't going to attract the beach resort hordes no matter how white the sand or how warm the water.'

• • • •

A decade later, when I finally arrive in Tripoli, Libya's capital, only one of Rowan's questions has been resolved satisfactorily. There are indeed lots more flights into Libya, including the Emirates 777 that brings Maureen and me in from Dubai. The night before, we'd dined at the Glasshouse, a trendy restaurant in the hyper-stylish glass-chrome-wood Dubai Creek Hilton. Our meal was accompanied by a very pleasant, if rather expensive, bottle of French Bordeaux.

Earlier we sipped a cold beer on a sightseeing cruise up and down The Creek. The tour beers and that bottle of wine would be the last alcohol we'd see for two weeks. Like Saudi Arabia (but unlike Syria and some other hard-line Islamic states) Libya remains a staunch prohibitionist. The Glasshouse meal would also be many Michelin stars better than anything we'd eat in Libya.

So flights, tick; booze, cross. What about visas?

Forget it.

For a start you can't make a solo visit to Libya. Lots of wanted and unwanted sub-Saharan Africans may traipse in across the border, legally and illegally, but for would-be Western visitors the only way to get in is to sign up for a group tour.

I'd got the names of a couple of reliable agents in Tripoli who could organise a two-person group tour for Maureen and me and sort out the visas. Getting the visas was not straightforward. The agent had to apply. Once this pre-application had been sorted, 'the visa invitation can be faxed to you within three to four days', emailed our agent Saif.

Then we just had to send the invitation to the Libyan embassy (or the Libyan People's Bureau as they tend to be called), get the official visa form (no photocopies or internet downloads available), get the important passport information translated into Arabic and written into our passports (although most people we would bump into in Libya could read our script perfectly well) and then apply for the visas.

There was, however, one more serious obstacle.

'There is a new law which makes it obligatory for travel groups to be at least four people', Saif's email continued. 'If you are just two people, you have to apply with two additional passports, even though only two of you will be actually travelling.'

'Well, the visa situation is certainly strange!' I emailed back. 'So I have to find two people who don't mind applying for a Libyan visa even though they are not going to Libya?'

Precisely.

We would only have to pay for the tour for two and we would only be charged for the work in making two visa applications, but there was no way around applying for four visas. Maureen and I both have dual nationality – could we each apply twice?

Not possible; it had to be four different people.

'Surely you have friends or relatives who hold valid passports and who would not mind having two pages of their passport stamped with the Libyan visa plus the translation of the passport?' queried Saif.

Some people might not find a Libyan visa in their passport too attractive, but eventually my 80-year-old mother volunteered to apply and we 'volunteered' our son.

At this point another obstacle popped up. Australia, we belatedly discovered, did not have a Libyan People's Bureau. The visa forms would have to come to us from the London bureau and our passports would have to be sent back and forth to Europe. The visa forms, however, did not come. Eventually I emailed Saif again and received an effusive apology for his delayed reply and the good news that a Libyan People's Bureau had just opened in Australia. Sure enough there was, but when I phoned the office a polite official apologised and said they could not yet issue visas. He suggested I apply to their diplomatic office in Kuala Lumpur, Malaysia.

By this time I had made the flight bookings to Libya, tagging the visit on to the end of a business trip to Europe. Time was rushing by. I emailed Saif: 'I've phoned the Libyan People's Bureau in Canberra and they are not yet issuing visas and do not know when they will be able to start. So we will have to make the visa application in London.'

Right, said Saif. I went off to the USA on another trip, expecting the forms to arrive while I was away. They didn't, and when I emailed Saif again he was 'terribly sorry for the long delay which is due to a long week of religious holiday we have had recently'.

He went on to explain that 'the London option is now too risky because of the time factor', but there was a new solution. The visas could be issued from Berlin because his agency had 'excellent relations with the Libyan embassy there'.

'OK, do it through Berlin', I replied, but again nothing happened. Finally, with time getting right down to the wire, Saif emailed me again to say Berlin was no longer necessary because the Australian Libyan People's Bureau could now issue visas. I phoned the bureau again and guess what? They still couldn't. I sent a final email to Saif: 'It seems to me that this is proving impossible to complete. Perhaps it is not possible for Battuta Tours to obtain a visa and I should approach a travel agent in London and see if they can organise this for me?'

There was no reply. I may have failed in Tripoli, but tours from London were quite easy to organise – given sufficient time, which I no longer had. They did cost about twice as much for precisely the same tour, but doing it through an agency in Tripoli wasn't intended to be a money-saving operation. I simply wanted to experience it that way. The forms arrived from London, I couriered the passports, forms and photographs back and 48 hours later followed them to London myself, travelling on my second passport. I still had nearly two weeks before I was due to leave Europe to meet Maureen in Dubai and then, a few days later, continue to Libya. Despite which the Libyan People's Bureau contrived to run me right down to the line. There were still no passports in my sweaty hands when I flew out of London. They caught up with me in Dubai.

· · · ·

There is love at first sight. I still remember waking up in a train from Talaimannar on the Jaffna Peninsula down to Colombo (we'd somehow snared one of the limited number of sleeper compartments), pulling the blinds up, looking out at this Arcadian vision of rice fields and palm trees, and instantly falling in love with Sri Lanka.

Tripoli doesn't do that.

The immigration official copies our passport data straight from the original page. The expensively procured Arabic translation does not get a glance. I'm watching. Then we're hanging around at the tail end of the passenger huddle, beginning to wonder whether our bags have been lost en route, when the conveyer belt reluctantly coughs them out and immediately grinds to a halt. The reason for their tardy appearance is plainly obvious. The straps have been pulled off my travel pack and someone has been trying to pull the zip open. The padlock on Maureen's bag has been ripped off, taking half the zip slider with it, and the bag is open, although the only sign that somebody has been inside is that the medical kit has been rummaged through. We're still seething as the minibus picking us up merges on to the airport freeway and immediately dials up warp speed for Tripoli. Twenty minutes of computer game highlights follow as we scream up behind taxis, dodge around Mercedes and slalom from one side of the freeway to the other. When I can drag my eyeballs away from the oncoming mayhem, the view from the freeway is not too exciting. Dusty apartment blocks draped with clotheslines seem to be the architectural statement for Tripoli. Satellite dishes (and big ones, not those dinky little things used for Sky TV in Britain) seem to adorn every apartment balcony. 'They're cheap and everybody's bored by the two Libyan channels', our guide in the minibus informs us. 'They'd rather watch Egyptian TV.'

As we approach the centre we pass what looks like a very modern and rather high-tech prison complete with guard towers at every corner and halfway along each wall, but also with a grand entrance.

'What's this – is it a prison?' I ask the guide.

'No, that is the home of our leader', is exactly the reply I expect.

Our hotel is a glossy new five-star affair. It opened as the Corinthia Towers, but the name was quickly changed to the Corinthia Bab Africa, the 'gateway to Africa', an indication of the Colonel's current Africa fixation. It's Tripoli's biggest, brightest, brashest new tourist trap, or it will be as soon as the tourists start to arrive.

Tourists or not, 'we're already running at 100 per cent occupancy', reports Tony Trabone, the dapper little Maltese chief concierge. 'Now if only I could get my staff to arrive on time', he complained. 'They think nothing of arriving three hours late and leaving three hours early.'

A relaxed attitude towards life can be a good thing. We hail a taxi outside the hotel to go to a restaurant just past Green Square for dinner.

'Great music. Who's the guitarist?' I query as the taxi drops us off at the restaurant.

'I have no idea. A friend made the tape for me', the driver responds, in perfect English. 'Here, have the tape', he continues, ejecting it from the player.

'No, no', I say, pushing the proffered tape away, and making a mental note to take those tales of Arab hospitality a little more seriously before I offer any more casual praise.

Walking back to the hotel we pass Green Square where the whirl of traffic still looks like Grand Theft Auto running at high speed, an impression underlined by a police car, a tow truck and an ambulance lined up side by side at the edge of the square waiting for the inevitable accidents to occur. The bus and shared taxi stations and a gaggle of restaurants, cafés and market stands cluster just beyond our hotel. The long-distance taxis are all Peugeot 504 or 505 station wagons, the 'car' of Africa.

I like Tripoli.

• • • •

The Jamahiriya Museum is magnificent, just as promised, even if four of the five floors are closed the first time we drop in. We do get everything from prehistory through the Punic, Greek and Roman periods with interesting models of the ancient sites and some superb Roman mosaics; I'm a sucker for mosaics. A big map of the country lights up to show prehistoric settlements, the Punic, Greek and Roman advances, and the trading routes into Libya from east and west and across the Saharan wastes to the south, but nothing happens when I press the button for 'Islamic Conquest'.

We don't get the Revolutionary Libya galleries, with all the images of 'the Man', 'the Colonel', the 'father of African unity', the 'knight of the revolutionary phrases' (according to Yasser Arafat), a 'mad dog' (according to Ronald Reagan) or simply the 'Leader of the Masses' (in his own humble opinion). We do get the battered green (everything to do with Colonel Gaddafi is green) Volkswagen he was beetling around in at the time of the great revolution. A few years ago I had a Beetle of much the same era as the Colonel's, although I'm pleased to report that mine was in much better nick.

The Colonel never saw a revolutionary movement or independence struggle he didn't like. His support for the IRA was notorious; he probably did more for terrorism in Ireland than anybody apart from the Irish of New York and Boston. Even the Welsh nationalists, a group principally known for their attempts to inflict unspellable and unpronounceable place names on the British, got a boost from the Colonel. Despite his enthusiasm for exporting revolution to the West, his greatest efforts were always reserved for pushing Arab nationalism and unity, in the name of which Libya entered into all sorts of completely impractical bonds with neighbouring states. The Federation of Arab Republics with Egypt and Syria in 1972 lasted in some fashion for five years, but others were much shorter. The merger with Tunisia in 1974 was probably a record: the Tunisians pulled out after two days.

There were plenty of other equally unsuitable tilts at Arab unity including one with Morocco in 1984. How was revolutionary Libya (led by the charismatic, if somewhat erratic, Colonel) ever going to hitch up with utterly conservative Morocco (led by a boring king)?

After 30 years of failing to unify the Arab world the Colonel switched horses and trained his sunnies on the south. If he couldn't guide the Arab world to unity, he'd give Africa the benefit of his leadership. In 1999 Gaddafi rolled out his grand plan for a second USA – the United States of Africa. Although it looks likely to be a long time before an African Union rivals the European one, the Colonel's African embrace quickly resulted in accelerated African immigration. Migrant workers from sub-Saharan Africa, particularly Mali, Sudan and Niger, have always found their way to Libya and the Libyans, happy to have somebody do the menial work they weren't interested in performing, were generally unconcerned. When people from Cameroon, Chad, Ghana, Guinea and Nigeria also started to pour in, the welcome quickly dried up. Riots in 2000 led to probably more than 100 deaths and were followed by mass deportations of illegal immigrants.

'We didn't get anything for all the money we put in to the other Arab countries', complained Abdel Chiouch, a young Libyan I met in the teahouse by the Ottoman clock tower in the medina.

'It was a complete waste. When we were hit by the embargo [UN sanctions were unrolled in 1992] nobody stood behind us. The prices of everything went up and none of the Arab states we'd supported did anything for us.

'After more than 10 years we're finally getting away from the embargo, but I think Africa is going to be the same mistake all over again.'

Wandering back from Green Square through the medina towards our hotel we seem to meet half the sub-Saharan population of Libya. There are an absurd number of barber shops down Sharia Homet Gharyan offering an exotic blend of 'Black Men's Haircuts'. Somebody somewhere in English-speaking Africa is turning out a great range of haircut posters. One cheerful hairdresser offers to cut my hair in any of the 40 or so styles on offer, but none of them suits.

Music shops offer pirated CDs of all the current American hip-hop, rap and pop chart-toppers as well as Kenny G. Pirated DVDs are equally popular and there's an interesting collection of West African titles, some of them labelled 'for sale in Ghana only'. I'm tempted by *Reckless Babes* (available as edition one or two) or *God Loves Prostitutes* (well, so does an awful lot of Africa), but *Emergency Wedding* sounds like it could be a big hit. The Western collection includes plenty of pop music video-clips, Hollywood blockbusters and sometimes a whole shelf devoted to Mr Bean.

There are a surprising number of internet cafés and passing travellers

are not their main clientele. There simply aren't enough of them. I look
into one café where every computer is in use, about a third of them for
playing games, some of them for surfing the net, but most for dealing
with emails. One guy is on something called Sudan Online, looking at
what looks like a Sudanese dating chatroom. Two other guys seem to be
composing one of those 'I need to get $17 million out of Nigeria and if
you give me your bank account details we can split the proceeds' scams.

• • • •

Having got our visas through a British tour company, we then had
a tour to go on. We tagged along on their standard one-week tour, but
added our own little two-person tours before and after. Apart from
Maureen and me, our group is 100 per cent British and even the two of
us, each with dual Australian-British nationality, are slightly British.
Neither of us is very used to group travel – apart from heading off with
a bunch of friends on trekking trips or renting a house somewhere – but
in some places a group is inevitable. North Korea, for example. Hardly
surprisingly our tour companions are a well-travelled bunch. Nobody
heads to Libya on their first trip abroad.

Although, by God, they are British to the core. There's eccentricity –
Richard is the prime example and as a result is also our group's clown,
tall-tale teller and naughty schoolboy. Naturally there are class issues.
With the British there have to be little frissons of tension across class
lines. And there's plain old British twitter. All the world may laugh about
the insincerity of a Californian's 'have a nice day now', but after a week of
l-u-u-u-vlys, w-u-u-u-nderfuls and a-m-a-a-a-zings, a simple 'have a nice
day' seems like complete reality.

To hustle the nine of us around Libya takes four people. Abdul
Shalgam is the guide, a quietly spoken, small and studious-looking man
in his early 70s, but looking much younger. He spent 40 years working in

the Department of Antiquities and clearly knows his stuff.

Salah Adem is the fixer and minder, making sure everybody is on the bus and has their room keys, and generally attending to all the other little problems forgetful tourists seem to generate. He's in his 30s, prematurely balding, very energetic and blessed with a permanent smile. Like Abdul he's from the Cyrenaica region to the east.

Sam-the-driver pilots the bus and is a model of smooth calm, always there and ready to go, never in a hurry, but equally never hanging around. And then there's Issei. At first I think he's Sam's offsider, the driver's general assistant, which seems to be a necessity in so many countries in the developing world, but then it's clear he doesn't actually do much assisting.

'He's our policeman', explains Salah. 'Every group of seven or more has to have one.'

'So what does he do?' There seems to be remarkably little for our very own policeman to accomplish, given that we're processed through checkpoints at regular intervals along every highway by Salah who has a stack of photocopies of his passenger list, detailing our names (in Arabic as well), our professions (either 'retired' or 'working'), dates of birth, passport numbers and nationalities.

'If we have any problems or the bus breaks down,' Salah explains, 'then he will help.'

I can't imagine what he would do. He doesn't have a weapon in the unlikely case we need protecting from somebody, he doesn't have a phone in case we need help and I'm positive if the bus broke down he'd be completely useless. In reality, Issei is just another example of Libya's huge programme of government make-work – somebody else who has been given a useless job to keep them busy.

Some of the group were already finding the trips too long, the toilets too dirty or the food too dreary, although to be honest we all soon found the food lived up to Libya's reputation for 'the dullest cuisine in North

Africa'. The only real dispute comes right at the end and of all things it's over tipping. A couple of Americans on board would have sorted it out immediately. It's partly word from above that we should tip and partly some feelings that tipping the secret policeman is definitely not our responsibility. I fall between the two extremes, happy to tip, but feeling no compulsion to tip the secret policeman – I didn't want him, he didn't do anything and if Gaddafi wanted to send somebody along to spy on me that was his responsibility.

• • • •

What is it about dictators and having their portraits – or better still their statues – everywhere? The Colonel's pictures are pretty ubiquitous in Libya, but they're a long way from high art. Quite often they're set up as revolving billboards, so two or three different likenesses are recycled every 30 seconds. There's a distinct style to Gaddafi portraits. The favourite is standing with arms folded, gazing upwards, so you always seem to be looking up his nose. Quite often he's wearing sunglasses, so that you can't tell if he's peering myopically at something – perhaps written on the ceiling? Some older photographic portraits show him dressed in the HMS *Pinafore* school of naval attire, always a favourite with dictators. The portrayal I like best, however, is on the one-dinar note, where he stands with one hand to the side of his face, looking like he's auditioning for a part in the Libyan production of *Queer Eye for the Straight Guy* and about to announce that this week's nerd has taste that is just too awful.

Like a surprising number of other dictators, Gaddafi soon realised that the brilliance that had led him to the seat of power had to be recorded for the benefit of the citizens of less-enlightened countries. In North Korea forests fell for the numerous books Kim Il-sung wrote to explain the earth-shaking importance of the *Juche* Idea, his formula for economic independence and wellbeing. China had Mao's *Little Red Book*, and in the mid-1970s Gaddafi retreated into the desert and came back with *The Green Book* – a slim volume easily available in a variety of languages from bookshops in Tripoli. Explained in just 120 pages, Gaddafi's 'Third Universal Theory' will, if we only take the trouble to apply it, solve all the world's problems. Presumably Libya's have already been sorted out.

The Green Book is divided into three handy sections, starting with 'The Solution of the Problem of Democracy'. The problem, so it seems, is that there isn't any out there. Democracy is all about representing the people and since we end up electing somebody else to represent us we aren't representing ourselves, ergo we don't have democracy. Political parties, parliaments, plebiscites and the press are all undemocratic and the solution, which you'll see posted up widely around Libya, is 'committees everywhere'. Once everything is decided by committees, we'll all have democracy, just like in Libya.

Having solved the democracy question Gaddafi goes on to sort out economics in Part Two, 'The Solution of the Economic Problem'. In a word it's socialism with the catchy slogan 'partners not wage-workers'. There's a detailed explanation of why getting paid for work is no different from slavery, a handy little example about producing 10 apples but not being happy unless you get to keep all 10 and some serious warnings about the dangers of employing domestic servants. It's also suggested that everybody needs to own their own land and their own house and preferably their own car. Since a surprising number of people in Tripoli own shiny new BMWs, Audis and Mercedes, this could be the kind of socialism we can all live with. Not Hertz or Avis, however. Gaddafi warns us that we should certainly not 'possess private vehicles for the purpose of hiring them out', because that's pretty much like enslaving the people who rent them.

196.
Finally Gaddafi really gets into his stride when he lays out 'The Social Basis of the Third Universal Theory' in Part Three. First of all he explains the pros and cons of 'Families', 'Tribes' and 'Nations' before getting down

to a serious think about women and why they're different to men. Part of it is that 'woman menstruates or suffers feebleness every month, while man, being a male, does not'. Having made this shattering discovery he quickly moves on to conclude that another big difference between the sexes is that women can get pregnant, in which case they are 'feeble for about a year'. Perhaps this is because men are 'strong and tough' while women are 'beautiful and gentle'. Much is made of the more liberated role of women in Gaddafi's new Libya, but in fact there's remarkably little of it to be seen. Women may not be invariably veiled and shrouded, but they're generally well covered up and what is much more noticeable is that they are simply not visible. In so many situations the crowd (in a teahouse, in an internet café, even on the streets) will be 100 per cent male. Gaddafi's 'female bodyguards', a favourite in most tales about the Colonel, are really just another little piece of showmanship. The real weaponry is packed by men.

Discovering how men and women are different and deciding what to do about it takes up the longest section of the book, but there's still room to ponder 'Minorities', 'Education', 'Melodies and Art' and, in some of the best gobbledegook in the book, the question of 'The Blacks' and 'Sport, Horsemanship and Shows'.

Sport could easily be sorted out if we all played it rather than wasted our time watching it. Then we'll all be down on the field kicking the ball around rather than sitting in the grandstands and as a result 'stadiums will be vacated and destroyed'. The black race is going to solve its own problem by the simple process of out-populating everybody else, due to the fact that 'their low standard of living has protected them from getting to know the means and ways of birth control and family planning'. Population increase is also lower among other races because they work too damn hard, unlike 'the blacks who are sluggish in a climate which is always too hot'.

197.

Travel-writing friend Jennifer Cox said that Gaddafi's *The Green Book* ideology also included the promise that everyone in Libya should get at least the basic essentials of life – a loaf of bread and a bottle of olive oil. I never saw it, but Jennifer said she saw piles of bread being dumped under half-built overpasses in Tripoli, left there to feed the hungry.

* * * *

Heading south from Tripoli into the desert, it's a couple of hours before we pull off at Qasr al-Haj, a wonderful fortified granary. The huge mud-built circle encloses 114 separate chambers, one for every chapter in the Koran. They were once used to store grain on the upper floors and olive oil in the basement level and are arranged in a charming higgle-piggle of ups and downs, looking like something that came from a child's scribble-pad rather than an architectural drawing-board. Further south there's another fortified granary at Nalut, a town perched on top of a plateau reached by a zigzag road from the plain.

The road runs through progressively more barren country – 'featureless' and 'waste' spring to mind. The imminent arrival of the occasional bleak little settlement of flat-roofed, block-shaped buildings is signposted by the litter of plastic bags and bottles, tin cans of varying ages, and general junk and rubbish that coats the roadsides in most populated parts of Libya. *The Green Book* may have set out to solve most of the world's problems, but it's clear the Colonel never got round to writing the chapter about keeping the Great Socialist People's Libyan Arab Jamahiriya tidy. Libya is one of the most comprehensively trashed countries I've ever visited.

We stop for lunch at a roadside filling station a little south of Sinoun. By this time the *ghibli,* the 'hot, dry wind from the south', is blowing at gale force and the usual overcast sky has taken on a uniform beige shade. Venturing out of the bus, you feel your eyes start to burn and the gritty sand on your teeth. Every couple of minutes through lunch the wind bursts the door open and one of us has to jump up to push it shut again. A small souvenir shelf offers a nice series of 'American Aggression' postage stamps, Gaddafi wristwatches in male and female models, and the first Gaddafi T-shirt I've spotted in Libya.

There's a final brief pause at Derj, a grotty little junction town brightened only by two excellent king-size Gaddafi billboards. I have to lean into the sand storm to run back down the road to photograph them. Meanwhile our group huddles in the Tsawa Company for Tourism café and watches what looks like 'Arab Idol' broadcast from Cairo. The weedy teenager from Syria wins and bursts into tears. On the final stretch to Ghadames, sand dunes have blown across the road in a couple of places.

At first glance Ghadames, the 'jewel of the Sahara', is just another jumble of block-shaped buildings and the Khafila Hotel is straight out of the cheap-and-nasty school of construction. Our ugly little room, with its squeaky metal door, is furnished with a collection of shoddy chipboard furniture including two lumpy beds. The bathroom features a shower but no shower curtain, so the floor is quickly awash and there's neither a fan nor air-conditioner. In late winter that's no problem, but the room must be uninhabitable in summer.

In contrast the old town, where Maureen and I head as soon as we've left our bags, is a Unesco World Heritage–listed delight. With one small problem: it's utterly deserted. Even tourists are absent for our impromptu evening circuit, although we're intercepted at the Bab al-Burr, the main entrance to the old city, by an utterly charming French-speaking guide who gives us a short introduction to what we'll experience at greater length the next day.

That night dinner (for the fifth meal in a row, French fries are a feature) is followed by a surprisingly good Tuareg 'cultural performance' for the predominantly Italian and Japanese guest list. Jerry-built or not, the Khafila has 100 per cent occupancy. A sextet of drummers beat tune to a wailing flute player's lead while six men (one of whom we'd chatted to earlier outside the Ghadames internet café) work through a repertoire of high-stepping, fast-paced, perfectly synchronised dances. There's a costume change between every dance and the exuberant ensemble's nifty footwork is emphasised by the beautifully embroidered slippers that are a Ghadames speciality. Next day Maureen buys a pair. The final energetic whirl, featuring one dancer dressed up as some wild beast, even convinces our skinny police minder Issei to join in.

The next morning the old city is populated by tourists, if not the citizens of Ghadames. In the 1980s the Libyan government decided to build a new town, presumably in the same building blitz as our tatty hotel. Within five years the old city's 6000 inhabitants had shifted to their new home.

'Voluntarily', insists Mohamed al-Houni, our local guide, who is just as charming, though English- rather than French-speaking, as the previous evening's equivalent.

'Nobody was forced to leave, but the new houses had electricity, running water and toilets,' he explained, 'so everyone kept their old homes and still sometimes visit them, but they all moved to the new city.'

That afternoon I track down Abdulgader Abufayed, the UN's project manager for the old city rehabilitation project. 'Moving out was purely voluntary,' he confirms, 'but a city without people is a monument. We have to find ways of bringing the city back alive.

'We are investigating many ways of doing that. I think in the end it will be a combination of handicrafts, tourism and investment. We have to find ways of making the city self-propelling. It has to be capable of sustaining itself. There is no taboo on new ideas. Some people may move back in but it will not be completely repopulated. The old city could not provide the facilities people demand today.'

200.

Lack of running water and sewerage are the key missing components, but there's no reason the old city could not be plumbed and have sewers installed without losing its character. The restoration that took place around 2001 is easy to appreciate at street level, but looking across the rooftops from our lunch stop it was easy to pick out the white-painted houses that had been restored among the other crumbling rooftops and towers. The beautifully decorated old house where we have lunch is clearly kept for just such occasions; it's a real highlight.

'What has happened is not so bad', Abdulgader concludes. 'It's not like the new city was built on top of the old and destroyed it. The old city is still all there.'

Richard and I had already kicked around one idea. 'A company like Aman Resorts could turn a series of the houses into a wonderful hotel. I can just see the tables and umbrellas set out on the roof terraces.

'Then we'll make a sunset drive to Algeria at gin and tonic time', Richard continued. 'We'll set up a little enclave just across the border.'

The Algerian border is not much more than 10 kilometres away and indeed we do head in that direction for sunset. Salah collects our passports before we leave – in case we stray across the border?

Close to the border we stop to climb to the summit of Ras al-Ghoul, the evocatively named Mountain of Ghosts. From the top of this crumbling desert castle we gaze down at the campsite where an Islamic force besieged the castle in AD 668. Just beyond the camp is a graveyard and from there the spectacular views roll away to the west. The sand dunes we can see are actually across the border in Algeria and we can also see to Tunisia, just to the north.

Descending from the castle, we drive a few more kilometres to a series of towering sand dunes, where our drivers engage in a bit of dune bashing, racing up the hills in our Land Cruisers although with less success than on a similar dune-hooning trip near Dubai a few days earlier. Our Land Cruiser in particular is arthritic and asthmatic.

Maureen, Salah, Issei-the-secret-policeman and I clamber up the topmost dune, floundering up through the fine sand to the summit. The afternoon wind is whistling up over the edge and abrading us with the windblown sand. We get back down to the cars just at sunset – our drivers have built a fire and are baking bread and making tea. Give us a billabong and we could be in Australia making damper and boiling the billy.

● ● ● ●

'Buongiorno!' A volley of greetings ricochets across the breakfast tables; Italians are far and away Libya's biggest tourist contingent, which is not surprising given it's only 500 kilometres from Syracuse in Sicily to Tripoli, only a two-hour flight from Rome. It is, however, also very surprising, given Italy's dismal colonial record. Like Belgium, that other European power that got into the empire game late in the day, the Italians didn't prove very good at it. Libya and Ethiopia both paid the price.

At the turn of the 20th century, Libya was another part of the rapidly decaying Ottoman Empire, which by the end of World War I would totally implode, leaving Turkey as its forward-looking replacement. By the end Iraq, Syria, Lebanon, Jordan, Palestine, Egypt and Libya had all gone their own ways or, more often, been gobbled up by somebody else. In unlucky Libya's case it was the Italians who did the gobbling. When the Italians booted the Ottomans out in 1911–12, they claimed it was to liberate the Libyans, ignoring the cold reality that the Libyans had been working very hard at liberating themselves from Ottoman rule for many years. It was nothing new. The USA had claimed to be liberating Cuba and the Philippines from Spanish rule in remarkably similar circumstances after the Spanish-American War in 1898.

For the next 30 years the Libyans struggled against Italian rule, most notably under the leadership of Omar al-Mukhtar, the 'Lion of the Desert'. Al-Mukhtar was finally captured and executed by the Italians in 1931. Today his statue tops one of the columns outside Tripoli Castle at the corner of Green Square. In the late 1930s Mussolini began to ship in

Italian settlers by the boatload and Italian control finally began to extend to all corners of the country. Italian domination came at enormous cost to the Libyans. It has been estimated that up to a quarter of the Libyan population died during the three decades of Italian colonialism.

Then World War II arrived and Libya became the battleground where the Afrika Korp of Rommel (the 'Desert Fox') slugged it out with the Eighth Army of Montgomery (the 'Full Monty'). When the sand settled in late 1942, the Germans had suffered their first major defeat of the war and by early 1943 it was the British rather than the Italians who controlled things from Tripoli. The war ended with the British Empire heading for rapid downsizing. There was certainly no incentive to add an impoverished and disgruntled new stretch of desert to the Commonwealth. The French had a go at grabbing a chunk of southwest Libya to weld on to Algeria, but Libya finally became independent in 1951.

For the rest of the 1950s Libya struggled to repair the damage of Italian colonialism and World War II, but the discovery of oil in 1959 quickly made it a very different place. Libya suddenly became the richest country in Africa and a succession of governments proved incapable of coping with the new-found wealth. The Six Day War in 1967 and the shock waves it sent through the Arab world probably triggered the upheaval that brought Gaddafi to power. Quite apart from popular anger with governmental excess, corruption and favouritism, there was now anger at a government that had paid loud lip-service to Arab nationalism, but in fact had done nothing to support the front-line Arab states.

The revolution in 1969 was remarkably peaceful (there were very few deaths) although initially a little puzzling (it was nearly a week later before Colonel Gaddafi popped up as the new leader and then went charging off at high speed). Gaddafi quickly nationalised businesses (proving his socialist credentials), redistributed wealth (pleasing the large percentage of the population who resented Libya's wealthy elite, which had profited from the oil boom) and set out on his quixotic campaign for Arab unity (pleasing those who thought Libya wasn't doing enough for Arab nationalism).

He also kicked out the remaining Italian settlers, dispossessed Libya's Jewish community and took an each-way bet on Islam by closing churches or converting them into mosques (which pleased religious hard-liners), but then stacking the mosques with compliant clergy (which didn't).

With his penchant for dressing up, Gaddafi was always the Peter Pan of dictators. One day he was taking his lead from Hollywood (desert sheikh followed by safari suit) and the next it was rock music (military uniforms from the Sergeant Pepper dress-up box followed by a lounge-lizard outfit from Bryan Ferry). Since Libya often seemed to be Neverland and the Colonel's behaviour was often as erratic as his wardrobe choices, there was also a definite flavour of Michael Jackson about the place. One day he was welcoming another terrorist group to Tripoli (although the IRA were never happy with a place where beer was unobtainable), the next day he was banning shops (all of Tripoli was briefly serviced by just seven government-owned supermarkets and Yasser Arafat flew in to cut the ribbon at the opening ceremonies). Then he was launching the Great Man-Made River project to turn the desert green or even changing the name of the country from simple old Libya to the Great SPLAJ, the catchy acronym for Socialist People's Libyan Arab Jamahiriya. Jamahiriya translates somewhat like 'state of the masses'.

In the 1980s Gaddafi's revolutionary impulses started to make him very unpopular outside of Libya. Part of the problem were the 'revolutionary committees', which, like Mao's Red Guard, began to have a life of their own. No Libyan who spoke out against Gaddafi was safe from these firebrands, not only in Libya, but also abroad. Assassination attempts took place all over Europe, reaching an extreme in London in 1984 when a sniper in the Libyan embassy fired on Libyan protesters outside on the street and managed to kill a police officer. The Libyans in the embassy were all sent home and Britain severed relations with Libya. America had done so three years earlier.

More assassinations, an expensive (in cash and lives) and ultimately unsuccessful border dispute with neighbouring Chad, attacks on passengers at Rome and Vienna airports in 1985 by Libyan-aided and Libyan-financed Palestinian extremists, and finally the Pan Am and UTA airliner explosions in 1988 and 1989 all elevated Libya to the top of the international most-wanted list. In 1992 the UN instituted sanctions, which would make life very difficult for the next 10 years.

Of course, as with all the Bad Lands, things weren't all one way and Reagan's missile strikes at Benghazi and Tripoli in 1986 weren't the only occasions the Libyans were attacked. In February 1973 Libyan Arab Airlines flight 114 departed Tripoli to fly via Benghazi to Cairo. The aircraft was chartered from a French operator and although the co-pilot, the flight attendants and most of the passengers were Libyan, the captain was French. Approaching Cairo the 727 flew into a sandstorm and the pilot lost sight of the usual visual approach markers and at the same time overshot a radio beacon. Air traffic control in Cairo warned him that he was approaching the Sinai, still under Israeli control following the 1967 Six Day War. The aircraft made a hasty U-turn and headed back towards Cairo, but not quickly enough to evade two Israeli Air Force Phantoms, which intercepted the airliner and shot it down, less than a minute's flying time from Egyptian air space. From the black box voice-recorder it appeared the crew did not realise they had strayed into Israeli-controlled air space and only realised the aircraft were Israeli, not Egyptian, at the last moment.

There were only five survivors from the 113 passengers and crew.

Of course, when trigger-happy military personnel shoot down civilian aircraft it's never a good look. So did the Israel government do some quick explaining and apologising? Over to you, Golda Meir: 'I want to tell you that I don't just appreciate you, I admire you!' she said to Israeli

Chief of Staff Dado Elazar, who had ordered the airliner shot down.

Well, they were only Libyans.

• • • •

It was Roman ruins that first attracted me to Libya. Of course, every visitor to Rome inspects the Coliseum and the other ruins at the centre of the empire, but at its peak Rome extended not just across Europe, but east into Asia and south into Africa. Years ago I walked across Britain from east to west, following Hadrian's Wall, which marked the northern extreme of the empire. I loved the feeling that the centurions stationed here were living life right on the edge, guarding the outer boundaries of the empire against the Scottish wild men to the north. One account I read commented how this was undoubtedly a hardship posting, but also tied up with excitement and danger. To the Romans, Scotland in those days was the equivalent of darkest Africa to the Victorian explorers.

Africa and Asia, on the other hand, offered warmth, wine and more than a touch of civilisation. I've been to the superb ruins of Ephesus in Turkey, Palmyra in Syria and Volubilis in Morocco, but Leptis Magna, on the Libyan coast about 100 kilometres east of Tripoli, is regularly cited as the most magnificent site around the Mediterranean.

Although Leptis Magna was first settled from the 7th century BC, it only became really important around the time of the birth of Christ, under the Emperor Augustus. The city became an important port and began to acquire those architectural symbols that distinguished an important Roman city, including a market and a theatre. Olive oil was a lucrative, although mundane, export through the port, but the trade in wild animals to appear in the Roman spectacles was a much more exotic activity. When Septimus Severus, 'the grim African', marched on Rome in AD 193, the centre of gravity of the Roman Empire shifted southwards and for a spell the new emperor had visions of Leptis Magna rivalling Rome itself. A long peaceful spell accelerated the city's growth, but then war returned and in AD 211 Severus was killed in battle in England.

For another century Leptis continued in undiminished splendour before floods, earthquakes and Roman neglect began to take their toll. The city fell into Byzantine hands in the 6th century and the construction of a wall around the city forewarns of the Arab invasion that followed a century later. By the 10th century the once-splendid city was deserted and disappearing beneath the sand.

We're certainly not disappointed with the ruins. Because no modern city was built nearby or, worse, right on top of the ancient Roman site, Leptis Magna is very well preserved. The triumphant Arch of Septimus Severus, the luxurious Hadrianic Baths, the Nymphaem – the 'Temple of Nymphs', the huge marble-floored Severan Forum with its many remarkably expressive Gorgon heads and the grand theatre all speak of the city's glory days. A party of schoolchildren arrive at the theatre at the same time as our group and, spotting the Western visitors, they line up on the stage to launch into that Disney number 'It's a Small World'.

We walk further east to inspect the extraordinarily well-kept 16,000-seat amphitheatre and the circus or hippodrome where wheel-to-wheel chariot races were once staged in front of up to 25,000 cheering spectators.

Despite its fine state of preservation, Leptis Magna still faces grave risks from the modern world. Exploring the market area Abdul Shalgam is dismayed to discover a missing piece of ancient balustrade. He's certain that it was there the last time he visited and tyre tracks across the paving to the spot underline his concerns.

'Look,' he points out, 'they've backed a truck up here, levered it out and taken it away. It looks like it's only happened in the last few days. The guards are simply not taking enough care.'

Of course sites like this are always threatened by greedy collectors and regrettably the danger is not a new one. Back in the late 17th century Claude Le Maire, the French consul to Tripoli, ransacked the site, shipping off huge numbers of marble columns to France. The Versailles chateau and the St Germain des-Pres church both feature pieces plundered from Leptis Magna.

Although Leptis Magna is Libya's most important Roman site, it's not the only one. We had already ventured west from Tripoli to visit Sabratha, a Roman city with an even more magnificent theatre than Leptis Magna (although without a troupe of school kids to sing to us). If our visit to Libya had been longer, we could have continued east towards the World War II battlegrounds of Tobruk and visited the ancient Greek ruins at Cyrene and Apollonia.

At lunchtime in Leptis Magna my soft drink comes from the 'African Bottling Operation, Tripoli, Great Socialist People's Libyan Jamahiriya under the supervision of Pepsico Inc'. US trade embargo? What US trade embargo? Pepsi is clearly the market leader in Libya, although Coke is also available. The principal Libyan soft drink is Bitter Soda, which looks and tastes remarkably like fizzy red mouthwash.

We finish Leptis Magna with a visit to the excellent museum. The penultimate room is a very unimaginative collection of pressies to the Colonel. 'It's all nothing', a young student who had attached himself to Maureen for some English conversation announces, with a dismissive wave of his hand.

'A revolution? We have not had a revolution', he continues, clearly unconcerned that any of the Gaddafi memorabilia was bugged. 'A revolution has to come from everybody. This was not a revolution, this was him taking over.

'But he has the weapons', he concludes thoughtfully.

The museum itself concludes with a huge two-storey-high cut-out image of the Man with arms raised exultantly and the happy throngs crowding at his feet. It would be fun to pose our contingent for a group photo on the balcony, gathered around him, peering over his shoulders and round each side of his head.

That night we continue a little further east along the coast to overnight at the port of Zlitern. Wandering back through the town to our hotel, I pause to gawk at the sheer number of satellite dishes tacked on to the tatty apartment blocks. In one shop I spot a 'super luxury size beach towel' sporting the English Arsenal football club badge so I buy it for my Arsenal fan son. As in shops all over Libya, lots of the outlets here are fronted by large displays of footballs. Clearly there's a big demand from local soccer players. Gaddafi's son actually captained Al-Ahly, one of the two major Tripoli football teams, and the Libyan national team, which still hasn't made Libya into one of Africa's great football nations. Even football can be political in Libya. In 1996 fans began chanting anti-government slogans during a game in which he was playing. His bodyguards proceeded to open fire on the crowd and killed at least 20 spectators.

The next day there's another foray into the desert before we return to Tripoli. We follow the coast for a stretch beyond Misrata to the east, then turn inland and finally on to a gravel road that runs beside the Great Man-Made River for 80 kilometres before finally turning off again to ancient Ghirza.

It's a minor site, a collection of tombs built in the Roman style, but probably by Libyans who had profited from serving in the Roman army. We picnic under acacia trees close to the larger group of tombs and wash our food down with bottles of 'Water from the Great Man-Made River'. Then we drive on a couple of kilometres to a smaller assortment of tombs, picturesquely perched close to the edge of a deep wadi with beautiful acacias scattered across its sandy floor.

At both sites Abdul frets that nobody is looking after these irreplaceable sites properly. Yesterday's discovery of the damage at Leptis Magna was a shock. Today there's a lintel fallen from the roof of a tomb.

209.

'I'm sure that was there last time', he worries. There have been so many police roadblocks. Why couldn't they pull some of them off that time-waster of an occupation and put them on duty looking after the ancient sites?

•　•　•　•

The rest of our group has gone back to England when Maureen and I head south to the Fezzan. In early spring the countryside is unexpectedly green and fertile for the first 100 kilometres out of Tripoli, then it starts to dry out and before the 200-kilometre line it's utterly barren – only at the occasional wadi is there much vegetation. The scenery is never without interest. The road climbs through dramatic rocky hills, then runs across equally desolate plains but the view is always punctuated by distant ranges, flat-topped mesas or curiously eroded pyramidal hills. Occasionally there's a scatter of camels or a telecommunications tower. At one point what looks like a Burmese pagoda pops up on the horizon only to resolve into another communications device, a bizarre stepped-structure fronted by a bank of solar panels. The infrequent settlements – always preceded by a denser roadside crust of plastic bags, frayed tyres, crushed water bottles and rusted tin cans – are dusty, drear little eruptions of half-built breezeblock buildings, a petrol station, a couple of teahouses (in one of them the proprietor is watching *Spartacus* when we drop in), a shop or two and the inevitable police checkpoint. The roads are smooth, the traffic light, the speed limit 100 kilometres per hour. The speedo needle sits at 150.

Further south, there's a lunch stop at Ash-Shwareef. After we stumble through a confusion of Arabic, English and French (the French works best) the meal is the usual salad-soup-chicken-rice-chips, but it's a cheerful place – it would be a good highway truck-stop in the US or Australia. Afterwards the country becomes extraordinarily barren. At times there is not a leaf or blade of vegetation as far as you can see, but the road parallels the Great Man-Made River for a stretch and crosses it a couple of times. After Brak we sail into the Idehan Ubari, the Ubari Sand Sea. This is serious sand-dune country and the afternoon *ghibli* whisks a film of sand across the road just a few centimetres above the road level. A dragon's backbone of dunes, regular as a sine wave, ripples away to the southeast.

Finally there's Sebha, a bustling metropolis with an old Italian fort and the airport. Just beyond the town is the truck park where grossly overloaded trucks labour in after long hauls across the empty desert from sub-Saharan Africa. In Australia almost every year a battered pick-up truck of Aboriginals grinds to a halt somewhere in the outback and before help arrives half of the five or 10 passengers have died of thirst. When disaster hits these African truckfuls of economic immigrants the numbers are likely to be 10 times as large. In 2001 a broken-down truck was found with 96 dead passengers. And 23 survivors.

From Sebha the road runs along the extraordinary Wadi al-Hayat, a green mirage in the heart of the Sahara. For 150 kilometres it's stony silence along the south side of the road and an intensively farmed strip along the north while massive sand dunes parallel the road only a few kilometres away. After the long, empty road south from Tripoli, this stretch is comparatively heavily trafficked. Finally we turn into the Dar Germa Hotel in Germa to be met by the equally extraordinary sight of Hassan Sharif, looking like a Tuareg garage mechanic, his *ashaersh*, the Tuareg turban, making a strange contrast with his Ferrari-red overalls.

Hassan learnt his English during a year-long spell in Dublin. The weather? 'Yes, it was terrible. There was rain, even snow!' Later he confides that it gets bloody cold in Germa during the winter as well.

The next morning Hassan is dressed Tuareg-style from the neck down as well as the neck up, his pale, mauve turban contrasting nicely with a black *galabiyya,* the full-length loose-fitting robe worn by men. Properly attired he looks even more dashingly handsome, ready to stride across any desert that presents itself. His endlessly cheerful offsider Mohammed sports a gold-brown turban and a purple robe. Mohammed is from Niger and speaks French, so for the rest of the day the conversation is a three-way Arabic, English, French melange.

We cruise a few kilometres back down the road towards Sebha, turn off through the farmed strip, stop to let air out of the tyres to cope with the sand, and almost immediately disappear into the sand dunes. Within minutes all directions disappear and I'm secretly glad I've brought my GPS along and set the coordinates for Germa before we left. For the next hour we swoop up and down over the dunes, sometimes stopping for Hassan or Mohammed to clamber up a nearby dune, possibly to reconnoitre the route, possibly simply to spy out a patch of *fish-fash*, the patches of ultra-fine sand that can bog even a carefully driven Land Cruiser.

If you've got a 'children's book' view of the Sahara – endless rolling sand dunes, the only sign of life a camel caravan plodding across the lifeless sand (of course, Toyota Land Cruisers are substituted for camels) – then this is it. We're even heading towards the postcard-perfect desert oasis – pools of clear water surrounded by green palm trees and then by the golden, burning sands. In fact the Ubari Lakes number more than a dozen. At Maharouba, the 'Burning' Lake, we come across a small party of Germans, two couples with some very small children. They've been dropped off here to camp by this little-visited lake for a week or two. Continuing west, with more stops to look around, we labour to the top of a particularly high dune and nudge our nose over the sharp edge of the sand ridge. The deep blue Gebraoun Lake appears directly below us.

'Ooooh', breathe Hassan and Mohammed in unison, as if they're amazed to have tumbled upon it.

'*Une bonne casquette*', announces Sher, the manager of the Winzrik campsite beside the lake. He's from Mali and he's spotted his home country on the map of Africa on my cap. It's easy to imagine the caravans pulling in to this desert oasis and in a sense they still do, except today the distant tribes are from Italy, the Netherlands or France and their camels have 'morphed' into Toyotas.

The village of Gebraoun itself has gone. The inhabitants were relocated to new apartments by the main road in 1991. At Ghadames I was told that everyone went voluntarily, but here there's no question that it took force to move some of the villagers from their remote homes by the beautiful desert lake. Today some visitors only stop for lunch and perhaps a quick dip; others hang around, perhaps renting a pair of skis or even a snowboard from Sher to try a little sand-skiing down the dunes.

•　•　•　•

The next day we head a few kilometres directly south from Germa, climbing up through the dark, stony range that backdrops the view. Then we turn west and for the next two hours race across a wide, featureless plain. Far to the south the view ends at a range of towering sand dunes, the start of the Murzuq Sand Sea. Later the dark trace of the Msak Settafet range emerges to the north. There's no trail to follow. The route could be a hundred or even a thousand lanes wide, despite which there is a police checkpoint in the middle of nowhere. Finally we leave the plain to make a short traverse of another stretch of textbook Sahara desert, race across some more featureless plain, and finally rock and roll over a corner of the Ocean of Stone before coming to a halt at Wadi Methkandoush.

The walls of the wadi and its southern extension, the Wadi In Galghien, form a remarkable gallery of rock art of the 10,000–6000 BC 'Wild Fauna Period'. It's a significant site for its remote location and for the extraordinary quantity of artwork, but also for the history so vividly illustrated. Global warming and climate change are such current topics that it's easy to forget how recently the Sahara was very different from the arid sandbox we've been cruising around. When the artists chipped out their illustrations on the wadi walls the Sahara was populated with animals that today are only found in the less extreme climates of countries far to the south.

The history of change the rock art illustrates is an eye opener, but the exceptional quality of much of the work is equally amazing. Elephants, ostriches and a variety of cattle and antelope appear regularly. There's at least one notable rhino and an equally impressive crocodile, but it's giraffes that really inspired these ancient Sahara artists. Even the complex patterns of the animal's hide are faithfully reproduced on some of the wadi's giraffes. My favourite, and it's equally popular on postcards, shows two giraffes and an elephant in a novel transparent style so you effectively see all of all three animals at once.

Driving back to Germa, we take a longer detour into the sand-dune country. Once again we're in picture-book Sahara, where sand rolls away in every direction and even a hubcap-high bush is a rarity. And once again we nose out over the top of a high dune and look down upon a lake, except this lake has disappeared, leaving just the rocky white pattern of its drying death throes. Once upon a time it must have been just like the Ubari Lakes. Now, like the water, the surrounding vegetation has totally disappeared. As we gaze out over this scene of utter emptiness, there is absolutely no sign of life between us and the horizon until, from behind a fold in the distant dunes, the tiny figure of a camel emerges. It's quickly followed by six more, trudging across the landscape towards some far-off water source known only to thirsty camels and their drivers.

It's a pleasure to get back to the Dar Germa Hotel and shower off the sand and dust that quickly coats you and everything else in the car. It's a particular pleasure in our room's extravagant bathroom. Although the hotel was described as 'very basic', a step down from the merely 'basic' hotel in Ghadames, in fact it's neat and tidy and illustrated with all sorts of Sahara photographs, pictures and maps. The bathroom is the same size as our entire room at Ghadames and equipped with a sink, toilet, bidet and a variety of fittings in an extravagantly kitsch gold-trimmed style. This is nicely counterbalanced by utterly utilitarian and completely exposed plumbing, which snakes and writhes its way from the wheezy water-heater mounted high on the wall. It seems to be a one-off; other rooms have much less extravagant bathrooms. The hotel's food is also several notches above 'very basic' – perhaps a function of the Sudanese cook, the staff from Mali, Niger and Egypt and the Italian woman who manages the show.

The following day we venture into the Ubari Sand Sea again. It's the same routine: down the highway a few kilometres, turn north through the farmed strip, stop to drop the tyre pressures and disappear into the rolling dunes. It's clear Hassan loves plotting a path through the dunes, careful never to drop too low into depressions, exhilarated when we top a big one. Once again we suddenly emerge at the top of a ridge to find a green-fringed lake below us. Mandara, like Gebraoun, once had a village, which was forced to relocate in 1991. Here the village would soon have had to leave anyway. In the early 1980s the lake started to dry up until today it's just a collection of pools and puddles.

'I think it's because of the agricultural projects', announces Hassan. 'They take too much water.'

Yesterday we'd driven by one of the projects. Its enormous irrigated circles of grain are fed by wells tapped into the underground desert aquifers. Is there any connection between that project's launch in the early 1980s and Mandara Lake starting to dry up at the same time?

Dried up or not, it's still an idyllic scene from the top of the sand ridge, but 20 years ago we would have been gazing down at a lake famed for its changing colours while the sounds of children playing drifted up to us. Now it's completely quiet. Down at the lake the pools and puddles are crusted with thin ice-like skins of salt.

'Too much water for agriculture', repeats Hassan.

We pause at the abandoned village mosque and Mohammed shins up a dead tree to break off some firewood. I have this absurd vision of driving through Los Angeles in our admirably beat-up Toyota with its Arabic licence plates. On the roof there's a line of jerry cans for extra fuel along with the pile of firewood; a goatskin full of water is slung on the side, while at the controls are two wild-looking Tuareg tribesmen with voluminous turbans swathing their heads.

It's only a few kilometres to Umm al-Maa, the postcard Ubari Lake and one that still has plenty of water. Long and narrow with dark blue swifts flitting between the palm trees and over the water and sand, the 'Mother of Waters' is even more picturesque than its predecessors, if that's possible. While Hassan builds a fire to bake bread and Mohammed fixes lunch, I go for a swim. Like the other lakes it's as salty as the Dead Sea although digging a well nearby always provided fresh drinking water. I glisten with salt crystals when I dry off and my swimsuit dries completely stiff, as if it had been hung out on a sub-zero winter day.

'I was bobbing around like a bathtub rubber duck', I explain to Maureen.

'You looked more like a rubber tyre to me', she sweetly replies.

Cruising back across the dunes in the late afternoon we finally meet a dune that beats Hassan. Despite surveying the route beforehand and breaking down the ridge top, we still end up teeter-tottering on the edge with all the wheels off the ground. Ten minutes of shovelling gets us back in control.

'That place is always difficult', Hassan grumbles. '*Fish-fash* too much.'

There's a final dried-up lake on the way home.

'There are wolves here', Hassan explains and as if on cue something emerges from behind a dune and trots down towards the lake on the other side. The animal spots us at the same instant we spot it and we all stop. There's plenty of time to study it through binoculars and although its large erect ears look more fox-like than wolf-like, that's the way wolves are around here.

Our final morning in the Fezzan we drive west as far as the town of Ubari, where Hassan lives. His wife and some of his children are away in Tripoli.

'Beyond here there is nothing for 240 kilometres until Ghat', Hassan explains. 'Or you can turn north and drive across the dunes for two days and then through the mountains for another two or three days until you reach Ghadames. I have done that trip several times, but you must have three or four cars. Today we navigate with GPS.'

We drive up to the top of the range overlooking Ubari, where we're perfectly aligned to look down at all the satellite dishes dotting the rooftops of the town far below. From here it's like the town is covered in white polka dots.

'I was born in Ubari,' Hassan muses as we look down on his home town, 'but then my father moved to Algeria and I lived there until I was 13. Then when Algeria became free all the Libyans had to move out.'

'Did your father work there?' I enquire.

'No, my father did not work. He had animals', Hassan replies somewhat enigmatically. 'He had camels. We brought them back to Libya to sell.' This was before cars, when camel caravans still travelled across the Sahara, ignoring the borders that now divide the sands.

'The trip took about 15 days each way', Hassan continues. 'Sometimes he did the trip twice in a year.'

• • • •

So where is Libya going? The Colonel has taken a step back from terrorism and a step towards a market economy, but where has 30 years of following *The Green Book* taken Libya? Not very far in some respects. For all the money poured into a multitude of revolutions the Israelis are still in Israel, Arab unity is still a nonstarter, African unity is unlikely to be any easier to create, and very few of those revolutionaries he funded have managed to achieve their revolutionary aims.

As for the economy, *The Green Book* or not, Gaddafi's recipe for a managed one has proved no more successful than any others. Libya still overwhelmingly depends on oil (and would be a sorry mess without it), the public sector is bloated and inefficient, and the private sector is not only tangled with restrictions and bureaucracy, it also suffers from the straightforward difficulty of interpreting what the hell Gaddafi means in his *Green Book* meanderings. Like Saudi Arabia and other oil-rich Arab nations, Libya has a native population that is remarkably unenthusiastic about a hard day's work. They crowd the public sector (lots of opportunity for sitting around there) and are notably absent in other areas, particularly in fields like tourism where slacking off isn't an option.

On the other hand, Gaddafi has made Libya a much more independent country and clearly made huge efforts to raise the general living standard and distribute the benefits of the country's oil wealth more equitably. From our perspective, shifting people out of their charming, if ill-equipped, old houses and villages may look unfortunate, but we're being chauvinistic, patronising romantics if we try to ignore the attraction of running water, flush toilets and electricity. Unfortunately Libya seems to have inherited the public housing curse of creating instant slums on a nationwide scale, but that's another story.

Dishevelled, tatty buildings and the nationwide problem of garbage make Libya look a much poorer country than the statistics indicate, but even the statistics aren't too exciting. Like Saudi Arabia, Libya is a country with so much money sloshing around that it clearly should have better figures in everything from infant mortality to literacy. So Gaddafi's school report isn't going to be a glowing one: 'tries hard, but easily distracted and end results not impressive'.

• • • •

Hassan drives us out to the airport to fly back to Tripoli. To the very end he's effortlessly charming. I don't think I've ever met anyone who looks so serenely calm, relaxed, dignified and competent. He waves away the money I try to offer him as we part – tipping clearly does not fall into the Tuareg code of conduct.

We'd heard that British tour groups could not use Libyan Arab Airlines because British travel insurance companies won't cover their flights, but for the first time in the Fezzan the tourist numbers are not almost entirely Italian – there's a healthy minority of Brits as well.

It's hardly surprising I miss the Tripoli pre-boarding announcement, it was probably only made in Arabic: 'We are now pre-boarding women with veils. Men and other women please wait for the general boarding announcement.' Twenty or so women and an assortment of children obediently head for the plane. The general scrum begins soon afterwards.

The next day we fly out. I'd met Donald Yorke, an old university engineering friend, at a party the year before. He worked in the oil industry in the post-revolution but pre-embargo era of the 1970s. 'When you left Libya you could fly with Libyan Arab Airlines or Alitalia', he recalled. 'There would be two flights departing simultaneously for Rome: one empty, one packed. Everybody on the Alitalia flight would be hanging out for a drink and the moment the door was shut, that was it. We were out of there, we'd left Libya – the flight attendants would be racing down the aisle handing out drinks before we'd even got out to the runway.'

We're well in the air and heading towards Egypt before the drinks trolley comes past us.

· · · ·

On our last morning in Tripoli there was one final surprise in an often very surprising country. I go for a last wander around the medina and drop in to the old cathedral. One of Gaddafi's first moves after the 1969 revolution was to turn it into a mosque, but today it's mainly used as a gallery. There's an exhibition by the French artist Marie-Elisabeth Mathieu titled Memento, sponsored by the old city of Tripoli and the French cultural association. There's no catalogue or explanation, but it's pretty clear what this exhibition is all about. It is memories of September 11 and would be a sadly evocative piece of art anywhere in the world. Here in Libya it's strangely moving. The centrepiece is an eight-metre-high World Trade Center tower, constructed of the little flat wooden trays used in Libya to transport and display vegetables and fruit. They're wired together with the plastic ties used to bundle electrical cabling. The centre of the tower is floodlit from below and pieces that look like aluminium foil origami – people, planes? – float down inside.

NORTH KOREA

CHINA

Mt Paekdu

Samjiyon

Orang

Chilbo

Sinuiju

EAST SEA
(Sea of Japan)

Gulf of
West
Korea

PYONGYANG

Wonsan

Sinphyong

Panmunjeom

SOUTH KOREA

'You guys really *are* the axis of evil', our guide splutters over his stein of beer in the Pyongyang duck restaurant.

'You're always leaning out of the windows and taking photographs when I tell you not to. You wander off without a guide to keep an eye on you. You giggle – giggle! – when the local guides are making speeches about the accomplishments of the Great Leader. I know there'll be a report made after this tour. I could lose my job. At the very least I'll be sent to Lake Chon to lead local tours for six months next winter.'

We fell about laughing. True, we had demanded that the bus stop every time we came to another really good billboard of the Great Leader, the Dapper Despot as I'd dubbed him, or his son, the Dear Leader, aka the Tubby Tyrant. Perhaps we were the tour group from hell, but what the hell? This was the country for suppressing giggles and our guide, Kim Myong Song, or 'Mr Kim' as I always called him, was always joking.

It's easy to fall for the international media's portrait of North Korea as a place alternating between horror and comedy, a Stalinist theme park, a gulag run by Monty Python. In fact it's hard to argue that any portrait of the country and its leadership could be too far-fetched when reports of the population facing starvation are counterpointed by tales of the leader's son trotting off to visit Tokyo Disneyland using a fake Caribbean passport. North Korea's recent elevation to the nuclear club has underlined that the antics inside this super-secret Communist state are no laughing matter.

•   •   •   •

My relationship with this enigmatic nation began by accident. I was in a lift in the former Portuguese colony of Macau updating my *Southeast Asia on a Shoestring* guide. The door slid open on the wrong floor and almost immediately I realised the office I wanted wasn't there, but it was too late, the doors had shut, the lift had already departed. I pressed the button to recall the elevator and glanced through the glass frontage of the Korean Tourist Office as I waited for its return. Fortunately the lift didn't return instantly because it took me a few minutes to realise what was wrong. This was not an ROK, Republic of Korea, tourist office. This was a DPRK, Democratic People's Republic of Korea, tourist office.

The word 'Democratic' in a country's name is always a giveaway. By definition any country that proclaims itself democratic is definitely not democratic and the DPRK is a fine example of that maxim. North Korea shut itself off from the outside world after the Korean War ended in 1953. Its only real supporters were Russia and China, both pretty reclusive places themselves.

'Hello,' I said to the smiling young lady, 'are you really a North Korea tourist office?'

'Oh, yes,' she happily replied, 'would you like to visit the Democratic People's Republic of Korea?'

'I certainly would', I shot back. 'I didn't know you allowed visitors. What do I have to do to make a visit?'

'There are no problems,' she went on, 'just fill in this form.'

I felt like I'd chanced on a wormhole into another universe, but my schedule was crowded and 10 years passed before I finally got around to joining a group visit to the Magic Kingdom. I am not a group travel person, but for North Korea there is really no choice. Technically you can make your own one-person tour, but you're still going to be stuck with guides and minders and have very little choice of what you see and how you see it. Going with a group at least gives you other people to bounce ideas and impressions off. And with a bunch of you running around, it's a little more difficult for Big Brother to be watching every minute of the day.

I meet my group at Beijing's main railway station. It's fitting that a place as isolated as North Korea should take a long time to get to. There had been a night at the airport hotel in Hong Kong, another overnight in a Beijing hotel and finally an overnight train journey.

Rolling out of Beijing in the late afternoon, we pull into Dandong, the China–North Korea border town, the next morning. The Chinese town sprawls back from the north bank of the Yalu River. On the south bank is Sinuiju, the greyer, quieter, poorer North Korean sister city. There's the usual Chinese hustle in Dandong, with neon signs and new buildings surrounding a giant statue of the Great Helmsman in the square directly in front of the station. The Mao cult has faded remarkably since its 1960s Cultural Revolutionary heyday and this survivor seems a brave relic, a signal from the citizens of Dandong that despite everything they've still got a soft spot for the old boy. Giant statues, as we would soon see, are definitely not an endangered species on the other side of the border.

We do some last-minute shopping at the food stands in the station entrance, but regrettably I don't go looking for a Kim Il-sung badge from the sidewalk vendors purveying North Korean maps, postcards and other tourist goodies. Almost everybody in North Korea wears a small, discreet Kim Il-sung badge but we soon discover they are impossible for an outsider to procure.

It takes a couple of relaxed hours to complete the border formalities on the China side. Meanwhile, the two Pyongyang-bound sleeper carriages, which had been hooked on to a standard train from Beijing, are disconnected, mysteriously rolled away and equally mysteriously reappear. We reboard them for the short shunt across the border where they'll be connected to a North Korean train for the journey to the capital. A few minutes after leaving the Chinese station we're rolling across the bridge, paralleling another bridge that was brought down during the Korean War. The Chinese chunk of the partially destroyed bridge has become a café and lookout point where Chinese tourists eye North Korea through binoculars.

'Cameras away', shouts Nick, our Beijing-based English tour organiser, comedian and all-round North Korea expert. It's the first rendition of what will become the standard North Korean order. The North Koreans are extremely touchy about what gets photographed in the workers' earthly paradise. Nothing that looks slightly unparadisiacal is to be recorded.

A children's fun park is our first sign of North Korea; it's dusty and disused – clearly nobody has been having fun here for a long time. Minutes later we're in the station at Sinuiju, where North Korean officials board the train and embark on an immigration and customs arrival process just as laid-back and relaxed as the Chinese on the other side of the bridge. Our first Kim Il-sung portrait gazes down at the platform. Two of our group have mobile phones, which are taken away and returned, much later, carefully wrapped and stamped with a customs seal to ensure they are not used in North Korea. Quite how they would be used is unclear.

After half an hour of poking around our bags, inspecting passports and visas (our visas, collected in Beijing, are assembled on one big sheet, not stamped into our passports) and chatting amiably, the officials allow us to ramble around the station, just as long as we don't go outside. We wander up to a rather sparsely stocked snack bar (all the drinks are from Singapore) where we can look down on the square in front of the station. A Kim Il-sung statue looks out over the square, which is hardly bustling but nor, on the other hand, is it deserted.

In our whole two-week trip we will see no fainting soldiers, no starving children, no obvious signs of the famine that has racked the country for years. Nevertheless on the six-hour journey from the border to Pyongyang there are plenty of signs that not all is well. The roads are empty. At one stage, a road parallels the railway and for an hour I only see one vehicle moving, a Mercedes Benz. Throughout my visit I will never see a bus carrying North Koreans outside of the cities and even the occasional trucks packed with people will look like they're on short trips only. Perhaps the government's tight control on movements plays a part. You don't go anywhere in the people's paradise without having a permit.

There are no goods on the go either. Empty highways tell tales of a country shut down, but there are also clear signs of the problems down on the farm. The North Korean countryside looks like one big disaster area. All the way to Pyongyang we're running through farming country and it's obvious the land is overworked. Every tiny patch is being used and it's clear a lot of it shouldn't be. When you start growing things on the sloping sides of riverbanks and drainage ditches you're asking for erosion problems. In Pyongyang I will pick up a booklet by Kim Jong-il titled 'Improving the Layout of the Fields is a Great Transformation of Nature for the Prosperity of the Country'.

Our train stops and people get off and line up to have their paperwork checked. Our North Korean guides, who will stick close to us for the next week, are waiting on the platform. There's the bespectacled Mr Kim, a fluent English speaker, who would make a good computer nerd in the West. His occasional exasperation (why can't we just accept that we shouldn't be taking photographs?) rarely overpowers his sense of humour. He's also very aware. We've been instructed to bring presents for our guides, but I soon see the kangaroo tie I present him with disdainfully passed on to our bus driver. The kangaroos aren't necessarily déclassé, but it's clear if a tie gift isn't silk it isn't worth having.

Mr O's English isn't as good and I soon begin to wonder if he's really a guide at all. Perhaps he's there to keep an eye on the real guides, just as they're there to keep an eye on us. Ms Park, on the other hand, is new to the job and a cheerful delight. She's young, sometimes slightly worried looking, but her English is just as assured as Mr Kim's. Physically and fashionably, if you'd whisked all three of them away to Seoul, they would have blended in without a hitch.

Our group is a curiously mixed bag. For a start they're not old. Sometimes 'last' destinations like this attract an older audience, people with money and time who've already been everywhere else. In fact half of this group is quite young and nobody is ancient. Are they anoraks, as the British refer to nerds with curious obsessions? The real surprise is how many are second-time visitors when I would have thought this was a 'been there, done that' destination.

Eugene, a solid, efficient-looking German engineer and long-term Japan resident, probably is a real travel junkie and Subrapta's Madras-based leather export business clearly gives him an excuse to travel widely. I guess I have to slot myself into that unhealthily addicted category as well.

Ivan and Jeanne-Pierre, on the other hand, are simply enquiring young travellers. They're both postgraduate students and you get the feeling they're here purely because they like going to unusual places. Ivan is really an American, but is travelling on a Slovakian passport, and Jeanne-Pierre is a French-Canadian, although the French connection comes courtesy of Belgium. Ian, a Scot, is also young and almost Japanese in his enthusiasm to be photographed everywhere. The rest of the British contingent are all unusual. John, from Northern Ireland, is in fact an anorak anorak, not even a travel one, while Camilla is not only very English (with a name like that she'd have to be) but also very very earnest. She has been in Beijing studying Chinese and this is her second visit to the DPRK. She's returning because her previous trip didn't coincide with the Mass Games. Also second-timers, Phil and Jaqueline soon become the weirdest of our weird little ensemble. Their enthusiasm for all things North Korean is so unshakeable that I find myself glancing over at them to see if they really are wearing those fabled rose-coloured spectacles. Digby, an Australian, is also a repeat offender.

Subrapta is the only Asian in the group. 'We don't need to visit North Korea', Jinghui, a Chinese friend, had commented in Beijing. 'Anyone who remembers China in the 1970s has already been there.'

The sun is just setting as we make our first, obligatory, stop en route to our hotel. Nick has thoughtfully brought a large bouquet of flowers from Beijing, their fragrance floating along the train's corridors. It saves queuing to buy a bunch from the flower-seller close to the foot of the giant Mansudae statue, a 20-metre-high bronze figure of the Great Leader looking out over the capital city of the dreamland he created. We're lined up to bow respectfully before this personality cult classic. 'If you can't hack doing it, then you should think twice about coming to North Korea', Nick had warned us.

The hotel lobby doesn't look enormously different to any other 43-storey international hotel's entrance foyer. The time at different international cities dances in lights above the reception desk and the cashier is ready to change your US dollars into North Korean won. The only immediate giveaway is the black-and-white photo exhibit to one side of the desk, detailing atrocities committed against the Korean people by the Japanese Imperialists (during the 1905–45 occupation) and by the American Imperialists (during the Korean War, which remarkably was not labelled with its better-known name, the Victorious Fatherland Liberation War). Oh, and this week's bestsellers in the bookshop included page turners like *Japanese War Crimes Past & Present* and *Kim Jong Il – Selected Works*. A sign above the bookshop reminds us that the *Juche* Idea 'is exerting a great influence on the ideological life of humanity', and at the same time 'gaining a strong sympathy from people all over the world'. Around midnight I finally crawl into bed, after one last look out my 40th-floor window. Across the Taedong River, the pyramid shape of the 105-storey Ryugyong Hotel dominates the city's skyline. The lights of a car cruise along the riverside road. It's the only vehicle moving in the city.

• • • •

Korea has always been the Hermit Kingdom. Today, under the absolute rule of the late 'Great Leader', Kim Il-sung, the man who single-handedly inflicted defeat on both the Imperialist Aggressor Japanese and the Imperialist Aggressor Americans (not to mention the Puppet Stooge South Koreans), the President for Life-and-Beyond, North Korea has become a modern version of that old nickname. It's an apt description for a country that manages to be isolationist and Stalinist and behave like a monarchy.

Squeezed between China and Japan long before they found themselves squeezed between Russia and America, both Koreas have suffered from being Big Power surrogates. In the late 1800s the Koreans panicked that their old enemies, the Chinese and Japanese, were being supplanted by even more frightening new enemies from Europe, America and Russia. Their response was to slam the doors shut. It proved hopeless. Poor Korea found itself battered between Russia and Japan until, with the defeat of Russia in the Russo-Japanese War of 1904, the country came under even stronger Japanese influence. By 1910 the Japanese were in control. By the start of World War II, Korean schools were forced to teach in Japanese and the study of Korean history was banned. Korean men were conscripted into the Japanese army, Korean civilians were shipped to Japan as virtual slave labourers (a large proportion of the atom bomb casualties at Hiroshima were Koreans working in the factories) and Korean women were forced into prostitution as 'comfort women' for the Japanese army. It's scarcely surprising that the Koreans, north and south, still carry a large chip on their collective shoulders against the Japanese.

At the same time, a divide started to open between the northern and southern halves of Korea. North Korea is colder, drier, higher and less fertile than the south. If a famine struck, it was always more likely to hit the north than the south, and during the periodic struggles with the Chinese it was the north that always bore the brunt of the onslaughts. The arrival of American Christian missionaries also played a part in the division, convincing many northern converts that their problems were caused by the effete Confucians in the southern capital of Seoul.

The guerrilla struggle against the Japanese during World War II was principally a northern endeavour. It may not have been quite as exclusively northern as the North Koreans will insist, but there's little question that, when it came to battling the Japanese, Kim Il-sung, even if he did not defeat them all by himself, played a major part. During the war the southerners continued to be better fed than their northern brethren, although it was the north that became the cog in the Japanese industrial tool.

After 40 years of Japanese occupation, the war's conclusion did not bring independence. The Russians only declared war on Japan on 8 August 1945, after the first atomic bomb had been dropped and less than a week before the war ended. Now they marched into Korea from the north at the same time as American troops entered from the south. Korea was divided at the 38th parallel. The unfortunate Koreans became the first Cold War pawn.

Both countries had been devastated by the Japanese occupation during World War II and then by the Korean War, which lasted two years and was fought out on almost every square centimetre of land. Fighting broke out on 25 June 1950 and the North Korean troops soon marched all the way to Busan in the southeast corner of the country. A couple of months later the South Koreans, with their American support (and the support of a small number of other nationalities), fought their way back north as far as the Chinese border before Mao sent his army in and pushed them back to the 38th parallel, exactly where the whole mess had started. The line has been the uneasy border between the two Koreas ever since.

With the Korean War, it's really irrelevant who fired the first shot – the South (according to the North) or the North (according to our side of the argument). Both sides were itching to start trading blows and America and Russia – paying the bills, supplying the arms and handing out the advice – were clearly ready to unleash things as well. The end result was not unlike what happened between Israel and the Arab world 20 years later. It's easy to forget that in 1967 it was Israel that invaded its neighbours, not vice versa. Of course, if they'd waited a few more days the Egyptians and Syrians might well have been marching across the border, but the truth is the Israelis fired first. The Korean War was going to happen – it didn't matter who fired the first shot.

After the war the Russians poured in aid to the North and created a Soviet-style economy of collective farming and gigantic state-run industrial concerns. The workers marched forward, led by the ideals of *Juche*, Kim Il-sung's home-grown blend of Marxism and self-sufficiency. For a while they were better off than their brethren in the south, but when the South Koreans put the pedal to the metal in the 1960s *Juche* was shown to be useless and South Korea pulled away from the North like a hotted-up Hyundai overtaking a worn-out horse cart.

• • • •

232. Our visit doesn't – like most – kick off with a tour of the Pyongyang sights. This is the 'mountain tour', and we've chartered a small Air Koryo aircraft to take us to the north of the country for a couple of days. Our bus pulls up at the Pyongyang International Airport terminal building and we all start to laugh. It's the natural reaction when you're confronted with the capital's international airport and find the car park deserted. To be honest, there were two vehicles, our bus and a car. It's OK to photograph it, so we scatter in all directions to record what an empty car park looks like.

Later that morning our bus winds down the dirt, but comfortably smooth, coastal road from the military airport at Orang to the mountain town of Chilbo. The coastline is beautiful with tiny bays, picturesque little fishing villages (which we're emphatically not allowed to photograph), soaring cliffs and mountains rising up further inland. Any place where land meets sea in anything less than a sheer, unclimbable cliff there's a continuous concrete wall, topped with spikes or broken glass and surmounted by a double-strand electric fence. Supposedly this anti–Imperialist Aggressor (and Puppet Stooge) fence continues right down both coasts, but the fear of invasion is clearly shared. Similar barriers line the coast in South Korea.

At the Outer Chilbo lookout there are beautiful pillar-like rock formations and our first encounter (there will be more) with Kim Il-sung rapture. A local guide pops up, something we will soon get used to, and launches into a description of the scenery, translated from Korean by Mr Kim. There is a standard routine to any description whether it's of a natural feature, historical site or monument. First there's a brief account of what you're looking at, then there's a longer report on when Great Leader or Dear Leader visited it. If they dropped by more than once then there will be a tale about each visit. If it's some sort of work site – a collective farm, for example – then you'll hear how Dear or Great instructed the farmers (or workers, fisherfolk or soldiers) how to grow more, produce more, catch more or kill more, this information being gratefully received with open-mouthed awe.

Here it was the mountains and the climate itself that were awestruck.

233.

When Kim Il-sung turned up the weather was lousy, but the mountains, clever mountains that they were, realised that their important visitor had a close connection to a more important mountain. After all, the Great Leader and Mt Paekdu, legendary birthplace of the Korean people and the highest mountain in the country, are good friends. So, recognising just how important the visitor was, it's hardly surprising that the weather cleared up instantly. This tale is recounted with such rapturous fervour and translated with such deadpan conviction, it's hard to suppress the giggles that become the norm for any North Korean tour.

Our hotel comes with a fairly standard feature outside Pyongyang – no running water. The bathtub was full of cold water and a plastic bowl is provided to scoop it out. Mix a couple of scoops of cold with the hot water from the vacuum flask, provided Chinese-style for making tea, and you have the ingredients for a shower. There's another very nonstandard feature – other guests. They're from a town in the northeast of China and by the time we get back they are already making serious inroads into the restaurant's beer supply. By dinnertime the all-male party is getting to the uproarious song stage and the restaurant staff begin to move a series of dividers between our tables to protect us from the sight, if not the sound, of Chinese party animals. Nick, whose fluent Chinese has already provided plenty of amusement in the train's dining car from Beijing, will have none of this. Leaping from his seat he seizes one of the dividers and pulls it aside, yelling 'We will have no divisions here!' A roar of approval goes up from the Chinese band, glasses are raised to our international group, and we're requested to add our songs to the festivities. Subrapta Das wins the contest with what he describes as 'a bawdy Sri Lankan number'. Subrapta vies with Olaf, one of the German trio, as the group clown. 'Beneath my coffee-coloured complexion,' he shyly announces when we compliment him on his winning song, 'I am blushing pink.'

234.

The next morning, after breakfast – which was remarkably like the rice, fish, vegetables and kimchi of lunch and dinner the night before – we board the bus and head back along the empty, winding road, requesting stops for photo opportunities and repeatedly being told not to take anything with people or villages in the frame. A half-dozen of the Korean War vintage MiG-15s at the airport are flying circuits. As our bus pulls on to the runway to take us to our waiting aircraft I look out the back window to see one of the elderly Russian fighter planes making its final approach. Presumably fuel is too precious to allow second circuits and our driver hurriedly pulls off the runway.

We fly north to Korea's most revered (and highest) peak, Mt Paekdu. Samjiyon Airport is not a purely military operation like Orang, but it's even quieter than the capital. Pyongyang International Airport had no passengers, Samjiyon has nobody. We unload our own baggage and march over to the empty terminal. The Tupolev on the apron has just flown in with an army contingent who are currently lunching at our hotel. There's not room for both army and tourists so we're ushered into the airport's VIP room (overstuffed chairs, side tables, the usual portraits) and handed what looks like a DPRK Japanese bento box prepared several days ago.

Beijing just two days ago was cooking, Pyongyang and Chilbo were warm. Samjiyon is distinctly chilly and as our bus carries us up towards Mt Paekdu it turns from chilly to cold to icy. By the time we've climbed above the tree line it's bloody freezing and I'm glad I stuffed a sweater and ski jacket into my bag. Mt Paekdu is a spectacular volcano crater with a lake straddling the North Korea–China border. In 1998 a young British backpacker in China set out to walk around the 14-kilometre circumference of Lake Chon unaware (his British guidebook hadn't warned him) that he would march straight across the border and into a North Korean diplomatic incident. No way I would want to be walking anywhere near the lake today. At the end of May it's still iced over and a bitter wind shrieks up the inner slope of the crater and spills over the edge with such ferocity that only a couple of us venture right up to the top of the lookout.

235.

Back in the bus, we roll down into the forests to investigate Mt Paekdu's Great and Dear Leader connections. This was where the Great Leader mounted his guerrilla attacks on the Japanese occupiers and where, in a humble log cabin, the Dear Leader was born in 1942. Except there are no records (outside of North Korea) of any anti-Japanese action here and, despite the tales of Kim Jong-il's arrival while shells whistled past and bombs exploded, the evidence is that he was born in Khabarovsk in Russia. The Western information is that Kim Il-sung was in Russia for most of World War II and returned to Korea on board the Russian warship *Pukachev* on 19 September 1945, well after he'd finished off the Japanese. Never mind, like any capitalist PR firm the North Koreans have never let the truth stand in the way of a good story and the Paekdu Secret Camp site is fronted by a magnificent billboard-sized mosaic of Great Leader and wife, with Kim Junior in her arms, all smiling warmly from the snowy scene with the log cabin standing cosily in the background.

Our attention is focused on our local guide, the charming Miss Lee, who is so irresistibly cute in her khaki outfit and so tiny (even her Kim Il-sung badge looked bigger than normal) you could have wrapped her up and taken her home as a Korean People's Army Doll. Once we've torn ourselves away from the mosaic, there is the Great Leader's log cabin from where he directed military operations and the family log cabin where little Kim theoretically greeted the world. Fortunately we later came to the rotting foundations of the 'real' log cabin where it is revealed the Disney-esque cabins we've just inspected are just rebuilt replicas. The slogan trees, however, are undoubtedly real.

Perhaps.

They're safely encased in Perspex cylinders and covered by canvas condoms, which, one day, will wrinkle back at the touch of a button to

reveal tree trunks bearing anti-Japanese slogans. In between ambushing the Imperialist Aggressors, the Great Leader's well-trained guerrillas took time out to burn patriotic slogans on to the trees. Since nobody had yet managed to wire up the electric motors to pull back the covers we are reluctantly allowed to pull them up manually. As if leaving tree graffiti wasn't careless enough, the guerrillas, clearly not too concerned about covering their tracks, were also inclined to leave the remains of their campfires to be found. At another possibly not-so-secret camp we are proudly shown countless campfire sites, each one encased in a tent-shaped glass box.

• • • •

The modern army contingent had moved on from the dining room by the time we arrive at the Pagaebong Hotel, a hidden-in-the-forest DPRK Fawlty Towers complete with 50 rooms, no guests (God knows how long since there had been another group) and once again no running water – to the sink at least. My room also has a TV, no doubt tuned to the DPRK's single channel, but since it has no power lead it's impossible to check. The fridge is similarly deficient, but at least one of the two bedside lights works. Much of the hotel (not all of it, curiously enough) is freezing cold. Half seems to be closed off, with piles of old furniture heaped along the corridors. The stairs and public areas are laid with fraying, badly cut carpet, which loops and sags down the stairs. Beside the second-floor bar is a pool room with a pool table, with no balls or cues, but the bar itself is well stocked with cans of Heineken for just 1.50 won, 75 cents in US currency. Where in the world can you buy a can of Heineken beer for less than a US dollar? The theory is that it's imported for the political elite and since nobody except that tiny group could afford anything so extravagant as a can of beer it's provided to them at cost.

We repair to the bar after dinner and proceed to have another raucously bizarre North Korean evening culminating in a game of musical chairs. Did I ever imagine I would end up playing musical chairs in a key centre of the evil axis? Remarkably we only manage to break one of the chairs and in the final round I take control of the cassette player and manage to rig the results so that the final chair is disputed between our charming Ms Park and the bar's equally charming Ms Kim. Clearly neither of them has experienced this Western children's game before and find it invigorating.

In the morning there's a visit to the Rimyongsu waterfall with a crumbling concrete pavilion plonked in the middle of it. The hotel dining room had a romanticised painting of the scene, everything magnified until the waterfall became Niagara in size. The visit has an unexpected bonus. The village by the falls has been turned into a huge housing construction site. It looks remarkably similar to suburban tract housing projects in the West. I half expect to see a display house decorated with flags and a sign offering 10 per cent deposit and low monthly payments, but a second glance indicates that this is definitely a Third World project with everything being done by hand and large groups with hammers squatting by the roadside converting rocks into tiny pebbles.

'Would it be possible to see inside a house?' I ask Mr Kim, not expecting for a moment that it would be. The senior guides confer, Mr Kim goes off and returns 10 minutes later to say it's been arranged. Even more remarkably, we find ourselves not in an almost completed or recently finished house, but in one that's actually inhabited. It's not going to win any architectural awards, and if you were over six-foot tall you'd be scrunching down under the low ceilings, but it's actually quite cosy, if bare. There are no chairs or tables. A long storage cabinet is all there is in the main room. The glass-fronted doors reveal quilts and blankets. They're rolled out on the floor to convert living room to bedroom, just like a traditional Japanese house.

The smaller second room just has a storage shelving unit. The floors are lino covered and the only decorations are the standard pictures of Dear and Great in one room, and a framed photograph of the dynamic duo in the other. There's a smaller storage room and a kitchen where everything is clearly prepared from scratch. There is nothing packaged or tinned, but everything is very neat and tidy, with stacks of pots and dishes in a cabinet. The sink and cooking equipment is all at floor level, the middle of the floor is at a lower level – you climb down to put yourself at waist level to the coal-fired cooking equipment. There's no running water – a tin bucket sits by the sink. The final room is the washing and laundry room, again without running water, or for that matter, a toilet.

After lunch some of us join in an impromptu football match with the construction workers labouring on an extension to the empty hotel. After a stop to pay our respects to another gigantic Great Leader statue, we fly back to Pyongyang and the Arirang Mass Games.

There's a dramatic 'clack' as 20,000 children slam their card books open on another page and, on the other side of the 150,000-seat May Day Stadium, the face of a gigantic Kim Il-sung pops up. There's a roar of approval while, down on the stadium floor, the dancing army proves they can march as well and stride off the grounds. I'm watching the Arirang Mass Games – or more correctly the Mass Gymnastic and Artistic Performances.

One side of the stadium is taken up by those carefully choreographed children, flipping open the pages of their card books to make patterns and pictures, including that huge face of the Great Leader. The activity is equally precisely timed and the numbers are nearly as big down at ground level where the evening kicks off with thousands of women in pastel green, yellow and purple dresses swooshing out on to the grounds. 'Mass' is clearly the appropriate word. A dozen or a hundred carefully coordinated hula-hoopers is one thing; a thousand of them, all dressed in blue, is visually quite another. Now feed in another thousand rope skippers (in pink) and yet another thousand tennis-racquet wavers (in white) and the effect is astonishing.

The effect can also be beautiful, when a sea of women in white swirl their blue cloaks to produce a shimmering then storming sea across which a red ship swiftly sails, mirrored by a second red ship moving in a flickering blaze of opening and closing card books across the stadium seats. It can be amusing, when rabbits, rice plants, chickens and (what came first?) eggs dance across in the 'increase production' number. Or it can be simply cute, when thousands of children, all toting flotation rings, race out on to the grounds while beach scenes materialise behind them.

And then there's the incredible dancing army. If a war's ever decided by which army does the best mass dancing, my money is on the North Koreans.

• • • •

For such a secretive society, North Korea has made a success of attracting global headlines. Giving the world the middle finger – the US and their southern neighbours in particular – has been a favourite pastime of North Korea, using somewhat unconventional foreign policy tactics such as assassinations, suicide missions, drug running, counterfeiting, kidnapping, missile launches and, since late 2006, nuclear tests.

In November 1987 Kim Hyun Hee, a 26-year-old woman from North Korea, boarded KAL 858, a Korean Airlines 707, in Baghdad. The flight continued to Abu Dhabi in the United Arab Emirates and then departed for the South Korean capital, Seoul. On board were 115 passengers and crew, 93 of them Korean workers returning from the Middle East. Unfortunately for those on board, Kim Hyun Hee and her 70-year-old 'father' had deplaned in Abu Dhabi and carelessly left some of their hand luggage in the overhead locker. Hours later, over the Bay of Bengal, KAL 858 exploded and plunged into the sea. There were no survivors.

Meanwhile Kim Hyun Hee and dad, travelling on forged Japanese passports, had flown from Abu Dhabi to Bahrain and were about to board a flight to Jordan when the immigration authorities became suspicious about their circular journey. Realising they were about to be arrested, the pair decided to have a last cigarette. It was indeed a last drag for Kim Sung Il, the father figure, for as well as the bomb, packed into a radio they had left on board the Korean aircraft, they were also equipped with cyanide-spiked Marlboros. Kim Sung Il, no relation to the Great Leader Kim Il-sung, died instantly, but his 'daughter' survived and was flown to South Korea for some extensive interrogation.

It turned out that she'd been recruited and trained in North Korea before starting her international activities from Macau, the centre of North Korea's most popular export – fake US hundred-dollar bills. In one four-month spell in late 1998 to early 1999, they were reputed to have funnelled more than half a million in counterfeit US bills through a front company based there. It also provided cover for Ms Kim's bombing operation.

In South Korea Kim Hyun Hee confessed (Kim Jong-il made me do it) and was pardoned on the basis that she was young, foolish and pretty and the nasty North Koreans had brainwashed her. So why had the nasty North Koreans, and Kim Jong-il in particular, dreamed up this crazy plan? To undermine the 1988 Olympics, due to be held in Seoul, of course.

The aircraft bombing wasn't the first crackpot plot designed to destabilise the South Koreans. In 1983 a South Korean government mission paid a visit to Rangoon (now Yangon) in Burma (Myanmar). North Korean agents left three bombs in the roof of Rangoon's Martyrs' Mausoleum. It was South Korea's president, Chun Doo-hwan, and his cabinet officers who were the focus of the assassination attempt, but the North Koreans mistook the South Korean ambassador, arriving in a large car, for the president, who was stuck in a traffic jam. Only one of the three bombs went off, but 21 people were killed including South Korea's foreign minister, deputy prime minister, two other ministers and a host of advisers, journalists and security personnel, all except four of them Koreans. Two days later a suspect was arrested, but in what seems to be the norm for North Korean agents when found out, he tried to commit suicide, using a hand grenade. Two more suspects also tried the hand grenade routine later the same day, one of them succeeding and killing three Burmese policemen as well.

In the 1990s North Korean activity shifted to submarines and fishing boats, although suicide remained part of the game plan. In September 1996 a North Korean submarine ran aground off the coast of South Korea and the heavily armed crew of 26 made it to shore, sparking off a manhunt that lasted 53 days and involved 60,000 South Korean troops. Rounding up the North Koreans led to the deaths of three South Korean civilians and five soldiers, but eventually 25 of the 26 were accounted for. One escaped, one was captured, 13 were killed and the remaining 11 committed suicide.

Remarkably, after initially threatening 'merciless retaliation' for the South Korean round-up, the North Koreans eventually apologised. The expression of 'deep regret' did, however, come at the end of a news round-up concentrating on the activities of the 'US Imperialists' and branding South Korean President Kim Young-sam a 'ruthless tyrant', a 'puppet' and a 'traitor'. Visitors to South Korea can see the North Korean submarine on display just north of the east-coast resort town of Jeongdongjin, otherwise noted for featuring in a popular South Korean television soap opera. Despite those 'deep regrets', two years later a North Korean miniature submarine got itself knotted up in a South Korean fishing boat's nets, well inside South Korean waters. When the crew of nine were unable to disentangle their vessel they all committed suicide.

In contrast to all the murder and mayhem of bombing missions, Kim Jong-nam's 2001 scheme to visit Tokyo Disneyland was light-hearted comic farce. The 29-year-old eldest son of Kim Jong-il looked like a younger version of his chubby pop when he – along with two women and his four-year-old son – were marched out to a China-bound plane from Tokyo's Narita Airport. Since there are no direct flights between Japan and North Korea (or almost anywhere else and North Korea for that matter) it wasn't possible to send the naughty lad straight home.

By the time he 'sauntered nonchalantly', according to the reports, out to his All Nippon flight, the Little General had been enjoying the Japanese government's hospitality for three days. The Japanese maintained a diplomatic silence about the affair, possibly to avoid inflaming relations with their touchy neighbours (next time the missiles might land right in Disneyland), but equally likely out of embarrassment for not noticing that a certain visitor from the Caribbean island of Dominica was more likely to dance to the rhythm of *Juche* than calypso. Kim confessed to paying US$2000 each for the passports for himself and his companions, but it wasn't a complete waste. The stamps in his passport indicated that this was his third stay in Japan in a 12-month period.

So why had he dropped by for visit number three? Reportedly so his son could enjoy that all-American Mickey Mouse experience, but cynical DPRK watchers noted that the Little General was a member of the North Korean intelligence service and believed to be a computer expert. The Disney excuse might have been simply to cover up some more sensitive pursuits.

Very little is known about Dear Leader's family life, but he is believed to have three (possibly four) children by three different women. Kim Jong-nam was born in 1971, but Dear Leader didn't bother to marry the Little General's mother, Sung Hae Rim. The Little General was followed by his half-sister, Kim Sul Song, born in 1974, and his half brother, Kim Jong Chul, born in 1981. Kim Sul Song is clearly the black sheep of the family. There were tales that she'd defected to South Korea, although it's now believed that she is in Moscow, being treated for depression.

In April 2003 Australian surfers at the popular Victorian beach resort of Lorne were witnesses to another North Korean botched operation. Wallowing in the waves dangerously close to shore was the Tuvaluan-flagged, 120-metre, 4000-tonne bulk carrier *Pong Su,* operated by the Pongsu Shipping Company in Pyongyang. The rusty vessel was just a few hundred metres off the notoriously tricky coast and had just dispatched a boat to shore. While trying to land through the heavy surf, one crewman drowned and the police turned up just in time to grab another, along with 50 kilograms of high-grade heroin. The *Pong Su* promptly sailed off and a comic-book four-day chase commenced up the east coast of Australia before the ship was finally boarded by commandos and sailed into Sydney.

Meanwhile the police had found another 75 kilograms of heroin, hidden close to the road outside Lorne, and presumably awaiting collection. Local treasure hunters took to scouring the woods around the resort, but who knows – the rust bucket had probably sailed right around Australia before the Lorne debacle, quite possibly dropping off shipments all over the place. It was all 'a sinister trick to tarnish the image of the dignified Democratic People's Republic of Korea', North Korea's official news agency reported. The shore party of four, from Malaysia, Singapore and China, were convicted, but remarkably all the North Korean crew from the captain down got away with it, including a 'political officer' who had worked in the DPRK's Beijing embassy. Somebody had fooled them into believing they were coming to Australia to pick up a shipment of BMWs for re-export to Malaysia. The final four were released in early 2006 and the 'unseaworthy' *Pong Su*, which had been costing the Australian government A$2500 a day for three years to look after, was towed out to sea and sunk by RAAF aircraft.

In 2002 kidnapping was added to the charge sheet. For years there had been sensational stories in Japan about abductions, backed up by testimony from captured North Korean spies and reports of sightings of the missing Japanese citizens in Pyongyang. Then, out of the blue, Kim Jong-il suddenly confessed that the wild rumours were true and 12 (a number later raised to 13) people had been kidnapped, although it is still believed that the numbers could have been much higher. The abductions took place in the late 1970s and early 1980s and included a 13-year-old girl, seized as she came home from school, and a courting couple strolling along a deserted beach. The people captured had no security, military or espionage value. They may have been taken to serve as Japanese-language instructors for North Korean agents or to provide identities for North Korean spies.

During the intervening years, eight of the kidnapped Japanese had died by natural causes or in a variety of accidents, a remarkably high death toll even in a country like North Korea. Furthermore most of their graves had been 'washed away in floods'. When remains of two of the kidnapped Japanese were returned to Japan, DNA tests proved they were not the people the North Koreans claimed so it's hardly surprising that years later this case is still running hot.

South Koreans were also kidnapped by the North, most notoriously the noted movie director Shin Sang-ok and his actor wife, Choi Eun-hee. In early 1978 she was kidnapped by North Korean agents while working on a film in Hong Kong. Six months later the director was also captured and whisked off to Pyongyang where he was told by Kim Jong-il himself that he had a new career awaiting him in the North. When he refused he was chucked into Prison No 6 to enjoy a four-year grass and rice diet. In 1983 he was hauled out for a second session with the Dear Leader and reunited with his wife. Kim Jong-il even apologised for taking so long to get back to him. He'd been 'busy at the office'.

This time the director decided that making North Korean movies might not be so bad after all, particularly when he was provided with a Mercedes and a salary of $3 million a year. There are 'fewer restrictions than is commonly believed', he would later tell a South Korean interviewer. In the next few years he directed five North Korean films and became so trusted that in 1986 he was allowed to pay a visit to Vienna, with his wife, where they escaped to the US embassy. He spent the next 14 years in the US, directing movies as 'Simon Sheen' and died back in South Korea in 2006.

• • • •

North Korea's background music, vaguely stirring patriotic sort of stuff, doesn't play in elevators, but drifts across the city, particularly early in the morning, and materialises from within bushes and trees at important sites. In the morning it greets me when I pull back the curtain to look out the window across the river. Despite the light traffic on its six- and eight-lane boulevards, Pyongyang is not as pollution free as promised. A smoky coal-fired power station belches a cloud of black smoke across the city. The unfinished Ryugyong Hotel's pointy shape wavers in the morning haze. In a command economy like North Korea's, where everything gets done from the top, building hotels and attracting tourists are two entirely unconnected operations. So huge hotels, like the one I'm in, stand three-quarters empty while even huger hotels, like the one I'm gazing at, stand half-built.

The massive Ryugyong Hotel is the supreme example of what happens when a command economy goes into meltdown. From almost anywhere in Pyongyang and for many kilometres outside the town, the 105-storey failure rises like a giant inverted ice-cream cone. If it had been finished, it would have been one of the world's largest hotels and added another 3000 empty rooms to the city's quota of unused bed nights. It would have been the ultimate symbol of the 1980s, when buildings and monuments sprouted like rice shoots, all designed to hide the fact that the emperor was really naked. In 1989, with the Soviet Union disintegrating, the flow of easy money suddenly stopped and so did construction. The Ryugyong remains an empty shell, which tourists are hustled past and discouraged from photographing.

We are billeted at the Yangakkdo International, which sits on an island in the middle of the river. Attractions here include a Chinese-staffed karaoke bar and a basement casino, also run by the Chinese, and with a 100 per cent Chinese clientele. At the bottom of the stairs leading to the second basement the entrance takes sharp descending twists and turns until anyone tallish has to walk hunched over. Eventually it leads to a host of attractions including a massage parlour, sauna, swimming pool, shop, hairdresser and shoe repairer.

At the end of this curious complex an exchange counter displays a sign with the prices for everything from a massage (including an 'itinerant massage'), every haircut you could imagine (bun, bob, loose hair) plus hair dyeing with a lower price quoted for 'guests who bring their own hair dye'. Men can opt for a regular shave or haircut or a rather cheaper 'hair trimming', which despite the lower cost still includes 'shaving behind the ears'. Finally there's a complete run down on shoe-repair costs including 'sticking down what has come off' with a price per centimetre of whatever it is that has to be stuck down. The grand finale, for both shoe repairs and this sign, is 'when fixing the men's heels to those of women's shoes'. This feat will set you back 4.70 won, a bit over US$2.

You can't step out of your hotel without a minder at your shoulder, except here. Since it's on an island it's safe to allow us out, so long as we don't try to cross the bridge. Or perhaps they only intended we wander around the hotel grounds at one end of the island. I decide to take an early morning stroll. When I try to walk along the riverside walkway I come up against a metal fence at the hotel boundary. I take the vehicle exit route and am firmly turned back at the security station, busily clocking in hotel workers for the morning shift.

I find another way out and walk along the riverside, past the Pyongyang International Cinema Hall (a festival due next month) and the Yanggakdo Football Stadium (they could have held a round of the 2002 World Cup here, but never bothered to even acknowledge South Korea's invitation), right up to the end of the island. Down here the land is divided into tiny strips of garden and two well-dressed women, front-desk staff from the hotel perhaps, arrive carrying bags and gardening tools. They pull out overalls from the bags to protect their office clothes while they tend their vegetable patches.

On the other bank, a greying rusting vessel is a floating symbol of

'Imperialist Aggression'. It is the USS *Pueblo,* captured while on an intelligence mission off the coast of North Korea in 1968. The 'Armed American Spyship', as the video shown on board calls it, was, according to the Americans, a marine research vessel, 'seized in international waters'. Despite US threats of retaliation, which included bringing the 'nuclear-powered', as the North Koreans underline it, aircraft carrier *Enterprise* up to the front line, nothing happened. Eventually the crew of the *Pueblo* went through the usual rigmarole of writing the sort of Communist-bloc confessions that Communist-bloc captives are always expected to write and nobody believes. The US made an official apology and after nearly a year's captivity the ship's 82 officers and crew (one was killed in the original capture) were bussed down to Panmunjom in the Demilitarized Zone (DMZ) and, one by one, got off the bus and walked across the border, all of it filmed by North Korean cameramen.

• • • •

Usually DPRK tours launch straight into Pyongyang propaganda, but our mountain interlude means we're four nights into the tour before we get our first bout of brainwashing. At the Victorious Fatherland Liberation War Museum the little lights are soon dancing down the map to show how, after the Imperialist Aggressors and the Puppet Stooges launched their unprovoked attack on the north, the People's Army soon crossed the border, liberated Seoul and advanced southwards liberating more and more of the country. They'd almost completed the job (move on to the next room and map at this point) before the Imperialist Aggressors shipped in vast numbers of troops and made their bumbled landing at Incheon. With the People's Army horribly outnumbered, the Great Leader made a rapid strategic withdrawal to the north and then turned round and, with a little Chinese help, pushed the Imperialists and their traitorous southern compatriots back to the south. Then there was a long stalemate during which time the monsters bombed the north unrelentingly and committed countless atrocities before finally, realising they were never going to win, admitted defeat and surrendered.

Next stop was the Great People's Study Hall, where the Great Leader's statue, sitting rather than standing for once, gazes out over the entrance lobby looking remarkably (except for the missing beard) like Abraham Lincoln's statue in his Washington, DC memorial. The library has, we are told, 30 million books in 60 different reading rooms. We're shown the one dedicated to the thoughts of Kim Il-sung; in between defeating Imperialists and advising farmers, workers and soldiers, he also found time to write hundreds of books. We're also shown one of the computer rooms, which, although it's not connected to the internet, follows that capitalist maxim that nobody went wrong by buying Big Blue. All the computers are IBM, although in this context it must stand for Imperialist Business Machines.

Like every other Pyongyang attraction there's a tourist shop in the Great People's Study Hall, but from a souvenir point of view the DPRK is turning out to be remarkably poorly stocked. Apart from the severe lack of badges, there's an equally great shortage of anything portraying the revolutionary kitsch that confronts you at every corner. Images of any of the countless Kim Il-sung statues that tower over odd corners of the country are unavailable, ditto for reproductions of any of the thousands of billboards that dot city and country alike, portraying father and son in a wide variety of images from the 'post-realist, neo-pop epoch of socialist romanticist art', also known as 'Commie kitsch'. It's the badges we really miss. Virtually the only North Koreans who don't sport a Great Leader badge are those fashionistas who have moved on to the double-portrait Great-and-Dear-Leader badge. Repeated shuffles through the postcard collections at every hotel, bookshop and tourist site finally yields one of the Arch of Triumph ('it's bigger than your petit Arc de Triomphe', I gloatingly inform a French friend) and a couple of the Monument to

249.

the Party Foundation, three gigantic hands holding up a hammer (the workers), a sickle (the farmers) and, convincingly one-upping the old USSR, a calligrapher's brush (the artists). Until that lucky find I was concerned that a 3D view of the Pyongyang Maternity Hospital might be the best on offer.

Daydreaming of the avid market waiting for the first capitalist to produce the Great Leader statue snow dome, I embark on a search for interesting stamps for my postcards. Even the Princess Di commemorative issues (the DPRK was no more immune to Di-mania than any other Asian country from Bangladesh to Bhutan) are only available through the stamp collectors shop and that's where I finally track down Kim Il-sung stamps for the cards I am going to send to Imperialist Aggressor Land.

'Where did you get these stamps?' the clerk at the hotel post office enquires when I go to mail the cards.

She seems content with my explanation – she should be, they cost twice their face value – but, it turns out, sending postcards portraying the country's dead (but still reigning) president is not so simple. North Korea may have a president for eternity, not just for life, but postage-stamp images of the Great Leader are clearly far too important to be used on postcards.

'After you left the post office there was a discussion about what to do', reported Camilla, who had been queuing behind me. 'They finally decided to put the postcard in an envelope with a box cut out to show the address. That way the Great Leader stamp wouldn't be displayed or defaced.'

• • • •

Pyongyang's metro is a subway designed by HG Wells. It looks and feels like a Victorian-era vision of the future, with huge platform areas surrounded by a heavy diet of revolutionary art and topped by kitschy chandeliers. Every station has an inspiring name that bears no relation to its actual position and on a ride from Reconstruction to Glory I board the carriage and, shock horror, realise someone has been scratching words on the windows!

Is this North Korean graffiti? The first sign of youthful dissent?

The guide quickly brings me down to earth: 'We bought all the carriages secondhand from East Germany. They came that way.'

We have half an hour to explore the consumer delights of Department Store No 1, five storeys of the output of the DPRK's finest factories and workshops, and just a stone's throw from Kim Il-sung Square. This is *Juche* self-reliance at its best. Nothing is imported. Like the metro, it seems to come from another era, the time when shops had counters and everything was kept behind them. If you want something, you ask for it.

I peruse the toy department, the record section (more 33⅓ LPs than CDs), the sports section (heavy on table tennis), the pen display (remember fountain pens and removable nibs?) and a surprising large space for stuffed birds and animals. The staff, strictly female and all in bright blue outfits, outnumber the shoppers, but they're friendly, greeting me with hellos and even, from the sports counter, an enquiry on my home country. Tour guides and the party elite are virtually the only people who speak any foreign language. What use would a foreign language be? Nobody's going anywhere. Yet you often hear 'hello' and 'where are you from?' In fact the North Koreans could easily be Californians; they'd quickly learn to say 'have a nice day now'. They're certainly not dour and unsmiling.

The musical instruments section offers everything from pianos to a double bass to a selection of the DPRK's finest electric guitars (I guess George W would call one an evil axe). It's the bike department that I find most interesting. Almost everything on sale in Department Store No 1 is crude or rough or outdated, but the bikes are on another strata of shoddiness. At first glance they look just like the classic men's single-speed, rod-brake machines turned out in their millions by Flying Pigeon or Phoenix in China or Hero in India. Close up it's a different story. These are the nastiest, crudest, roughest, most badly made bicycles I have ever seen. Everything about them looks inferior, from the rough welding to the bent brake rods to the uneven paint. Back at the hotel for lunch, I head straight for the employees' bicycle park. Contrary to many Pyongyang visitors' reports, the city is not bicycle free. Some of the bike park machines are Japanese, most of them Chinese. There's not a DPRK bike to be seen.

Musing about those shoddy bicycles, I can imagine the DPRK missile salesman at work: 'Mr Hussein/Gaddafi/Musharraf/Assad, we have an Axis-of-Evil special this month. With every Rodong 1 missile we're throwing in 100 of our finest bicycles.'

'That's how you make bicycles?' queries the potential weapons-of-mass-destruction customer. 'Look, I think I'm going to have to cancel that missile order.'

Our shopping interlude over, it's back to the monuments. We whisk by the Arch of Triumph (commemorating the Great Leader's defeat of the Japanese in 1945), the Monument to the Party Foundation and the tower of the *Juche* Idea (complete with a wall of plaques put up by *Juche* admirers from all over the world – there's even one from New York City). Then it's out to visit Kim Il-sung's humble peasant home on the outskirts of town. Somehow it alone survived the Japanese occupation and the destructive power of the Korean War, which flattened Pyongyang, and Seoul too for that matter.

It's the obscenity called Mangyongdae School Children's Palace that really does it for me. Our group is led around a half-dozen rooms (and one Olympic-size swimming pool) where smiling, rosy-cheeked children dance, play accordions, strum the curious stringed instrument known as a *kayagum* (its sound is 'tender, elegant, but plaintive' according to my local guidebook), work on their calligraphy, embroider or, in the swimming pool, plunge from the high board.

These rooms are only a selection, a tiny sample, we are assured, of the 500-odd rooms in the palace, where every day 5000 pampered school kids hone their skills and sing the praises of the Great Leader. And those 500 rooms are only an adjunct, a side game, a mere appendage to the grandiose, over-the-top, ostentatious, obscenely extravagant horror of this marble-pillared, soaring-ceilinged, sweeping-stairwayed, statue-tiered monstrosity of a building.

When the fat cats in Pyongyang decided to construct this ugly symbol of their arrogance, how many farmers did they decide to leave planting their fields by hand and ploughing them with an old cow? How many road workers did they decide to leave by the side of the highway breaking rocks with a hammer? It's no wonder aid workers pull their hair out when they're confronted with this contradiction. In the country people starve while in Pyongyang their masters play games in palaces. The idiots then let us gather the evidence for their conviction. They're so ashamed of what they've done to the workers that they have a fit if a tourist photographs someone doing real work, but photographing another colossal stone and bronze monument to the Tubby Tyrant is OK. So aid workers try to feed the starving, living in textbook Third World conditions, while children dance in a marble palace a whole world away.

That night some of our group embark on a tour of Pyongyang by night, which essentially means looking at monuments by floodlight, although in Kim Il-sung Square the Great Leader's illuminated portrait turns off at precisely 9pm, just as we arrive. Some of us end up at the Taedonggang Diplomatic Club, which seems to be run by the North Koreans, not the diplomats, since it has all the standard North Korean signs: portraits of the deadly duo, photos of recent events in Pyongyang with the dumpy despot's face smiling from the centre, no running water in the bathrooms and so on. There's a video room, cinema, restaurant and karaoke bar as well as the billiards room and bar where we repair to.

Arabic music is oozing out of the speakers. 'Sounds Libyan', says Camilla, an identification quickly confirmed by Digby who recognises one of the billiard players as someone from the Libyan embassy, having met him in the basement Egypt Palace Karaoke Bar at our hotel. Libyans seem to lose their distaste for alcohol once they're outside their own country. The other billiard players are from Laos and Pakistan and for once every fluky shot I make goes in, so it's a fine DPRK evening.

· · · ·

We're off across country. The road to Wonsan sweeps across the central mountains, diving through dark tunnels, the last one of which, the Rainbow Tunnel, is 4 kilometres long. The highway activity is just like I observed from the train down from the border: nobody and nothing is on the move and there are clear signs of a highly stressed environment with fields cut into steep hillsides, erosion and deforestation.

Overuse is a short-sighted approach, but 'North Korea has always been very short-sighted', a Western diplomat I bumped into at the Diplomatic Club had mused. 'Before the collapse of Communism, Russia and China paid for everything. The Koreans didn't need to worry about rice production because China covered any shortfall. While other Asian countries were double-cropping and introducing new improved varieties of rice, they didn't worry about raising production. Having full employment was more important than how much they produced.'

Just past halfway there's a pause at Sinphyong where, according to the guidebook I bought in Pyongyang, Yellow Serpent Liquor is the specialty. 'The nonpoisonous yellow serpent is tasty and effective', the guidebook declares. 'A yellow serpent is put into over 60% alcohol and buried until the medicinal elements come off. The liquor makes the organs of the body work smoothly. It is said to do wonders for ageing male virility.' A bottle of this potent tipple costs US$10.

A long pedestrian causeway, punctuated by a couple of swaying suspension bridges, leads out from beside our hotel to Jangdok Islet. At night it's populated by fishermen toting quite professional rods. In the morning they've been replaced by a solitary snorkeller and a large collection of women foraging around for shellfish. Some fishermen are floating their lines out with the aid of square wooden floats topped by sails, but my favourites are young guys paddling energetically out to sea on inflated truck inner-tubes, trailing a long fishing line baited with hundreds of small lines dangling below. A fellow fisher pays the baited line out from a neat box on shore. These guys are miniature long-line trawlers.

Regrettably we don't get to wander the traffic-free streets of Wonsan – lack of city wandering time is the number-one complaint for the whole group – but we do visit a fine old temple ('extensively damaged by American bombers during the war') and the Chonsam Collective Farm, where there's another local home visit. This one is clearly pre-selected, but it's remarkably like the house to which we'd made a spur-of-the-moment visit. There's the same kitchen with a sunken central area, the same coal-fired cooking range, the same sparsely furnished rooms, the same double portraits as the only form of decoration.

● ● ● ●

The DMZ is in fact the world's most heavily armed frontier. On the drive south to Panmunjom in the DMZ, our bus stops in what would be a freeway service centre in the West, except there are no fuel pumps. The building, complete with restaurant and souvenir shop, straddles the six-lane freeway and from the balcony I take a photo of the empty highway. I have to wait 10 minutes for a vehicle to come by, otherwise the image would be totally traffic free.

255.

Can we visit the North's DMZ village, just to confirm that the southern puppet's lies that it's actually uninhabited are indeed an outrageous slander? No, sorry, that won't be possible. We can, however, make an excursion to see the Korean Wall, the solid concrete structure that extends 280 kilometres from one coast to the other.

'They claim it is an anti-tank wall, but if that is true why is it so high?' proposed the DMZ soldier-guide. 'To stop a tank you only need a wall 50 centimetres to a metre high.'

'Is it true that there's also a 30,000-volt electric fence on the North's side of the DMZ?' we bounce back.

'Perhaps', comes the enigmatic reply.

And what is that designed to stop? It won't hold up tanks, will it?' we persist.

In fact fences, walls, concrete obstacles and electric wires are completely unnecessary when it comes to shutting the South out. The crippled state of the North's economy provides all the restraint necessary.

The bus pulls into the Armistice Building, something DMZ tours from the south are never going to see. These are the buildings where the protracted negotiations took place – they went on for two years, nearly twice as long as the entire first stages of the war – and where the armistice was finally signed. They are firmly in the northern sector of the DMZ.

Our soldier-guide gives us the standard spiel: the American Imperialists arrived in Korea on 8 September 1945, claiming they had liberated the country from those other imperialists. 'This was clearly a lie since the Great Leader Kim Il-sung had already liberated the country on 15 August.' Then the Imperialist Aggressors and their Puppet Stooges built up their strength for the next three years before launching their assault on the North. Fifteen other countries joined the one-sided attack on the DPRK (there's conspicuous silence on Russian support and the flood of Chinese 'volunteers') before finally the American warmongers, realising the hopelessness of their situation, begged for peace. From the starting point of the negotiations in mid-1951 the mess could have been sorted out in a couple of months, but instead the Imperialists dragged it out for two years and 718 separate meetings before they finally admitted defeat.

Well that's one interpretation.

• • • •

There are always two sides to every story and, wherever we are, one side is always much louder. Not many of us get to visit these pariah states, so it's hardly surprising we've taken the standard Western perspective on board. North Korea is so clearly a Bad Land – forget any blather about Weapons of Mass Destruction and terrorist activities, the way the DPRK treats its own citizens is shocking.

The government Kim Il-sung installed in North Korea may not have been very nice (even before the shooting he was the one who shut the border to stop an exodus south), but nor was the system the US installed in the South. For the best part of 40 years the South was saddled with a series of dictatorial, draconian and decidedly undemocratic governments.

We hear a lot about the North's million-plus troops, more than half of them within 80 kilometres of the DMZ, and how they outnumber the South Korean army nearly two to one. Yet if the North's energies are so focused on plans to invade the South, what are those walls and electric fences along the North's coast all about? Is it possible the North is equally frightened of an invasion from the South?

There certainly are North Korean incursions into the South, but the traffic is not one way. There was the USS *Pueblo* in 1968, which I'd seen moored on the riverside when I'd made my early morning stroll from my Pyongyang hotel. And was the EC-121 reconnaissance aircraft shot down in 1969 an innocent victim of North Korean aggression? There doesn't seem to be much question that other US aircraft flew over North

Korea in subsequent years, and the Fatherland Liberation War Museum in Pyongyang has a whole basement section for shot-down aircraft of the American Imperialist Aggressors. There's even a mint-condition helicopter complete with a photograph of the offending machine with its American crew standing beside it, hands raised and looking very surprised about the whole matter.

We hear a lot about nuclear weapons the North may have, far less about the nuclear weapons the US definitely did have (and, who knows, may still have) in the South. Back in Washington, Dubya musing loudly about the virtues of 'regime change' and calculating the costs of just marching in and changing things for countries that haven't got the sense to do it themselves was hardly encouragement for a little disarming.

When Kim Il-sung met with US negotiator Selig Harrison in 1994 he announced, 'What would be the point of making one or two nuclear weapons when you have 10,000-plus delivery systems that we don't have?'

Whether they need nuclear weapons for defensive (or offensive) purposes, the North Koreans certainly know how to use them as bargaining chips. Eight years before the 2006 crisis, the Pentagon decided there was an underground nuclear-processing facility under construction at Kunchang-ni near the Chinese border and demanded to have a look. 'Sure,' said the North Koreans, 'you can come and have a look, that'll cost you US\$300 million.'

Eventually the price was bargained down to 600,000 tonnes of food, and a team of 14 American nuclear inspectors turned up and spent three days looking round no less than 10 kilometres of tunnels, none of which, it turned out, had anything to do with nuclear weapons. The suspicion about this nonexistent facility had screwed up relations on the peninsula for the best part of 12 months, but nobody at the Pentagon got their knuckles rapped. The economy may be in tatters, they may have trouble feeding the population, but there's no question the North Koreans have an admirable ability to perform one feat. The *New York Times* recognised it clearly in a March 1994 article: 'They have mastered the art of dangling Washington on a string.'

So, what about unification. Could it work? First of all the Americans have to leave the South, that's clearly the starting point from the Northern perspective. Jimmy Carter suggested doing exactly that way back in 1975, even before he was elected, but was eventually shot down by the Pentagon sabre-wavers. Simply pulling all the American troops out is hardly likely to make everything instantly OK, but it would help.

For a decade at least, the South has adopted an official policy of rapprochement but the two Koreas would face a huge information, understanding and attitudes headache. Nobody from the North travels south and for years anybody from the South who travelled north, via a third country or whatever, had committed a criminal offence and could expect to be imprisoned when they returned.

'The two sides would elect a Supreme National Assembly', our guide explains. 'It would handle international diplomacy and the military, but everything else would be administered by the two regional governments. They don't want to change their system and we don't want to change ours so we would have one country, but with two different forms of government and two different economic systems.'

'Would there be freedom of movement between the two halves?' I ask.

'Of course', he responds. However, he's much less certain when I ask if the North will be able to access world news, southern media, mobile phone systems, the internet and all the other avenues of communication and information that are so rigorously blocked off at present. After all, if the North was really genuine about opening up to the outside world, there's no reason they couldn't stop jamming the South's radio and TV broadcasts right now.

'Aren't you interested in outside news?' I asked one of our guides. 'Wouldn't you like to hear the news from South Korea?'

'That does not interest us,' he staunchly replied, 'it does not meet our socialist standards.'

'Well, when the Dear Leader's son was arrested in Japan, trying to visit Disneyland on a fake passport, did you hear about that?' I queried, knowing very well that he had not.

'I do not know if the Dear Leader has any children', he replied.

Nor, it turned out, did he know where the Dear Leader lived. 'You do not know where your leaders live, do you?' he countered. The White House? Ten Downing Street?

The Dear Leader's Pyongyang hideaway may be really hidden, but it would have been hard to miss the Great Leader's humble abode. On the way out to the zoo (for some of our group) and the Revolutionary Martyrs' Cemetery (for others) we'd passed the Kumsusan Memorial Palace, the mausoleum where the remains of the Great Leader, like other Communist heroes from Beijing and Hanoi to Moscow, are preserved like a wax model at Madame Tussauds. Prior to his departure to the workers' paradise in the sky this was his personal palace and, as befits one of the great heroes and inspirations of the century, it was considerably bigger than the White House or other lesser leaders' official homes.

'And what about photographs?' I continue. 'We can photograph anything we want in the South. Will that change in the North after reunification?'

'It's not just the government', he answers. 'You ask those people out there,' he says, waving at the pedestrians on the roadside, 'they don't want to be photographed either.'

'Oh, sure,' I shoot back, 'they're certainly told they shouldn't want to be photographed, but why should we believe they really don't?'

There's no answer.

From what I've seen, it's crystal clear what the fate of 'one country, two systems' would be, if it actually happened. Within days the South Koreans would have filled North Korea's shops with the spoils of consumer society. Who would be shopping for the shoddy products of the North's earthly paradise when the glittering prizes of the South's *jaebeol* (business conglomerates) were on offer? How long would Air Koryo last in competition with Korean Airlines? How long before the North's handful of secondhand Toyotas had been replaced with shiny new Hyundais, Kias and Daewoos?

• • • •

'What does surreal mean?' asks Mr Kim. We have made that final dawn trip to the giant statue of the Great Leader and while we'd been photographing the early morning pilgrims he'd read the line in my guidebook that visiting North Korea was 'too surreal to be believable'.

I proceed to dig myself into a hole that proves difficult to get out of. 'Surreal means something that, on the surface, looks very realistic, but when you look more closely you realise that it is not real at all', I explain. 'It's a word often used to describe a style of art in the West.'

'So how does it apply to North Korea?' he continues.

'Well, it's like all the exploits of the Great Leader and the Dear Leader that we're told about', I say, strolling nonchalantly out on to very thin ice.

'We're told the Great Leader visited a farm and taught the farmers how to grow more rice, that he went to a factory and instructed the workers how to increase production, how he meets fishermen and they quickly discover, with his expert tuition, that they could be catching more fish. Obviously this is not true, nobody can be an expert on everything.'

'When did you meet Kim Il-sung?' says Mr Kim and I can see the veil drop, surrealistically, across his eyes. 'If you have not met him, how do you know he is not an expert on all these matters?'

It's the final surreal experience of a decidedly surreal trip.

Of course the North Koreans are not dull automatons, characters from a real-life Orwellian *1984* – they're people who laugh and play and want a better life – but what we see is what their government wants us to see and

261.

any attempt to sneak a peek at anything else, or worse photograph it, is energetically circumscribed.

The next day we fly back to Beijing: Air Koryo to Shenyang, Air China from there. As we taxi in to Shenyang's big, glossy new airport terminal (a steel, aluminium and glass construction that could be anywhere in the affluent West) a Korean Airlines flight from Seoul rolls in right behind us. The governments of the North and South may be barely talking to each other, but minutes after clearing immigration the Seoul bags are spilling on to the carousel, mixed in with the Pyongyang ones. I toy with the idea that you could jump on the Seoul flight when it returns to the South Korean capital and 24 hours later be right back on the DMZ, toeing the line from the opposite side.

SAUDI ARABIA

'Swap oil for carpets and it might all be different', said Don George, Lonely Planet's US-based global travel editor. 'If Afghanistan had oil and Saudi Arabia had carpets, which country would have been bombed?'

There's no question that having a barrel or two of oil around the place does ensure you get treated with some respect. What was Afghanistan after all? Just the post office where the letter bomb was sent from and where, foolishly, the letter-bomber hung around after delivery.

When somebody mails you a letter bomb do you attack the post office or the place where the letter bomb was put together? September 11's letter was written in Saudi Arabia, the letter's author was from Saudi Arabia, its contents (15 of the 19 hijackers) came from Saudi Arabia and the cash for the postage came from Saudi Arabia. So why did Afghanistan get bombed and not Saudi Arabia? Carpets versus oil may have something to do with it.

I knew Saudis weren't the most popular people in the Arab world. Nobody in the Arab world likes the Israelis, but once that dislike is out of the way they can concentrate on not liking each other very much either.

Only the Kuwaitis challenge the Saudis for most unpopular Arabs. It's partly wealth: the Saudis have it, most of the Arab world doesn't, and many Egyptians, Palestinians, Syrians and other less-wealthy Arabs end up working in Saudi Arabia where they're often poorly paid and badly treated. It's partly Islamic arrogance: Saudi Arabia has the two holy cities and Wahhabism is the purest, most conservative form of Islam (it's what the Taliban modelled themselves on). The Saudis look down their noses at everybody else's Islam. Even the 7 or 8 per cent of Saudis who are part of the Shiite sect rather than the mainstream Sunni sect are severely discriminated against.

Finally, though, it's sheer hypocrisy. How austerely pure can you be when you're spending up on every luxury brand from Armani to Ermenegildo Zegna? Nor are the Saudis quite so Islamically pure once they venture beyond their borders. The Arabian Gulf city-state of Bahrain is joined to Saudi Arabia by a causeway and every weekend Saudis flock in for a short spell of R&R. A wave of political liberalisation in Bahrain in 2001 raised the prospect that religious clerics might push to ban alcohol. 'Unlikely', thought the more cosmopolitan Bahrainis, 'We make too much money from being the closest bar to the world's thirstiest country.'

• • • •

You don't whine about being misinterpreted and misunderstood, but then keep the doors firmly shut to anybody who might want to come in and do a little understanding. The Saudis keep their house locked so securely it's hardly surprising that the outside world believes they're ashamed of what goes on indoors. This is a country that beheads, mutilates and flogs people; that keeps women locked away and disenfranchised in almost every way possible; that has zero democratic rights, zero religious freedom and strict state censorship and media control. As Geraldine Brooks points out in *Nine Parts of Desire,* if Saudi

Arabian society were divided into blacks and whites rather than women and men, there would be international trade sanctions and worldwide outrage at the appalling treatment of one half of the population by the other. As she also points out, if there were 90 million small boys who were forced to have their penises amputated, there might be an outcry about that as well. Clitoridectomies remain a predominantly Muslim rite.

Saudi Arabia is not just two holy cities and a whole lot of desert, and it does get some tourists. What we think of in the West as tourists that is, not just the three million Muslim pilgrims who make the haj to Mecca each year, or the *umrah*, which is a Mecca pilgrimage made out of season. A small number are Gulf-state Arabs, who don't need a visa, or *umrah* pilgrims who take advantage of visa regulation that lets them stay on after their pilgrimage.

There's not a lot of domestic tourism. 'When Saudis travel they want what they can't get at home, so nightlife and shopping are the most important things', said a hotel manager. Considering the amount of shopping available in the kingdom it scarcely seems necessary to go overseas to look for name brands, but the Saudi shopping instinct is well known. When the king did a 45-day trip around the world in the 1990s, his two 747s didn't have enough shopping capacity. A Saudi Air Force Hercules flew out to each stop to cart purchases back to Riyadh and would then catch up at his next stopover.

'Nor are they very interested in anything pre-Islamic, so you won't see many Saudis at Madain Saleh for example', my hotel manager informant continued. 'If the Prophet's not involved, they couldn't care less.'

Nevertheless some tourists are nonbelieving foreigners, not just pilgrims. There are lots of foreigners in Saudi Arabia. Perhaps six or seven million of the population of around 21 million are expat workers and their families. The greatest number are from the Third World, including over a million each from India and Egypt, and large numbers from Pakistan, the Philippines and Bangladesh. Few will have their families with them and they often only get home to see their wives and children for a month or so every couple of years. In contrast, the First World workers are highly paid and often bring their families and take time off to travel around. After all, there's plenty to see – great desert and mountain country for off-road camping trips and the Red Sea for scuba diving.

There are probably also a handful of tourists like me, business visitors who stay on after they've done their business. Once you are inside you can pretty much go wherever you want, although if you're not a Muslim you have to stay out of the two holy cities. I'd had a previous incarnation as an engineer so it was a fairly simple job to find a friend with an air-conditioning company in Jeddah who could arrange for his company to 'sponsor' me – that is, to ask the Saudi embassy to issue a visa.

Prior to September 11 there had also been a limited number of tightly controlled and fairly expensive tours for Westerners to Saudi Arabia. September 11 certainly scared that contingent away.

'We used to get 10 to 15 tour groups a month', lamented the hotel manager. 'In the six months afterwards we had two.' Today that limited and fairly exclusive business looks like it may be kicking into gear again, but you can forget about joining one of those rare tour groups if you're a 44-year-old orphaned widow, divorcee or spinster. Women are not allowed if they're under 45 unless they're accompanied by their husband or father. A responsible male is required to keep an eye on them and make sure they behave themselves.

Absurd? Well, a lot of things about Saudi Arabia are absurd. Presumably once women reach 45 they're sterile, dried up, on the shelf and unlikely to pose a serious danger to the stability and morality of the kingdom. A 35-year-old unaccompanied woman, on the other hand, could be a real danger. The prophet might turn in his grave, the Kaaba in Mecca could shatter, the kingdom could fall.

There are lots of problems for foreign women quite apart from the need to have a man to watch over them. For a start there's the *abaya*, the all-enveloping black shroud that all women are obliged to wear. Technically non-Saudis are not required to wear the *abaya*, but if they don't the *mutawwa* are likely to get them. The 'Committee for the Propagation of Virtue and the Prevention of Vice', which is more or less what *mutawwa* translates as, are 'a squad of moral vigilantes out to enforce Islamic orthodoxy as they understand it', according to my guidebook.

After my first couple of days in Riyadh I was disappointed I'd still not seen a *mutawwa*. 'How do I find one?' I asked an Indian expat.

'Wear shorts and you'll find one very quickly', he replied.

In fact the *mutawwa* are recognisable by their short ankle-revealing *thobe*, or robe, their full bushy beards and long hair and the fact that they do not wear the usual *gutra* or headcloth. They also carry around a stick to whack wrongdoers. A website on the miserable state of human rights in Saudi Arabia commented that they are 'empowered to investigate, search, arrest and detain citizens and foreigners, and their abusive practices, including physical attacks and beatings, have been widely noted' (Human Rights Watch – http://hrw.org/backgrounder/mena/saudi). The Australian foreign affairs department warns their citizens, 'particularly females', that 'incidents of assault have been reported' and that they should end any encounter 'as quickly as possible – if necessary by leaving the area immediately'. 'Steer clear of them', suggested my guidebook.

So if a woman doesn't wear her *abaya*, a *mutawwa* is likely to attack her with a stick.

'"Close your face!" they'll shout, "Close your face!"' a Sudanese taxi driver had demonstrated in Dubai.

'It's part of the government's method to keep down dissent', suggested one liberal Saudi I spoke to. 'If people are worrying about being hassled by the *mutawwa,* they have less time to worry about the profligate spending of the wealthy.'

In mid-2002 a government official announced that the *mutawwa* would be cracking down on manufacturers whose *abaya* did not come up to standard. The regulations for 'decent women's cloaks' required that they be 'thick and not revealing, loose so they do not show the body, and open from the front only. The black dress should cover all the body, be devoid of decoration, drawings, writing and other marks and different to male dress'.

In fact *abaya* and the necessity to wear them vary quite considerably. A Saudi woman is likely to wear the whole head-to-toe outfit with the face completely covered or with only a slit for the eyes. Wearing your glasses outside the slit can look quite comical. Really serious Saudi women even wear black gloves so if they have to hand money out, or take something in, not a square centimetre of flesh will show. Foreign women can get away with showing their faces, but not their hair. Even a wisp of hair is completely verboten.

Riyadh – the capital, in the religiously conservative heartland – is 100 per cent *abaya* country. Certain other centres are also very conservative, but some cities are much more freewheeling and although foreigners will still have to wear one they may not have to cover their heads. Get out in the desert or way off the beaten track and foreign women (none of this applies to Saudis) can dress conservatively, but pretty normally. There are unlikely to be any *mutawwa* poking around the un-Islamic ruins of Madain Saleh. The strictly foreign 'compounds', where most Western expats live, are also much more free. Even Wilfred Thesiger, the Englishman who crossed the burnings sands of the Empty Quarter soon after World War II and wrote the desert-crossing classic *Arabian Sands*, pointed out that it was principally a city extravagance. In the desert women have to work and they can't do that in an *abaya*.

Apart from branding women, the *abaya* is also uncomfortable, hot and quite possibly dangerous. Perhaps it's just as well women are not allowed to drive. Saudi roads are unsafe enough already without people trying to drive with a black bag over their heads.

'The Japanese tourists are amazing', said a Moroccan tour guide I spoke with. 'They actually get *abaya* made in Tokyo so they can get off the plane already wearing them. Other visitors don't buy one until after they arrive and then they're always asking, "Do I have to wear it now? Can I take it off now?" I think Japanese women even wear their *abaya* in their hotel rooms.'

The Saudis not only keep a tight grip on who comes in to the country, they also tightly restrict the news that filters in. While the *Arab News*, the principal English-language newspaper, daily rails about the 'Jewish dominated' American media, the Saudi censors are busy blacking out anything that offends them in publications from outside the country.

'Religion, politics and sex are the three things they don't like', said a bookshop manager. 'The trouble is the responsibility for wielding the black marker-pen on incoming publications goes to the most junior staff and they can get into trouble for letting something through, but they won't be reprimanded for censoring too much.'

Of course, it's pictures that are more likely to get blacked out than text, so in a liquor ad on the back cover of *Outside* magazine, the bottle is blacked out along with the two blondes' cleavages and legs, but Hugh Hefner escapes untouched. In another magazine a picture of the *Sex and the City* stars requires heavy blackout work on arms, legs, navels and cleavages.

The absurdity is that, while countless marker-pens run dry covering up Britney Spears' navel in magazines, she can flaunt it at will on MTV. With so much satellite TV beamed down, the Saudis have simply given up trying to keep questionable TV out. Once upon a time the *mutawwa* were likely to stone offending satellite dishes so owners either hid them away or stone-proofed them with wire fences. Eventually satellite dishes were simply banned, and then the ban was not enforced. Today there are even 'dish *souq*',– markets devoted to satellite dishes and their paraphernalia.

In early 2002 the *mutawwa* determination to ensure no women went out uncovered contributed to a tragedy in the city of Mecca. A fire in a run-down, badly designed and overcrowded girls school led to the deaths of 15 girls and injuries to many others. As the girls attempted to escape from the blaze they were pushed back inside by the *mutawwa* because they were not covered by their *abaya* and there were no responsible males to accompany them out. Furthermore when police and firemen tried to enter the blazing building they were blocked by the *mutawwa*, since men, even firemen, should not be mixing with unrelated women. The Interior Minister Prince Nayef said that the *mutawwa* had only been there to 'stop the girls being mistreated', but people I speak to do not think it unlikely that they would have been quite capable of such idiocy. 'They're the most hated people in the kingdom', is a sentiment I hear expressed more than once.

• • • •

I've heard that getting through immigration and customs can be tedious so I'm not surprised when there's an undignified scramble for the door before the 777 has even come to a halt at Riyadh's King Khalid Airport. The haste is even more evident inside the terminal, but I'm fairly well placed in the line until, when I'm just two from the head of the queue, our immigration official stands up and walks off the job. After 15 minutes another official comes by and tells us he ain't comin' back, so it's back to the end of another line. After a while I start timing how long it takes to process each passenger – about two minutes – which means a 30-person line takes an hour to work through, nearly as long as the flight from Dubai.

272.

The Englishman in front of me goes through in less than 30 seconds, however, and I follow suit, grab my bag and get whisked through customs with equal alacrity. After all the stories about zealous officials going through women's fashion magazines looking for 'pornographic' bra ads, I was wondering if they'd check what you had stored on your computer.

The speed-up continues when I emerge because my hotel has sent a driver and a few minutes later we're zooming along the freeway towards Riyadh, the speedometer warning-chime occasionally informing us we're exceeding 120 kilometres per hour. Despite my Indian driver complaining about death and carnage due to speed and simple craziness, the drive into town is actually fairly calm. Sure, a few cars zoom by at what must be closer to 200 than the 110-kilometre-per-hour speed limit, but we only encounter one accident all the way to the Al-Khozama Hotel.

Right next to my hotel, and a useful landmark for my next few days in Riyadh, is the new Faisaliah Tower, looking like a slightly pregnant version of San Francisco's Transamerica Pyramid. It's the work of English über-architect Norman Foster and discreet engravings both sides of the entrance doors reveal that it was built by the bin Laden group. Riyadh's other signature skyscraper, the Kingdom Centre, has a hole right through it. 'It's used for practice flights' is the Saudi joke.

Having dumped my bag, I find an ATM and soon I am in the Faisaliah Shopping Mall. The flashy centre has lots of familiar Western brands, including labels such as Miss Selfridge, Harvey Nichols, Donna Karan, Etam lingerie, Liz Claiborne, Hugo Boss, United Colors of Benetton, Mango, Guess and even French Connection UK, with its racy acronym proudly displayed across the back of the shop. Do those all-enveloping *abaya* wandering out of the shop enshroud teenagers with 'FCUK' inscribed across their T-shirted breasts I wonder? The Western kids, with their jeans emerging from the bottom and their faces on display above, look like they're appearing at some engowned graduation ceremony, but the Saudi women, totally covered up, resemble a scene from *Star Wars*.

I walk down the next street stopping for a cappuccino in a Dr Café, which feels just like a Starbucks except there are no women either side of the counter and the exclusively male clientele is more than 95 per cent

273.

traditionally dressed. A few doors down I discover that the standard red-and-white check *gutra,* which makes Saudi men look like they've just had a collision with a French bistro's red gingham tablecloth, isn't so standard at all. A menswear shop advertise that they have Valentino, Dunhill and Givenchy *gutra.*

• • • •

I quickly discover that the capital's taxi fleet is almost without exception piloted by Pakistanis – and a nicer, gentler bunch of subcontinental taxi drivers you could not ask to meet. Many of them speak at least some English and are keen to talk about cricket (Pakistan's team is doing pretty well) and, quite unlike the way taxis work on the real subcontinent, none of them is at all pushy about the fare. They use their meters without hesitation and often seem keen to round fares down to the nearest five riyals!

Between taxis I walk, particularly around the Al Baatha old city area. I go there in the early afternoon to visit the Masmak Fortress only to discover the Saudi siesta can really stretch. The fort's closed from noon to 4pm. I return just after four only to be told that today is family day and since my family aren't with me I'll have to come back tomorrow, which is a men's day.

The fortress plays a key role in modern Saudi history and at least I get to see one clear piece of evidence to demonstrate just what a dramatic day 16 January 1902 was. Less than a century earlier in 1818 the Al-Saud family's rule came to a disastrous end when the Turks, who reckoned the sandy wastes of Arabia were just another part of the mighty Ottoman Empire and that these local upstarts were getting too big for their *thobe,* decided to reassert their authority. Dir'aiyah, the Saud family capital just outside Riyadh, fell to the Turks and it looked like it was all over for the Al-Sauds.

Not quite. Within four years they'd regained control of Riyadh, but for years internal squabbles sapped the family's power and finally in 1891 Riyadh was taken by their rivals the Al-Rashids, strongly supported by the Turks. To this day Turkey is not very popular in Saudi Arabia. The 12-year-old Abdul Aziz ibn Abdul Rahman al-Saud was smuggled out of Riyadh, hidden in a saddle-bag on a camel, so the legend goes, and grew up in Kuwait intent on restoring his family's power and getting rid of the Al-Rashids and their Turkish patrons. Ibn Saud, a shorter version of his name popular in the West, rode back across the sands in late 1901 leading a band of just 60 supporters on what would undoubtedly be the most successful raid in Arabian history.

Hiding in a house near the Masmak Fortress, Ibn Saud and 40 of his warriors waited until the fort's commander left the stronghold at dawn. Rushing out from their hiding place the Al-Saud band overpowered and killed the commander and soon controlled the fort. In the melee a spear hurled by one of the band lodged itself so firmly in the wooden fortress door that the broken spearhead can still be seen today. I take a photograph of that notable chunk of metal before departing to wait for men's day. It's an arresting thought that if the fort commander had managed to get back inside and slam the door shut the Al-Saud raid might have failed and today the country might be named after an entirely different family. I'd be in Rashid Arabia.

The fortress isn't Riyadh's only piece of history. The next morning I grab a taxi soon after dawn. I see a lot of dawns in the next 10 days. The first couple of hours of daylight are cool and delicious before the heat starts to pound on you like a white-hot sledgehammer. On the outskirts of Riyadh are the ruins of Dir'aiyah, the Al-Saud's capital until the Turks destroyed it. Much of the dried mud architecture is picturesquely crumbling, but there are a couple of palaces and the old bathhouse that have been restored along with most of the extensive city walls and some of the guard towers. Wandering around this spellbinding ruined city in

275.

the morning cool, I also experience something that will become very familiar in the days ahead: I have the whole place to myself. Repeatedly in museums, forts, palaces and ruins I will be the only person there.

Having Dir'aiyah all to yourself is great and the previous day I'd also been the sole visitor in Riyadh's magnificent new National Museum. Saudi Arabia's near total inexperience with tourists is not so convenient when you need a permit to go somewhere. Officially you must have a permit from the Ministry of Antiquities to visit any archaeological site, but Dir'aiyah is permit-free and it's very unclear which other sites need permits or even where they are. Madain Saleh, my next stop, definitely needs a permit, and later in the trip I come across another permits-only site and I'm simply not allowed to see it, even though I might have been the only visitor for weeks.

After inquiries, phone calls and shuffling from desk to room to office at the museum, I'm eventually led to a large, spacious office where half a dozen men lounge around looking bored. It's unclear what gets done here, if anything, but having a solo tourist turn up to apply for a permit is clearly not part of the everyday agenda. Not much English is spoken, but eventually I'm told to apply in writing and the letter, preferably in Arabic, should be stamped by my sponsor. I patiently explain that I'm not working here, I'm just a business visitor and my office is on the other side of the world so I can't go back there to get the letter written. Can't I just write the letter right now?

Eventually this proposal is reluctantly agreed to and I tear a page out of my notebook, note down my name and passport number and write 'please give me a permit to visit Madain Saleh'.

Come back tomorrow I'm told.

The next day there's no discernible change in the office and the official I spoke to before isn't around but, remarkably, my permit is found and after a long delay while somebody important enough is found to sign it, I go away clutching it tightly.

That evening, after my men's day visit to the Masmak Fortress, I continue on to the Murabba Palace. Unfortunately men's day at Masmak is family day at Murabba. Fortunately, even though I have no wife or children to give me respectability, I am allowed in.

The men and family ruling causes lots of complications. Unless a restaurant has two separate areas – one for men and one for families – women are simply not allowed in. It's understandable. Women are not allowed to uncover their faces when unrelated men are around and eating when you've got a bag over your head would not be easy. At lunchtime I'm in a quite respectable, but male-only, Lebanese restaurant when I notice a woman outside waving what looks like the same menu I'm holding. She's come to order food to take away, but she is not allowed inside to order it. My waiter in his coat and bow tie goes outside to stand in the sun on the busy pavement and take her order.

Furthermore 'men' does indeed mean 'men', but 'family' doesn't necessarily mean 'women'. At the entrance to the family room at a branch of an American fast-food outlet, a sign announces that no single women are allowed in. Of course men by themselves are banned, but so are women either solo or with just another woman. She needs a man or child to be allowed entry.

'It can get very confusing', said an American expat. 'I was taking a friend's daughter out for a pizza before I met the rest of our group. She hadn't reached puberty so she didn't have to wear an *abaya*, but as a man with a child did I qualify as a family, even though it wasn't my child?'

The answer was no. They were not allowed in.

• • • •

At 6am, the sun just up, I'm boarding a flight to Medina, probably the only nonbeliever on an MD90 full of Muslims. It's one of the two Muslims-only holy cities, but the airport is outside the infidel-free zone so it's OK to fly in. I'm then going to rent a car and drive north 400 kilometres to Madain Saleh. The airport is actually the other side of Medina and I'd been concerned about accidentally straying into the city, but everybody, including the rent-a-car desk, assures me there's no chance I'll do that. Sure enough a few kilometres down the road an exit sign announces 'All Non-Muslims Take Next Exit'. I peel off and head north.

Never heard of Madain Saleh? Well, if you've seen Petra in Jordan or even its appearance in *Indiana Jones and the Last Crusade,* you'd certainly recognise Madain Saleh. The stone-cut tombs, which are all that remain of the ancient Nabatean centre, date from 100 BC to AD 100, when this was a great city on the frankincense-trading route and second in importance only to Petra itself. Today there's one major difference between the two ancient cities. Petra is overrun with tourists (or at least it is when the Israelis aren't shooting it out with the Palestinians and scaring everyone away) and has over 70 hotels. Madain Saleh has hardly any tourists at all and just two hotels.

I no sooner arrive at my hotel than I'm adopted by a little group of Canadians, two of them Riyadh-based expats, the other two visitors from back home. They're being guided by Hamim, an extremely capable young Moroccan guy. Moroccans are well regarded as guides in Saudi Arabia because they're used to dealing with tourists and they generally speak English and French as well as Arabic.

The ruins are superb. The stone-cut tombs are not as ornate as at Petra and instead of being concentrated along a narrow ravine they're scattered in a variety of outcrops. The iconic Madain Saleh tomb, the Qasr Farid, stands isolated, a single mighty lump of rock swelling up out of the sand. We arrive just before sunset and sit atop a nearby dune to watch the sun sink beyond the hills off to the west, dappling the red rock of the tomb an even deeper colour.

Earlier in the afternoon we'd stopped at the old Hejaz Railway station at the northern end of the site. Once upon a time this was a station on the line that carried pilgrims from Damascus to Medina. Opened in 1908 the line was a favourite target for Lawrence of Arabia during World War I although his railway-sabotaging activities never got this far south. The crippled line never recovered from the war and was finally abandoned in 1924. There were some half-hearted attempts to revive it during the 1960s and 1970s, but today it's quietly and picturesquely rusting away.

At the hotel that night I meet Patrick Pierard, a longtime, French resident in the kingdom who has written a book about off-road trips in the Hejaz region and is the local expert on the line, the old Turkish forts built to protect it, and the solid-stone station buildings that pop up beside the road about every 20 kilometres to Medina. The next day, on my way back south, he leads me off the road to the ruins of a fine old railway fort and later, following his instructions, I divert to another abandoned station with a locomotive and line of carriages still standing outside.

Flying out of Medina includes one of those weird little experiences that has you scratching your head and wondering if it was something cultural you'd missed or some deeper misunderstanding. I get back into Medina earlier than I expected, early enough that it seems possible I might get a flight out to Jeddah that evening and not have to wait for the flight I'm booked on the next morning. I've got no urge to stay in a city I'm not even allowed in, even if there is a hotel just outside the Muslims-only ring of protection.

So I drive to the airport and leave my bags in the rented car in case I can't get on, and go to the check-in desk. It's 6.15pm, there's a flight at 7pm, but I'll have to go standby. Come back in 15 minutes. I go back to the car park, retrieve my bag, hand the keys in to the Budget desk and clear up the paperwork and I'm back to the check-in desk at 6.30pm. They still don't know if there's a seat available. Come back in another 15 minutes. At 6.45pm I'm told the flight's in final boarding and it's full. I'm not worried, there's another flight at 9.30pm and I can hang around the airport and grab some food.

279.

At the ticketing counter my ticket is taken and the agent goes into such an interminable bout of keyboarding I'm beginning to think there's something wrong with it, but finally he emerges from behind the counter, tells me to come with him and marches off through security and into the departure area. I trail behind, still toting the bag I intended to check in as well as my carry-ons. At the gate desk the agent goes into another marathon bout on the computer, but finally (by this time it's about 7.10pm) hands me a boarding card and tells me I can get on the 7pm flight after all. So up the steps I run, still carrying the bag I intended to check in.

Business class is half-empty. If they'd have upgraded me, I could have got on easily. It's only a short flight and I would probably even have offered to pay the extra if they'd asked. However, when I step into economy I'm mildly shocked. Where are all the passengers? This plane is not full. Around 100 of the 250 or so seats are empty. So why was I told to wait 15 minutes, and then another 15 minutes, and then told it's full and to try my luck on a later flight?

• • • •

There's a definite Indian flavour to my Jeddah hotel. The check-in clerk asks for my 'good name' and the porter is then told to 'do the needful' with my bag. The hotel turns out be part of a subroutine of the Indian Oberoi chain.

Jeddah's importance as a Red Sea port made it the big city of Saudi Arabia until Riyadh finally overtook it when air travel ended the capital's desert isolation. Not until then did the foreign embassies relocate from Jeddah and Riyadh become the national capital in more than just name. The historic port city is still a more cosmopolitan place than straight-laced Riyadh, and Al-Balad, the old town centre with its multistorey houses, although dwarfed by the relentless expansion of the new city and distanced from the sea by land reclamation, remains one of the most interesting city areas in the country.

With its intricately fretworked wooden windows and coral-rock construction, old Jeddah's architecture is instantly recognisable although many of the Al-Balad buildings are like dishevelled, pot-bellied drunks. A couple of storeys up, the walls lean precipitately backward to counterbalance their bulging lower storeys, swelling out closer to street level like overhanging beer guts. At the same time the whole building sways drunkenly to one side or the other while the windows lean sideways or fall forward like the torn and peeling coat pockets on a drunk's jacket.

Wandering round the *souq* – the generic term for a market – I ask one stallholder, his wares limited entirely to Saudi-style sandals, if I can take his photograph and I'm invited in to sit and sip a cup of tea. It turns out he's from Yemen. I've been warned so forcefully about the dangers of taking photographs in Saudi Arabia that I have, to date, been very cautious about taking my camera out of my daypack. There is no question that taking photos of women is totally off-limits. I think even taking pictures of streetscapes with women in the frame would be off-limits. The few requests to take photographs of men have not been welcome either. In a square near a mosque I was amused to see the park benches had signs, in English as well as Arabic, insisting that you did not use them during prayer time. Two young Saudi boys were sitting on a bench beside the sign, but when I asked if I could photograph them they refused.

I'm the only passenger on the Red Sea Palace Hotel's bus tour of the city's further flung sights and it's a pretty perfunctory affair: 'there's the king's palace, there's another palace, there's the old airport, this is the Corniche', and finally, just before we got back to the hotel on the edge of Al-Balad, 'this is chop-chop square'.

Every Saudi city has a chop-chop square, where capital punishment is administered in Saudi style. There's no advance announcement, but on the appointed day the executioners come to the square and spread out a blue plastic sheet. The condemned man or woman arrives in a police car, hands bound, eyes covered, tranquillised. He or she is led out to the execution spot, made to kneel down and is beheaded with a swift sword stroke. It's usually just chop, not chop-chop. Nor is murder the only crime that leads to beheading. You can also pay a one-way visit to chop-chop square for rape, armed robbery, drug smuggling, sodomy or even witchcraft. In 1996 a Syrian citizen was executed for sorcery although it's believed his real crime was knowing too much about the questionable business practices of his employer, a Saudi prince.

Chopping hands off (for theft) and floggings (for drunkenness or homosexuality) are other popular Saudi punishments and in 2002 Englishman Gary Nixon was sentenced to eight years imprisonment and 800 lashes for running a booze business. Now that might have dissuaded Al Capone in the prohibition era. Usually the lashes are administered 50 or so at a time with 15 days between instalments. Nixon can be thought lucky he got off so lightly. A few years before, nine transvestites were sentenced to between 2400 and 2600 lashes each.

My second night in Jeddah I eat at Abou Shakra, an Egyptian restaurant overlooking the Corniche. It's Thursday night, the equivalent of Saturday night in the Christian West and it seems half the town has come to the seaside for a stroll.

The Arab world loves its mobile phones. Earlier in the day I'd passed a coffee bar where a group of Saudis were sitting around a table, their mobiles piled in the centre like logs on a boy scout campfire. Tonight the restaurant doesn't need muzak, there's a constant jangle of ring tones. Sometimes the jingles harmonise, sometimes they clash, but nobody is willing to answer the bloody things until their selection has played right through to the bitter end. I'm happy to leave and join the other weekend strollers along the Corniche. In a car park between the road and the beach, families have spread rugs on the tarmac and are having picnics. It seems a strange place to picnic, but further along the feasts are taking place right on the sidewalk with six lanes of traffic whipping by just a parked car's width away.

In the distance I can see strange lighted objects moving back and forth just out to sea. Jeddah is noted for its peculiar 'sculptures', which seem to pop up at every junction, in the middle of every roundabout and in any other sufficiently conspicuous position. My first thought is that this is some sort of mobile, illuminated sculpture.

The moving sculptures turn out to be horse-drawn carriages parading the beach, each festooned with strings of Christmas-like coloured lights. In between the carriages are camels and horses, taking beach-goers for a ride. The beach is also lined with rows of swings womaned by a chorus line of *abaya*-clad mothers pushing their children. So there's noise, colour, confusion and camels, enough to make the complete Saudi experience as soon as one more vital ingredient is added to the mix: danger. A couple of hundred miniature versions of those fat-tyred four-wheeled motorcycle devices supplies that. Some of their pilots are adults, but many more of them are children. Some simply hurtle along the pavement or beach, crouched low over their machines; others race around the beach, weaving in and out of the horse-drawn carriages, horses, camels and strollers. Others perform high-speed slaloms along the front.

This is clearly an accident begging to happen yet somehow it doesn't. In the half-hour I sit and watch this bizarre scene, doing my best to keep out of the line of fire, no high-speed racers collide head-on or chop a camel off at the knees; no beach moto-crosser mows down a strolling family; no slalom-ace spins out and wipes out an entire picnicking group. One day they will!

There's a final touch of Saudi surrealism back at the hotel. Usually the lobby reflected the country's cosmopolitan mix, with a group of Indian expats at one table, a party of British engineers talking loudly about 'Saudi-fucking-Arabia' at another, and a mix of Saudis and Western businessmen at a third. Tonight all the foreigners have been swept out and the lobby is wall-to-wall white *thobe* dotted with red-check *gutra*.

Regrettably Jeddah's most famous long-term expat resident was relocated even before he died in 2003. Big Daddy Idi Amin ended up in Saudi Arabia after his despotic rule of Uganda ended in 1979. His conversion to Islam had made him friends like Libya's Gaddafi and Saudi Arabia's King Faisal although it was unlikely that Faisal's successor, King Fahd, was so happy about his long-term guest. Idi may have been a lousy human being but he was a good Muslim, so the Saudis provided him with a home and swimming pool in Jeddah, a late-model Chevrolet Caprice, and a monthly allowance of about US$1500. Although he gave occasional interviews to African newspapers, he knew the deal depended upon keeping a low profile – trying to ship arms to northern Uganda in 1998 didn't fit that bill. He was promptly relocated from sophisticated Jeddah to straight-laced Mecca.

• • • •

'It's good business', said the manager of the Jeddah internet café I ducked into. He didn't seem concerned about government censorship and hadn't even heard of women's internet cafés being closed down, although I looked the story up on one of his computers. Like everything else in Saudi Arabia, internet cafés are sex-segregated. The 'women's café shut down' story didn't make it clear why it was shut down. Using the café as a meeting place? Looking at sites they shouldn't have? Accessing banned sites is a likely reason for a Saudi café to be shut. The government's censors have blocked off over 400,000 websites because they're 'anti-Islam' or they are a 'danger to state security'.

My next stop is Taif and a quick surf for hotels turns up an unbeatable 'one night only' bargain at the Taif InterContinental. When I get there it turns out to be not such a great deal because the hotel is way outside the town.

'We can call a taxi from town', suggests the doorman, but adds that I

284.

might find a taxi on the road outside. It's more freeway than road, but a couple of taxis flash past so I venture down the slip-road where Osama bin Laden's miniature twin brother in a beat-up old Peugeot stops almost immediately. Grow a bushy beard and slap on a *gutra* and almost any Saudi looks like Osama. His driving is very un-Saudi – he's slow and cautious, for which I'm most grateful, and he seems quite happy with what I pay.

Prayer time pops up five times a day and although the pre-dawn one, Fajr (sunrise), doesn't interrupt much (apart from perhaps waking you up) the other four – Dhuhr (noon), Asr (afternoon), Maghreb (sunset) and Isha (night) – certainly can. Since the times are determined by the time of sunrise and sunset, wherever you are they differ from day to day and from place to place and are listed for main centres in the paper each day.

At prayer time everything is supposed to stop, but that seems to be open to some interpretation. Planes don't stop flying, buses don't stop driving, taxis don't stop picking up fares, but shops and restaurants do close their doors. At prayer times you'll see the McDonalds staff lounging around outside, waiting for the 'all clear' to sound from the mosque, 20 minutes or half an hour later. Or sometimes longer. If you're hidden away inside, some places will let you carry on with your meal, but if you're in plain view you're likely to be hustled out on to the street. Dreaming over my coffee one day I didn't notice the café empty and, when I stood up to pay, discovered I was not only totally alone, I was also locked inside. The staff were grabbing a smoke outside. Hearing noises upstairs, I climbed the stairs to investigate and found a pool hall with all tables in action.

• • • •

Looking down the Abha-bound bus, there are half a dozen Saudis, but **285.** the other 50-odd passengers are probably a representative selection of Saudi guest workers. Developing world guest workers that is – wealthy

Western workers would be flying or driving. There are no women either, although the previous day's bus had half a dozen, including a couple of brazen older Filipinistas with uncovered hair. Today's passengers mainly come from the hard-working Middle Eastern neighbours or the subcontinent, apart from a scattering of Africans.

The first 100 kilometres from Taif pass by at suitably rapid Saudi-freeway pace, but then the road narrows and begins to twist and climb. The countryside also becomes noticeably greener, hardly lush Irish-green, but the sort of green that would not be out of place in parts of Italy or Greece. It's also surprisingly densely populated. One scattered small town is quickly followed by another, places that could boast a bank or two with ATMs, a car dealer and a host of shops and workshops.

In between the more modern buildings – square, flat-roofed places whether they are smaller homes, bigger ones or four- and five-storey buildings – are square watchtowers, signs of an earlier unsettled age when tribal feuding was common. They go on for hundreds of kilometres, sometimes popping up every kilometre or so. Fortress-like homes or even groups of buildings like small walled villages also appear from time to time.

I've had remarkably few real conversations with Saudis over the past week. So much of the everyday tourist contact is not with Saudis, but with Egyptians, Syrians, Indians, Pakistanis or Western expats. This time, however, I find myself sitting next to an English-speaking Saudi. Eventually I steer the conversation around to September 11 and its effect in Saudi Arabia.

'Nobody wants to talk about it or even think about it. They want to close their eyes', he says, gesturing with his hands across his eyes.

'Nobody knows why they did it, although most of the hijackers came from Asir', exactly where we are heading towards. 'We saw their pictures on the television.'

'What you are saying to me, you should not say to anyone in Riyadh', he concludes. 'It's OK to talk with me this way, but in Riyadh you must be very careful who you talk with.'

The man in the street wasn't the only one with an *abaya* on when it came to seeing what was going on. When the Saudis finally and reluctantly admitted that 15 of the 19 hijackers were Saudis – although Saudi newspapers still tend to say 'were alleged to be Saudis' – the Interior Minister Prince Nayef claimed 'Saudi Arabia bears no responsibility at all' for September 11. As for the whereabouts of that well-known and much-searched-for ex-Saudi all the prince had to say was, 'we have no information and we have no interest in this subject'.

In fact I'm going from one hijacking centre to another. At least one of the hijackers hailed from Taif, but it was the Asir region, and most particularly Abha, where most of them came from. Abha was the home town for four of the 15 and it's speculated that the town's firebrand cleric Safar al Hawali may have helped to convince them of their holy mission. So it's remarkable that hordes of high-powered Western journos hadn't taken this same bus south. This should have been the town where packs of reporters from the *New York Times*, *Time* magazine or the *Daily Telegraph* descended to doorstep the families of the September 11 multiple murderers. Abha was 'ground zero' for hijacker recruitment, but had there been any Western reporters on this bus, intent on chasing the story back to its starting point? I don't think so.

The trip to Abha had been 'guesstimated' from six to nine hours, but by late afternoon it looks like even nine hours is wishful thinking. Apart from the winding road, there is also a subcontinental routine to the stops. Someone would shout for the driver to stop, would get up and farewell his friends, the driver's assistant would swing up the luggage compartment doors and retrieve the passenger's bags and off we'd go again only for the process to be repeated a hundred metres down the road.

Just when boredom was really setting in we get there, right on nine hours. Though we're not at Abha. Somehow we'd zoomed by Abha half an hour previously and I end up 25 kilometres further along at Khamis. A taxi whisks me back to Abha for precisely half of what it has cost to get all the way from Taif. My guidebook says there's only one hotel in the centre of town. It turns out to be a dive, but I'm too exhausted to care. When I wander out for food – chicken shwarma yet again – I find three other hotels.

If I have one superstitious travel fear, it's tied up with grubby hotels like this one. I'm not particularly worried about my bus falling over a precipice, or my boat going down soon after I discover there are no life jackets on board. I hate the thought of dropping dead in some nameless dive. It's stupid, because if you're dead you're not going to care, but when I'm travelling alone the thought of having a heart attack or dying in my sleep in some dismal hole like this one really freaks me. The next morning I shift hotels, although my bill turns out to be somewhat less than I was quoted at check-in, which makes it seem not quite so dive-like.

I go in search of a rent-a-car. Jamal, an Egyptian, offers me a choice of battered Mitsubishis and points out that the rate doesn't include insurance.

'Can't I pay extra for insurance?' I ask.

'Sorry, we don't have insurance. Don't worry about it, you're not going far from Abha.'

Well, *enshallah*, nothing will happen, but Saudi driving comes from another universe. It's not aggressive like Italy, it's not flat-out speed like Spain or Germany, it's not utter chaos like Cairo or Delhi, nor do Saudi drivers display the sort of pig-headedness you can encounter in the West from Manchester to Melbourne. No, Saudi drivers are completely random. They'll overtake and then simply not pull back in until they're suddenly surprised by somebody approaching head-on. They'll hurtle up behind you at warp speed and either try to squeeze past or decelerate a centimetre behind your back bumper.

288.

All too often Saudi drivers discover warp speed is too big a figure for the next corner, as the black rubber streaks on the way in and battered guard rails and coloured concrete on the apex repeatedly illustrate. On the road from Taif there are regular sightings of battered vehicles far down the hillside below those traumatic corners.

The keynote driving manoeuvre, however, is the unsignalled multi-lane change. Using indicators is never popular with Saudi drivers, but it has a special frisson of excitement when a driver suddenly decides he wants to turn off to the left and he's three lanes over to the right. No problem, he simply turns and most of the time everybody misses him.

'Double zero', announced my Pakistani taxi driver in Riyadh as a Saudi Chevy swung abruptly across our bows.

'Their *agal* [the double-looped cord that holds their *gutra* in place] makes two zeros,' he explained, 'and that's how intelligent they are.'

Their driving may be erratic, but they're remarkably tranquil about the sort of driving that would inspire road rage in the West. The only time Saudis consistently use their horns is the instant a traffic light turns green, even if they're 10 cars back. My Saudi driving technique is simply to give every other car a lot of space. And I constantly watch my rear-view mirror for anyone about to ram me from behind.

'Don't have an accident, you'll always be at fault', an English resident had advised me.

'Even if the local driver is going too fast and not looking when he runs in to you from behind it's still your fault', he went on. 'This is his country, he belongs here, you don't and if you'd not been here the accident wouldn't have happened.'

Everywhere in Saudi Arabia there are plenty of Mercedes and BMWs and in the big cities like Riyadh and Jeddah it's clear how important this market is to companies like Rolls-Royce, Ferrari and Porsche. It's also one of the last places outside North America where Detroit can still flog its wheels, although curiously all the Chevrolet Luminas so popular with the Saudi police force are really from Australia. Ditto for the ubiquitous Toyota taxis. The real Saudi car, the one you'll see parked side-by-side-by-side in town-centre parking lots, or gathered by the dozen at Bedouin encampments in the middle of the desert, is the Toyota pick-up truck. Sure a Nissan or Mitsubishi will do, but, just like the Taliban, oh-what-a-feeling the Saudis have for a Toyota Hilux, so long as it's in the standard Saudi pick-up colour scheme, that is – white with an orange flash down the side. It's said the king dispensed thousands of them to the Bedouin at the start of the Kuwait Gulf War, to ensure their loyalty.

My Mitsubishi is not only battered, it's also worn out I realise as I chug up the first hill heading south to Habalah. The road climbs up to the very edge of the escarpment, from where the mountains tumble down to the Red Sea. Some of the villages I drive through have more of the characteristic square mud houses with their sloping walls and decorative slate ledges. They're interspersed with watchtowers, but unlike the square ones between Taif and Abha these are round, with stone for the lower section, mud for the upper. The house and the watchtower design elements are reflected in much of the modern architecture around Abha.

At Habalah an abandoned village clings to the steep rock face, 300 metres below the plateau top, but still hundreds of metres above the dry valley bottom, which slopes away towards the coast, disappearing in a shimmering grey heat haze. It's a fantastic sight and once again I have the whole place to myself. If I'd come at the weekend, however, I wouldn't have been so alone. Perched at the top of the escarpment is an amusement park, a Luna Park as the Saudis (and Australians) call them, complete with a cable-car running down to the abandoned village. A row of stone enclosures allows Saudi families to picnic and enjoy the view without seeing each other. To complete the desecration there's a dense coating of soft-drink cans, mineral-water bottles, plastic bags and other modern debris over everything. Great view, though.

290.

In the afternoon I take another direction out of the city and drive to another escarpment-edge view. It's only as I reach the top I realise why my rent-a-car is so gutless – the altitude is just under 3000 metres, which also accounts for my breathlessness when I climb a little hill. On the way back into town I divert off the road looking for a view down on Abha and find myself, judging from the armed military guards at the front gate, at the entrance to some Saudi prince's weekend mountain escape. Saudi Arabia is littered with the royal family's many princes' many palaces, escapes, weekenders, retreats and hideaways. The high walls around this one seem to stretch for about a kilometre and what I took to be a neat row of pine trees turns out to be an equally neat row of furled green garden umbrellas peeking over the wall, presumably on a terrace where you could sip a nonalcoholic sundowner at beer-o'clock and watch the last rays dapple the town below.

Keeping the extended royal family in palaces, executive jets and limousines consumes a large part of the budget (King Ibn Saud had 44 sons from his 22 wives, for example), but Saudi Arabia still manages to get by without any income tax although a modest (perhaps 2.5 per cent) tax on foreigners is mooted from time to time. After all, they send home around US$18 billion annually so they could presumably pay a bit to their hosts.

I'd had a glimpse into the spending habits of Saudi princes and their entourages over a cup of coffee at a ski resort in Colorado. I'd met a British executive aircraft dealer on the chairlift and he'd given me a brief background on the used-jet market.

'I don't deal in the little stuff like Learjets,' he started, 'I handle G5s and up.'

Usually he didn't buy and sell like a used-car dealer either. His business was more like a real-estate agent, the middleman. Sometimes, however, it was worth putting up his own money.

'It was an about-to-be-deposed dictator's DC9', he explained. 'Low hours, forced sale, a great buy. I had to find a crew, get them into country X and get the aircraft out before the mob at the palace gates got too restive. Eventually I found a buyer for the plane in Saudi. The king has a

291.

747, with an operating theatre downstairs just in case he has a heart attack at 30,000 feet. The top princes will also have widebodys and then as you move down the royal pecking order it's smaller passenger aircraft before you get into the executive jet territory. Members of a top prince's entourage would also have their own aircraft and I eventually sold this one to the Lebanese business adviser of one of the high-level princes.'

A popular myth held that the king's 747 not only had an operating theatre, but also a live transplant donor on board each flight, ready to be sacrificed just in case a fresh heart was needed.

• • • •

Stephen Ulph, the editor of the Jane's Information Group's *Islamic Affairs Analyst*, wrote that, 'a staggering two-thirds of Saudi PhDs are now awarded in Islamic Studies – a qualification that leaves their bearers effectively unemployable, disenchanted, and in many cases with little else to do but go in search of a "higher calling".'

On my final Saudi excursion, in Najran, just north of the border with Yemen, I test that research on the ground. Once again I find myself sitting next to an English-speaking Saudi, a university student on holiday from the US and, presumably, slumming it travelling by bus. When I query him on the statistics he agrees.

'The percentage is probably even higher', he suggests, but then pops up with the old Arab world Coca-Cola-and-the-Zionists urban myth. 'Ten per cent of the price of every can and bottle of Coca-Cola goes straight to Israel', he announces. 'The fact is suppressed in the West so you don't hear about it, but in the Arab world everybody knows.'

At lunchtime we pause in Zahran, a small town where I'm told some of the September 11 hijackers had connections. Nobody seems to be looking for would-be pilots today and a couple of hours later I'm in Najran. It's a curious place, essentially one long main road stretching for 15 kilometres from the isolated Holiday Inn at one end to the fairytale castle in the heart of the *souq* at the other.

The next morning I am picked up by Saeed Jumaan, quite the most charming tour guide you could ask for. As a young boy he went off to work for Aramco, the Arabian American Oil Company that propelled Saudi Arabia to the top of the petrodollar charts. He learnt English with Aramco, but returned to his home town, still a teenager.

'One day in the market I saw this Western woman having difficulty making herself understood', he tells me. 'I offered to translate and she immediately asked if I wanted a job. I ended up working for her company for the next few years, but that first afternoon she asked me to come back to her company's encampment. I went with her, but I remember being terrified. I had no idea what was going to happen to me, whether this was the end of my life.'

In the shadow of Najran's enchanted castle is the basket *souq*, full of baskets and curious stone-turned pots from Yemen, and close by is the 'ladies *souq*'. Special dispensation allows women to work in this market. The goods spill out of the stalls and across the wide, dusty aisles – baskets of spices, heaps of kitchen utensils, piles of pottery, incense burners, boxes of tribal jewellery, all of it jumbled together with no discernible order, much of it piled up on boxes and stands that give the whole *souq* the look of a rolling, colourful hillscape, dotted by the black peaks that are the women, squatting among their wares. It is absolutely the most disorganised, chaotic, untidy, higgledy-piggledy market I have ever seen. There's no way they can pack things away at the end of the day's business, a tarpaulin or a plastic sheet is simply hauled across the goods.

One woman is selling goat skins sewn up at the head and anus with a stopper plugged into one of the legs to be used as a water container or, in this case, to carry cooking fat. I can't imagine anything I'd less like to carry home with me, but my 'what the hell is this' interest prompts her to offer a lower price every time I pass her position. Later I see a man making larger ones, strictly for carrying water with a tap shoved up the opening where the anus would have been.

• • • •

Queuing up for security at Najran Airport, I peek surreptitiously over the shoulder of the woman in front. What would her identity card show? Clearly if a Saudi woman went overseas she must have her photo on her passport. Other countries are not going to accept a picture of someone disguised as a black sack. Here the question of photo identification on a driving licence never arises, but what do they show on their local ID?

Answer: their husband's picture.

The flight to Riyadh skirts the edge of the Rub Al-Khali, the Empty Quarter. I'd toyed with the idea of making a foray out into the Empty Quarter from Najran, but it's two hours each way before you really get into the sand dunes, too long for my short stay. Halfway to Riyadh the desert – generally beige, featureless with occasional black, rocky outcrops – suddenly gives way to a huge agricultural project. The circular irrigated fields (technically known as centre pivot irrigation systems) look like someone has sat down with a stack of giant CDs and slung them out one by one on to the sand. The Saudis used a big chunk of their oil wealth to build up a major agricultural sector, proving that if you pour enough water on a desert you can grow grain even if it isn't necessarily a very ecologically or economically sensible idea. This realisation is beginning to sink in and some cutting back is going on.

The Empty Quarter may be the world's biggest sand desert, but in fact it isn't that big. The state of Western Australia, which is nearly all desert, is 25 per cent bigger than all of Saudi Arabia – in *Dirt Music*, Australian author Tim Winton described his home state as being rather like Texas, 'only it's big'.

In the Riyadh boarding lounge, waiting for my flight to Dubai, I'm suddenly not the sole nonbeliever in sight and some of the Western women have already cast their *abaya* aside.

'I have this vision of expat women dropping their *abaya* at the departure gate when they finally leave Saudi', I'd said to one of the Canadians in Madain Saleh.

'I'm burning mine at my going-away party', she'd replied. 'I'll be on my way out, they can't do anything then.'

• • • •

So much of the Saudi experience revolves around women: their presence, their exclusion, their appearance, their restricted lives. This is the country that taught the Taliban how to treat women and much of women's role in Saudi Arabia is well documented. They can't drive (which introduces a whole new category of guest worker to the equation, the women's guest-worker-chauffeur), they can't work except in strictly controlled female-only situations, they can't go into certain shops (CD shops and video shops are both strictly forbidden to the fairer sex), they can't even ride on a bus without a responsible male to keep an eye on them.

They can't even get a haircut. Saudi Arabia is overstocked with barbers, but hairdressers for women simply don't exist. A woman can't have her hair cut by a man and working as a hairdresser is not an occupation open to women.

'It's not a problem for the rich Saudis,' said a British expat, 'they'll fly in a hairdresser from Paris when they want their hair done. Of course, there are secret hairdressers, the taxi drivers know where to find them.'

'What about Kingdom Tower?' I asked. Riyadh's new super skyscraper included a pioneering women's floor with shops purely for women and operated by female staff. 'Why couldn't they have women's hairdressers in a women-only environment like that?'

'Well, Kingdom Tower is still pretty experimental', she said. 'Anyway there are female *mutawwa* as well. They've been in there trying to ensure that women keep their hair covered.'

In fact I do see women working. In smaller towns, further from Riyadh, there were often women selling things in a *souq*, but not in the shops themselves. While the men lounged back in the comfort of stalls, the women squatted on the ground, often on the pavement or out in the sun. The special ladies *souq* in, remarkably, ultra-conservative Najran was the one exception.

The most unusual thing about the women was that most of the time they just weren't there. Early in the morning you might see the occasional woman, but most of the time in most of the country they simply disappeared for the rest of the day, reappearing like black-cloaked vampires as the sun went down. For much of the day you could almost forget this was a country that treated women like enslaved second-class citizens, only to wake up with a start as their sinister forms reappeared in the evening. Like 'death out for a walk' as French author Guy de Maupassant famously described them.

So why do Saudi men treat their women so abjectly and why do they brand them with this absurdly uncomfortable and impractical outfit? It's not like the ritual tattooing of the Pacific, the stretched lower lips of the Surma women of Ethiopia, or the long necks (actually depressed collarbones) of the Padaung women of Myanmar. Those ritual appearances are looked upon locally as a sign of beauty, not something to be hidden away and disabling.

There was, however, another time and place where women were deliberately handicapped, just like in Saudi Arabia today – China. Every time I go back there the speed of change seems to have kicked up another notch. In Guilin the hustle, the bright lights, the crowds, the fashions, the traffic and the restaurants would have had Mao spinning in his grave faster than a CD. In the restaurant I went for dinner (busy, noisy, very

Chinese, terrific food, especially the noodle-thin stir-fried potatoes with green peppers) the next table had three young guys and a girl. Shortly after I arrived a second girl turned up – she was stunning, wearing very tight, faded blue jeans and a silvery top. Then the sixth member of the group rushed in, looking equally à la mode and finishing a phone call on her mobile as she pushed through the door. A couple of days later I was leaving the country and at Beijing airport I was suddenly whisked back to a much older China. A small group of Chinese were moving towards the check-in counter, gently helping a very old lady who was hobbling painfully. I realised instantly why she was having such trouble walking – she had bound feet. I'd seen the shoes, read the description of how it was done, but surely it was centuries ago, something associated with the opium trade, something that had died out long, long before Mao or even Chiang Kai Shek? Yet here we were, at the start of the 21st century and there were still people alive with bound feet.

That's what *abaya* remind me of. They're the Saudi equivalent of bound feet, something that ties people down, makes them helpless, deprives them of freedom, restricts them, binds them, hobbles them.

And black. Why would anyone want to wear black under that pitiless Saudi sun?

'So why did the men end up all in white and the women in black?' I asked a Saudi.

'Well, we men had the first choice, of course,' he replied, 'and in this climate you'd be crazy to wear black.'

Given that women can't work, except under the most constrained circumstances, and are severely restricted in what they can do and where they can go, how do they pass the time? Things aren't all that great for men either. You're certainly not going to meet your friends in a bar (since alcohol is banned), male or female you won't be going out to the cinema (they're banned too) and as for clubs, dancing and discos… So Saudis do what lots of people do when there's nothing else to do. Make babies.

Fertility rates have come tumbling down in many countries. In Japan and Italy the average number of children per woman has dropped below the 2.2 generally reckoned to be what's needed to keep the population static. In Bangladesh, once looked upon as an international basket case, the fertility rate has dropped to just over three children and even Kenya, the world's fertility horror story in the late 1970s when the average Kenyan women had eight children, has brought its rate down to around five children.

For all the BMWs and Mercedes Saudi Arabia is more like the Third World when it comes to contraception, birth control and fertility. Until recently the average Saudi woman had more than six children, although that has dropped to something between three and four in recent years. In the same period the total fertility rate in Iran has had one of the most dramatic drops anywhere in the world; after a baby boom following the Iran–Iraq war, fertility today has dropped to Western European levels.

The resulting population boom means 60 per cent of the population is under 18 and unless oil stays at sky-high levels, simple demographics will eventually undo things. The post-oil-boom baby bulge is looking for jobs and in turn creating its own baby boom. Eventually something has to give. New job-seekers appear on the market far faster than new jobs are created and it will inevitably get worse if the government does not institute big changes, but the Saudi government has never moved fast. A continuing fall in per-capita income and a drop in living standards could lead to some emancipation of women, a window could crack open to a democratic breeze. Or it could lead nowhere at all. There's still a lot of oil and at current price levels the government has lots more breathing space.

So the government seems to be edging towards real employment change in only the most gentle and delicate fashion. My guidebook discreetly notes that, 'two generations of generous public assistance have not inculcated the country's youth with a strong work ethic'.

That's putting it mildly. It was a joke during the Kuwait Gulf War that you'd get a thousand-dollar prize if you spotted a Saudi carrying anything heavier than money. When I queried why the 'no women working with men' rule didn't seem to apply to Saudi Arabian Airlines' female flight attendants I was told: 'They're probably Moroccans, you certainly couldn't have a Saudi woman employed as a flight attendant. Anyway if you see anybody working, they're probably not Saudis.'

Saudis dominate the government jobs. About three quarters of the million or so people employed in that sector are Saudis, but there are an awful lot of non-jobs in that sector, a lot of offices full of people pushing paper from one side of a desk to the other and then having another cup of tea. Meanwhile in the harder-working private sector, the proportions are reversed. The sector is much bigger, employing over six million people, but over five million are expats. That's a tough statistic for the government to live with when unemployment among Saudis is already conservatively estimated to be 15 to 20 per cent and set to go much higher.

The government has instituted a policy of Saudisation. Seventy-five per cent of a company's employees should be Saudis unless, of course, there are not enough 'competent nationals' available. 'Some firms employ Saudis to sit around to meet the numbers', an Indian business manager in Riyadh told me. 'We can't afford to do that, but it can be difficult to find Saudis who'll stick with a job. They're keen to be managers, but they don't want to start at the bottom and work their way up. If they speak good English, they're likely to be paid more in a government job as well.'

Indians, making up 1.5 million of the expat-worker pool, have recently been subjected to a blanket ban except in certain categories. Osama al-Kurdi, Secretary-General of the Council of Saudi Chambers of Commerce and Industry, in trying to get the recruitment ban lifted, stated that 'all studies on Saudisation emphasise that there are certain areas which Saudis do not like to work in, while in other sectors the number of Saudi workers are far fewer than the number required.'

Of course, spurning the menial jobs isn't unusual in most First World countries. Would a table get cleared in the US without Mexican bus boys? Is there still a Brit employed in a London hotel? Even Japan depends heavily on its frequently illegal arbeits to keep its economy functioning. In Saudi Arabia, however, the problem isn't just at the bottom of the job basket. 'They simply aren't turning out enough graduates with the right qualifications and until they do they'll have to keep importing labour', said an expat doctor.

· · · ·

There's a lot I don't like about the country, but everybody I met, Saudi or expat, was polite, helpful and often friendly, and it was an intriguing place to visit. There have been so few visitors and so little written (and even less filmed or photographed) that places often came as pleasantly jolting surprises. If the Saudis were to free up their visa requirements, they could easily have many more visitors – there's plenty to see, getting around is quite easy and the facilities are more than adequate. The jobs created could also help reduce their mounting unemployment problem. More importantly, though, it could form a channel of communication in both directions. And that's what Saudi Arabia badly needs. For all the whining about how unfair the world is to Islam, it's the country's inward-looking, tightly constrained, narrow-minded view of its religion and its position in the world that is the real cause of the Saudi problem.

THE EVIL METER™

Measuring 'badness' is not an exact science. Countless times in my Bad Lands travels I was reminded that every story has two sides and very often one country's terrorist is indeed another country's freedom fighter. Balancing up the varying perceptions of what constitutes immorality or wickedness is like trying to compare rotten apples with bitter oranges. Nevertheless I'm going to have a go at it. I've devised my very own 'Evil Meter™' and I'm going to run it over each of my Bad Lands to gauge which really is the baddest of them all.

Three things give a country marks on my Evil Meter™ – how it treats its own citizens, if it is involved in terrorism and if it is a threat to other countries. We'll look at how each measures up to those requirements and rate them from zero (perfect treatment) to three (evil personified).

In a perfect world people should have a say in who rules them. So if they have no access to democracy, and decisions about their lives are made at the whim of a monarch or a dictator, that's going to rack up points. As well as the right to vote governments in or out, people should also be allowed to criticise them and not risk getting thrown in jail, or worse. They should also be allowed to get on with their lives without undue government interference. Sure the government can tax you, fine you if you drive too fast or drink too much, require that your kids go to school and generally make you jump through dozens of other hoops. If, however, you want to start a legitimate business, move from town A to town B, marry or take up a weird religion, then you should be allowed to do so. Finally you should expect to be treated fairly by the government. If you do something wrong, you should get a fair trial and the punishment, if you're convicted, should fit the crime. My Evil Meter™ records up to three points in this category.

Terrorism, and how a country handles it, also includes a number of factors. A country may be an outright supporter of terrorism. There are places that think for various reasons terrorism is a good idea and support it directly. That might mean training and financing its own terrorists. Or it might mean offering support in some form for an independent terrorist group or a terrorist group in another country.

Supporting terrorism doesn't have to be direct in my point count. It can be a result of some other policy or it can even be completely inadvertent. Pouring too much military equipment into a country for one reason or another can easily result in excess equipment spilling over the edge and getting into the hands of a terrorist group. Or the government can turn a blind eye to support from the general population for various forms of extremism. It may see this as a way of allowing people to let off steam or exercise their free will, but the end result may be support for terrorist activities. My Evil Meter™ can also record up to three points in the Terrorism category.

Finally there's External Threats – outright national aggression towards another country. For some reason country A simply decides it has to bomb, attack or invade country B. Three points are available in this category too, making nine points available thus far.

Of course, nothing worthwhile is measured on a scale of nine. We all know 10 is the number to aim for so my Evil Meter™ also dispenses a bonus point for a good Personality Cult. No Bad Land can be really awful without a superlative collection of statues and portraits of the leader. A strong personality cult isn't a prerequisite for Bad Land status, but a decent collection of statuary and portraits of the great leader certainly helps. Iraq clearly ticked that box during the Saddam era and Libya still has a nice collection of Gaddafi billboards, but I was very disappointed in my visit to Albania to find that Enver Hoxha statues had totally disappeared.

Far and away the best Bad Land statue collection is, for now at least, in North Korea and I desperately hope the fall of that regime won't also lead to the fall of all those Dear Leader and Great Leader figures and portraits. The Chinese could show them how to let the political artwork gently fade into the background. Big Mao images remain – they're simply in the shadows; either the spotlights have been turned off or statuary is simply lost among billboards for mobile phones, cold beers and pricey perfumes.

Working from bottom to top, the merely slightly bad to the outright appalling, here are the scores.

CUBA
1.5 POINTS

Poor old Cuba is an also-run when it comes to evil. The only place Fidel is tough on is Cuba. There's only ever one candidate to elect (the maximum leader, of course), there's no chance you can say anything critical about him, and the only free-enterprise is prostitution. The USA may have worked hard for nearly 50 years at impoverishing the country, but Fidel's worked even harder at the same task.

On the other hand, when it comes to public health and education Cuba doesn't do so badly – infant mortality figures in Cuba are comparable with the far wealthier USA. This pulls the two points Cuba would score for being thoroughly bad to its own people back to a 1.5.

Externally the country is no threat to anyone. Apart, that is, from the Cuban national baseball team's ability to beat almost anybody, including the USA, and Fidel's ability to bore anyone to death with his endless speeches. Once upon a time aircraft hijackings were pretty much a 'take me to Havana' speciality, but terrorism is really not a Cuban talent.

Despite those trademark military fatigues, the bushy beard and the big cigars, Fidel doesn't get off the ground in the Personality Cult bonus category. Images and statues are almost all reserved for the even more photogenic Che Guevara.

BURMA
2.5 POINTS

Despite all the fingers pointed at it, Burma is really nowhere when it comes to evil on my meter. There's no evidence the generals have ever tried to foment revolution, export terrorism or invade other countries although their slack attitude towards opium poppy cultivation means they're a major supporter of First World drug problems.

When it comes to grinding down Burma's own population, however, the generals are champions. They've slaughtered students, imprisoned a Nobel Prize winner, devastated minority ethnic groups, beaten up democracy campaigners, flattened and relocated villages and forced children to work building roads and railways. Twenty years ago, when their policies also included mad socialism, they could have scored a full three points in this category, but shops full of electronic gear and streets jammed with Japanese cars indicate that mad socialism has been consigned to the economics wastebasket.

The generals do score a half-point in the Personality Cult bonus category. Apart from dressing up in Ruritanian military outfits and pinning ridiculous numbers of medals across inflated chests, they wouldn't look like contenders. Although, given there are those billboards proclaiming what a wonderful job they're doing, how much everybody loves them and how all the country's problems are the fault of 'that woman', for sheer outright delusion they get a half-point.

ALBANIA
DURING THE ENVER HOXHA ERA
3 POINTS

Today Albania is a reformed nation, simply waiting for the outside world to realise all those image problems are part of the distant past. Even in the worst years of poor deluded Enver Hoxha's regime, Albania was really a nonstarter in the evil stakes. To the outside world it was simply reclusive; it was certainly no threat to anyone either through terrorism or directly. Actually, scared little Albania was convinced the outside world was a threat to it, hence all those bunkers scattered around the country. Britain and America probably did plot to help Albanian opposition forces overthrow Hoxha in the early 1950s, about the time he kicked off his bunker-building spree.

Internally, however, Hoxha ensured that Albania was right up there in the evil stakes. You didn't vote, you didn't criticise (unless you wanted a lengthy stay in a prison modelled on Joe Stalin's gulag originals), you enjoyed the most impoverished lifestyle in Europe and for entertainment you could help build those crazy concrete bunkers. Or enjoy a spell in the chrome mines.

Hoxha-era Albania scores a bonus point for a good Personality Cult. Unfortunately the statues and busts have all disappeared. The only hint of the bad old days is Hoxha's awful (in architecture, design and construction) pyramid ex-museum in the centre of Tirana.

SAUDI ARABIA
4 POINTS

Well, the Saudis certainly aren't going to invade anybody. Back in the Kuwait Gulf War it was a standard joke for coalition military that the only thing you'd ever see a Saudi soldier lift up was a bag of money. Nor is a country so dedicated to hiding statues, pictures, films, drawings, painting and any other depiction of the human form going to have a chance of scoring a Personality Cult bonus point.

When it comes to terrorism, however, the Saudis are right up there. Encouraging terrorism may not be government policy, but the Saudi government is hand-in-glove with Wahhabism, the extremist form of Islam, which believes that it's right and anybody else is an infidel deserving death with no virgins lined up in the afterlife. Add that to an educational and economic system in large part dedicated to turning out Islamic scholars and then having to spend the oil money on importing people to do the hard work, and you're heading towards a situation where the only calling for too many bored young men is a spell of jihad. That could mean trotting off to Afghanistan to help the Taliban oppress women, or trotting off to the USA to hijack aircraft and fly them into buildings. The Evil Meter™ reads two points.

Saudi activities may not be too much fun for other countries, but it's not much fun if you're a woman either, having to put on a black sack anytime you go outside, not being able to drive, only being allowed to work under extremely limited circumstances – in fact not being able to do most things without a 'responsible male relative' to keep an eye on you. Many of the country's guest workers don't get treated too well either. Throw in near-zero democratic rights, a medieval punishment system, strict government censorship and the morals police wandering around waving big sticks and Saudi Arabia scores another two points for not being very nice to its own people.

LIBYA
BEFORE GADDAFI REFORMED
4.5 POINTS

Today it's an all-new user-friendly Libya, although they've still got a long way to go before the doors are really open to Western visitors. Visitors from other (poorer) countries in Africa, planning to turn up as refugees in Europe as soon as possible, don't face anywhere near as much difficulty getting in to Libya. It's hardly surprising, since Gaddafi has given up on unifying the Arab world and now concentrates on unifying Africa, with himself at the helm of course.

Libya's treatment of its own citizens has not been terrific. In the bad old days Gaddafi was prone to chasing his opponents wherever they went. The most notable downside of this policy was in London in 1984 when a Libyan sniper, firing on Libyan protesters in the streets outside the Libyan embassy, managed to kill a London bobby instead. Complaining isn't a good idea in Libya either. In 1996 a riot broke out at a football match in Tripoli and when the shooting stopped there were at least 20 dead. The shooting had started after spectators began shouting slogans against either the Gaddafi government or, equally possibly, Gaddafi's football-crazy son Saadi Gaddafi, who is said to have ordered his personal security guards to fire on those foolish fans. Of course, the slaughter wasn't widely reported in Libya so it's hard to tell exactly what happened.

The positive side of the equation? Well Gaddafi does believe in his socialist duty to feed and shelter his people. A visitor reported seeing bread dumped under bridges and underpasses every morning for the hungry as part of this programme. Nevertheless Amnesty International continues to have grave reservations about the human rights situation in Libya so even today the Evil Meter™ scores would give him a point in this category.

Terrorism? Well, the reformed Gaddafi wouldn't think of that sort of thing, but in his bad old days he not only funded any terrorist organisation who wandered by Tripoli with their hands out, he also did some terrorising of his own, most famously by sabotaging a French DC-10 and an American 747. So although the new good Gaddafi may not go in for that sort of thing, the old bad Gaddafi certainly did and scores two points.

307.

Gaddafi wasn't above making the odd direct external threat and sending the Libyan troops in when he felt they were needed. Fortunately for the outside world they weren't too effective. His support for Uganda's Idi Amin didn't save that notorious bad lad, although his escape to Saudi Arabia was probably engineered by Gaddafi. He supported a variety of other African hopeless cases including the Central African Republic's Bokassa and Liberia's horrific Charles Taylor, but it was in Chad where Libyan military might played its longest-running role. When the French Foreign Legion turned up, however, they soon scooted home to Libya. So despite his efforts Gaddafi only scores one as an External Threat. He might have liked to be threatening, but he wasn't.

Finally Personality Cult bonus points: a good effort, but not up with the best is probably the most you can say for Gaddafi's billboard collection. The problem is he always looks like he was trying out for a position on *Queer Eye for the Straight Guy*: not the ideal look for a Great Bad Land Leader role. Half a point.

AFGHANISTAN
UNDER THE TALIBAN
4.5 POINTS

Outside the Taliban's own ranks and the equally misguided enthusiasts of Wahhabism (the Taliban with credit cards), nobody has much enthusiasm for the Taliban and their treatment of the long-suffering citizens of Afghanistan. It's hard to find anything nice to say about people who hate music, art, film, kite flying and women. Plus they were so completely focused on forcing their interpretations of how the world should work upon everybody else that simple little things like feeding people just didn't come on to their screens. Those things could be left to Allah (or the UN, or foreign NGOs) while they concentrated on stoning adulterers, burning books and blowing up Buddha images. So a solid three points for being horrible to the people of Afghanistan.

Sadly it has to be admitted that the Taliban were not all bad. They came into existence as a reaction to how much bad was already out there.

The mujaheddin may have helped to topple the Soviet Union, may have several nice positions in the new democratic government of Afghanistan and may have created a genuine poster-pinup national hero in Ahmad Shah Massoud, but the reality is that much of the time rape, pillage and destruction were their chief talents. The Soviet Union may have trashed the Afghan countryside, but it was the mujaheddin who trashed the cities and heaped more years of suffering upon the already long-suffering Afghan people. So we'll pull the Taliban back half a point, horrible though they were.

Which is remarkably like how I feel about the Western world's best-known Taliban: Australian David Hicks. Anybody who supported all the ridiculous stuff the Taliban believed in can't be a very pleasant person. If he'd turned up back in Australia, I would definitely have wanted to cross the street if he was strolling by. If he'd been handed over to a bunch of radical feminists for a little re-education after he returned home, that would have been entirely fitting, but getting shoved into a no-charges, no-communication, no-defence, no rules-of-law, utterly wrong prison camp like Guantánamo Bay is just as bad. Worst of all, when your own government does the Pontius Pilate act and washes its hands of you and says some other country can do whatever it pleases with you, then definitely the Evil Meter™ has to balance things up. So, unhappily, I have to say David Hicks' sins are balanced out by the sins against him.

Given a clean, uninfluenced reading the Evil Meter™ would probably produce the same result for America's best-known Taliban, John Walker Lindh.

Irrespective of which, the Taliban can rack up another two points in the Terrorism category. They may not have engaged in it themselves, but they put up with and sheltered people who did. They took in a bunch of people who not only used Afghanistan as a launching pad for the September 11 attacks on the USA, but also brought their particularly single-minded hatreds to bear on parts of the Afghan population like the

Hazara. And women in general.

Personality Cult bonus score? A big fat zero. The Taliban didn't like images of anybody and they were so reclusive there's hardly anything known about Mullah Omar apart from the fact that he only had one eye.

On the other hand Osama definitely generated a Personality Cult, but he was a Saudi, not an Afghan…

IRAN
5 POINTS

Like many visitors to Iran I've come away with some passion for the place. As a tourist destination it's fantastic and the people can be terrific too. They have the right blend of enthusiasm and cynicism and they're smart enough to have thought-out opinions about their position in the world, what the world thinks about them and what they think about the world.

'You can talk to the man in the street and you'll get a thoughtful judgment', mused Andrew Burke, a Lonely Planet writer who has covered the country. 'That wouldn't happen in, say, Laos. The average man-in-the-street in Laos wouldn't have a clue what was going on and certainly wouldn't think it was his right to say something about it.'

It's called democracy and, while democracy Iranian-style certainly isn't up to the standards we're used to in the West, it is probably ahead of any other country on my Bad Lands list apart from today's Albania. Even Iraq, despite its good-as-it-gets-under-the-circumstances brand of democracy, was probably a long way behind Iran until recently. In the last few years, Iraq's elections, despite the associated violence, seem to have been reasonably fair, while the 2009 election in Iran was a disaster. Nevertheless, the Iranian reality is that lots of people may be a long way from 100 per cent enthusiastic about the ayatollahs and the religious influences on their life, but they're also very unenthusiastic about the United States (or anyone else for that matter) nosing in and suggesting that 'regime change' should be on their agenda.

So, although the Iran government is a long, long way from being nice to its citizens, it's also far from the worst around: score one point in the first category.

Where Iran is definitely not nice is the Terrorism category. Although they've probably not become directly involved, they have certainly supported lots of organisations who have put their Iranian money to bad use. They put much more effort into promoting terrorism than Iraq and, what's more, they're proud of it. Two points.

External Threats? Well, there's lots of talk about destroying Israel because the Holocaust never happened so for hot air alone they score a point here. In fact, despite their 'we'll make a bomb if we want to' threats, they don't have the wherewithal to turn all this posturing into bad actions so no more than a point here.

Remarkably Iran can scratch up a half-point in the bonus category. Given the Islamic abhorrence of graven images it would seem unlikely, but in fact, as any visitor to Iran can confirm, the country is well stocked with some very artistic Khomeini billboards.

Finally, since it's my Evil Meter™, there's going to be another half a bonus point for the Ayatollah's fatwa on Salman Rushdie. I don't like to see writers being threatened, particularly for books the threateners have not even read.

IRAQ
UNDER SADDAM HUSSEIN
6 POINTS

No question about it: Iraq under Saddam was not a nice place. He slaughtered and gassed his own citizens, murdered his political opponents, set his son Uday loose on a losing football team and killed thousands more Iraqis by sending them off to fight ridiculous wars. The Evil Meter™ reads two in the first category.

For External Threats Saddam scored even higher, a perfect three. He launched a war against Iran that went on for eight long years and then repeated the feat with his invasion of Kuwait. In the course of the Kuwait Gulf War he also hurled a bunch of badly aimed Scud missiles at Saudi Arabia and Israel. Having Saddam as a neighbour was clearly not a good idea.

On the other hand, despite the Coalition of the Willing invading Iraq as part of the War on Terrorism, Saddam scores a big fat zero in the Terrorism category. If Saddam didn't like you, he'd launch the Mother of Wars – he didn't mess with mere terrorism.

Saddam does score a solid bonus point for Personality Cult. He built statues and posted portraits with the best of them. If bad taste could earn another point for a Bad Land, then Saddam would have scored with every good-taste magazine from Architectural Digest to Wallpaper for his collection of over-the-top palaces.

NORTH KOREA
7 POINTS

No way round it, the DPRK is the only country to score points in every category including a clear Personality Cult victory.

The unfortunate citizens of North Korea have no choice about their government and absolutely no right to say anything about it. There's minimal economic freedom, no choice in where you live or work, and religion simply doesn't exist (apart from worship of the Great Leader and his progeny of course). Plus countless North Koreans have starved to death in recent years and if you try to escape and get caught, things can turn really bad. So three points.

Terrorism: with blown-up aircraft, kidnapped schoolchildren, fake US hundred-dollar bills and assassinations on its scorecard, North Korea fully deserves two points in this category.

External Threats is a difficult one. After their 2006 nuclear test (if it really happened) North Korea is more likely to have those dreaded WMDs than Iraq (of course, these days we all realise Lichtenstein was more likely to have WMDs than Iraq). It also has a penchant for driving tunnels under the DMZ towards South Korea and there are those provocative missile-tests and submarines full of suicidal commandos. Plus there's all the bragging about exacting terrible revenge upon imperialists and puppet stooges. On the other hand the coastal defences indicate that they're just as frightened of being invaded and how effective would a North Korean attack be in any case? Their air force dates from the Korean War, their army is half-starved and half a head shorter than their South Korean equivalents and from what I saw in Pyongyang they can hardly build a bicycle, let alone an accurate missile. So the Evil Meter™ only scores them one point in the External Threats category.

The bonus point, however, is clearly theirs. There is no Personality Cult like the North Korean Personality Cult and I really hope we can all one day enjoy the great Dear Leader/Great Leader Statue & Billboard Amusement Park.

SOME CONTROL COUNTRIES

Any good instrument needs a control test to make sure it's working properly so let's think about how my Evil Meter™ would react to some countries that don't feature as a Bad Land: like the USA.

You'd be hard pushed to complain about American treatment of American citizens. Come the next election you know whoever is in power will pack up and depart if he or she is voted out. There is no way an American president is going to call in the army to extend a stay in the White House. Plus you can certainly say whatever you like about any politician including the president and get away with it. Just imagine what would have happened to Michael Moore or Graydon Carter (the editor of *Vanity Fair*) in, say, Singapore.

Starting up a business and making a lot of money is an American birthright, marrying who you want (well, perhaps not if they're the same sex in some states) is also a right and you can certainly join any religion you choose. You can even dream up your own nutty religion and encourage others to join up. Anything new in the religious line, from Mormonism to Scientology, seems to be an American invention.

Of course, you're far more likely to end up in an American prison if your skin is black or your language Spanish. And when it comes to prisoner numbers the USA is a world leader per capita or in outright statistics. Capital punishment is also a US favourite, but overall the Evil Meter™ would still have trouble giving the USA a reading in this category.

Unhappily, despite George W Bush's War on Terrorism, the USA is not lily-white in this field. There's plenty of evidence of direct US support for terrorist activities – remember Ronald Reagan, Colonel Oliver North and undercover arms sales to Iran in order to fund the Nicaraguan Contras terrorist group? And didn't the CIA try to blow up Fidel with exploding cigars?

What about all the civilian deaths from the US military's trigger-happiness and bad aim as well? Quite apart from civilian deaths in Iraq the 290 crew and passengers on an Airbus flying in to Dubai in 1988 discovered the US military could be as trigger-happy as any real terrorists when the guided-missile cruiser USS *Vincennes* shot the aircraft down with the loss of all on board.

Then there's indirect US support of terrorism. A large slice of the financial support for the IRA's terrorism in Ireland came from hats being passed around in Irish bars and clubs in New York and Boston. Most of the dollars collected no more went to Irish widows and Irish education than the Saudi equivalent ended up supporting peaceful study of the Koran in Pakistani madrasahs. The War on Terrorism has, at least, stymied that sort of terrorist support.

Unfortunately the USA today is an outright winner when it comes to encouraging and recruiting terrorists. Driving down a freeway in Tehran I saw some wonderful terrorist recruitment billboards: ad agency, the US Army; studio, Abu Ghraib; model, Lynndie England. Could Al-Qaeda have produced anything better even if they'd had J Walter Thompson working for them?

Furthermore every image of the USA's own gulag, Guantánamo Bay, encourages more jihad supporters. Every story about 'rendition flights', grabbing suspects and flying them off to a nameless destination for a little incarceration and torture, inspires a few more suicide bombers. Every time a US government spokesperson like Colleen Graffy opens her mouth and says something so incredibly stupid as her description of a triple suicide by Guantánamo detainees as a 'good PR move', terrorism chalks up another win.

Or perhaps not. Perhaps Colleen Graffy and Rear Admiral Harry Harris, Guantánamo Bay's commander, with his equally asinine comments about hanging yourself with clothing and bed sheets being 'an act of asymmetrical warfare waged against us', had another aim. Perhaps they were simply trying their best to make the place so distasteful even the most blindfolded neo-cons will campaign to close it down.

So overall I'm pretty sure the Evil Meter™ would score some points for the USA in the Terrorism category.

Finally I suspect my Evil Meter™ might go off the scale if the USA was tested in the External Threats category. Just run through the Bad Lands and think what has happened to them, courtesy of the USA.

Afghanistan – flooded with arms that fuelled the devastating years of mujaheddin turmoil, bombed by Clinton and Bush, bombed and invaded by Bush.

Albania – nothing much, although Hoxha must have built all those bunkers because he was terrified somebody was going to invade.

Burma – boycotted.

Cuba – almost 50 years of isolation, boycotts and embargoes and plenty of threats, although the Bay of Pigs affair probably fits the terrorism rather than the invasion category.

Iran – any number of threats to try the Iraq regime-change experience again.

Iraq – bombing, invasion, boycotts, embargoes, more bombing, another invasion, occupation.

Libya – boycotts, seclusion, embargoes, bombing.

North Korea – war, invasion, threats, boycotts, embargoes.

Saudi Arabia – now there's a country the USA has always loved. OK, they're somewhat democracy-free, they do treat women rather shabbily and they did finance, plan and man the September 11 attacks but, hey, any country can make mistakes.

Of course, any story has two sides, so we should try not to forget that although the USA may be a serious danger to any country it doesn't agree with that can still be a good thing. The European nations would still be sitting around twiddling their thumbs and saying 'oh dear' as ethnic cleansing went on in the Balkans if the US hadn't led the way in Kosovo.

Personality Cult? Well, it's true that portraits of the president do seem to be a much more common sight as you're lining up to clear US immigration these days, but there's certainly not enough of them to score a point in the bonus category.

How would the Evil Meter™ react to some other 'good' countries, like Australia, the UK or France?

Australia and the UK were both willing to join in when it came to rounding up the forces for the Iraqi mayhem so they're in there with the USA on that one. On the other hand neither has been quite as keen as the USA on throwing out centuries of well-founded laws or in kidnapping people and flying them off for a spell of electrics-to-the-genitals treatment.

For a long spell Australia remained one of the few countries in the

Western world, apart from the USA of course, that continued to believe that Guantánamo Bay was a good thing. It's worth noting that Britain insisted that none of its citizens were left in a Caribbean gulag and Major Michael Mori, the US Marine lawyer for Australia's Guantánamo inmate David Hicks, has correctly pointed out that in the USA there would be national outrage if any American citizen was being subject to the sort of treatment meted out to his legal client.

France, of course, resolutely said 'non' to the Iraq idea, but I'm fairly certain my Evil Meter™ would produce a reading if it was applied to *la belle France*. After all, France has had a long tradition of propping up nasty African governments so long as they made an effort to speak a little *français* or invest the money they'd beaten out of their population in chateaus, champagne and Concorde charters. And if things began to look really bad for some of their Bad African Land clients, France had the Foreign Legion always ready to ride in to the rescue, successfully keeping the rebels away from the palace door.

Finally, even the worst of the Bad Lands would have trouble competing with France at getting caught red-handed in the state-sponsored-terrorism competition. In 1985, spooked that Greenpeace might disrupt French use of the Pacific as a convenient nuclear-testing spot, a batch of French agents were dispatched to Auckland, New Zealand, to sink the Greenpeace vessel *Rainbow Warrior*. The ship sank and a Portuguese photographer on board died, but the French agents were clearly not James Bond material. Two of them ended up on trial, but New Zealand was curtly reminded that it was Paris who pulled the European Union strings in Brussels and economically things wouldn't be very nice for the small Pacific nation if the incompetent French agents weren't promptly released. They were.

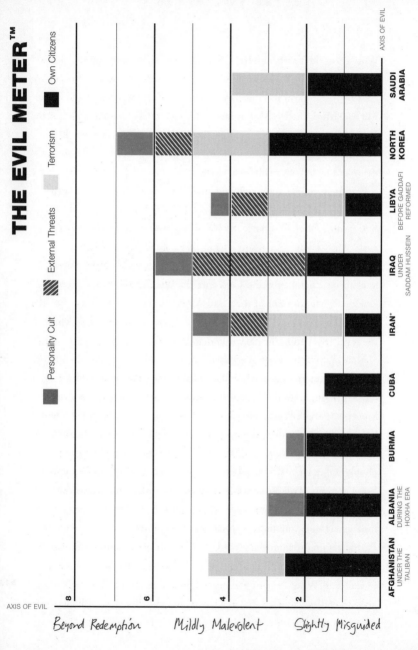

THE EVIL METER™

Personality Cult   External Threats   Terrorism   Own Citizens

AXIS OF EVIL

8 — Beyond Redemption

6 — Mildly Malevolent

4 — Slightly Misguided

2 —

AFGHANISTAN UNDER THE TALIBAN   ALBANIA DURING THE HOXHA ERA   BURMA   CUBA   IRAN*   IRAQ UNDER SADDAM HUSSEIN   LIBYA BEFORE GADDAFI REFORMED   NORTH KOREA   SAUDI ARABIA

AXIS OF EVIL

* Iran scores an extra 0.5 bonus points for issuing fatwas

OTHER
BAD LANDS
THE EXTENDED LIST

I described my journeys through nine Bad Lands, but of course there are many other places in the world that could easily qualify for that status. Here is my 'Top Ten' extended list of countries that, like the others already chronicled, derive their Bad Land status from an assortment of causes ranging from colonial-era mismanagement, involvement in other countries' proxy wars and governmental failings to outright corruption.

Somalia defines better than anywhere the description 'failed state' and has been effectively written off and forgotten since the 'Black Hawk Down' disaster in 1993. Forgotten, except that over the following years many of Somalia's warring warlords have been quietly funded by the USA, because the alternative, an Islamic state that might become a new home for Al-Qaeda, was too horrible to contemplate.

The end result? In June 2006, after 15 years of anarchy, an Islamist force took over Mogadishu, the capital, and kicked out the assortment of warlords. Why? Because the general population was completely fed up with endless violence and, as a result, no government, no schools, no health care, no life. Inevitably the Afghanistan comparisons have been made: for squabbling Somali warlords read squabbling Afghan mujaheddin and for Somali Islamists read Afghan Taliban. Don't forget the Taliban were, perhaps reluctantly, welcomed at first and the Somali Islamists might have learnt some lessons from how the Taliban squandered that welcome.

The dramatic rise in pirate attacks launched from the Somali coast, with vessels captured and held for ransom, has succeeded in bringing Somalia back into the news. Sorting out the country's failed-state status is once again on the international agenda.

Remarkably Somalia has a Kurdistan-like northern region, known as Somaliland, which has cut itself off from the rest of the country, elected its own government and been relatively stable and safe. You can visit Somaliland from Eritrea and be fairly confident of getting home to tell the tale. Despite the chaos and lawlessness, Somalia as a whole also has one modern business: mobile phones. There's a workable and reliable cellular phone system, just like in Afghanistan and assorted other Bad Lands.

With the mess in Darfur regularly popping up on our TV screens and in newspaper editorials Sudan, separated from Somalia by Ethiopia, could also join my list. But there are plenty of other African Bad Land candidates including Congo/Zaïre, the country that two centuries ago defined the term 'darkest Africa' and remains one of the blackest black holes in a continent well endowed with disaster stories. From 1867 until 1908, this great slab of central Africa was known as the Congo Free State, with Belgium's King Léopold II as the utterly ruthless ruler. International outrage over the king's mindless brutality – he knew all about terrorism – led to the creation of the Belgian Congo. Independence arrived in 1960, but Patrice Lumumba, independent Congo's first elected prime minister and to this day a hero of African independence, was deposed only 10 weeks later, imprisoned, brutally beaten on more than one occasion and finally killed in early 1961. Belgium played a part in his overthrow and, naturally, the CIA are also accused of lending a hand.

Joseph Mobutu, the chief of staff of the army when Lumumba was deposed, soon took over and ruled for the next three decades. For the full story read Michela Wrong's *In the Footsteps of Mr Kurtz,* accurately subtitled *Living on the Brink of Disaster in Mobutu's Congo.* Mr Kurtz was Joseph Conrad's character in *Heart of Darkness.*

The reader alternates between horror and laugh-out-loud amazement as Mobutu, who ran Zaïre as his personal fiefdom for 32 years, leads France, the USA and the World Bank down every blind alley on offer. While his people starved, Mobutu chartered Concordes from Air France so he could zip to his chateau in France at supersonic speed. In the last swirls of the final downward spiral, as his international friends abandoned him and the rebels closed in, Mobutu discovered he couldn't even call in his air force. The fancy supersonic Mirages were never going to return from a visit to France for maintenance – they'd been surreptitiously sold off to finance a Zaïrean air force commander's European retirement.

Mobutu departed in 1997, but never got to enjoy his own retirement in France. Within months he died of prostate cancer in Morocco. Congo/Zaïre has abundant natural resources, including huge diamond deposits, and it's one of the most important sources of tantalum, a vital ingredient in the manufacture of mobile phones and computer chips. So with Mobutu gone things soon improved, right?

Sure things improved, just like getting rid of that nasty dictator Saddam Hussein made things much better for Iraq. Far from improving the country's hopeless situation, Mobutu's departure made things far worse. Laurent-Désiré Kabila, the new dictator, proved equally rapacious and it soon became clear that Mobutu's overthrow was simply an excuse for a proxy war between rebel groups supported by Rwanda and Uganda.

Soon other African nations joined the melee including some, like Zimbabwe, that did not even share a border with the Congo. Kabila was assasinated in 2001, only to be followed by another Kabila, his son Joseph. Africa's First World War, as the civil war has been described,

321.

brought a soaring death toll, as many as four million by 2006, which has made it the most deadly war anywhere in the world since World War II. A ceasefire between the assorted rebel groups and elections in late 2006 may have brought some stability to the unhappy country, but after nearly 50 years of unremitting post-independence misery it's hard to believe.

Further south, Zimbabwe is not quite such a disaster area as Congo/ Zaïre, although it clearly could be if President Robert Mugabe has his way. Once upon a time Zimbabwe was fairly well-off by African standards and one man has managed to piss that all away. I have to admit that on the first occasion I went to Zimbabwe – back in 1989 – I was told Mugabe would eventually wreck the place and I dismissed that view as ex-colonial paranoia. They were right; I was wrong. Power-sharing with Morgan Tsvangirai, instituted in 2009 following the disputed 2008 election, has enjoyed very limited success, but completely dumping the Zimbabwe dollar (I've got a 100 trillion Zimbabwe dollar note in my wallet) and using the US dollar as the regular currency has revived the economy to some extent.

Poor Angola had the bad luck to be a Portuguese colony and become another of the world's proxy battlefields when the Lisbon dictatorship collapsed in 1974. Marxism-Leninism would have won, but the US certainly didn't want that domino falling and through the 1980s the CIA poured military aid into the country, often via the apartheid government of South Africa. The greenbacks went to Jonas Savimbi and his UNITA (National Union for the Total Independence of Angola) rebel group while on the other side the USSR financed Cuban mercenaries for the MPLA (Popular Movement for the Liberation of Angola). Just like Israel in southern Lebanon, South Africa itself was ready to shift troops into southern Angola anytime the struggle seemed to be going the wrong way. The result was death, injury or refugee status for hundreds of thousands of unfortunate Angolans.

The collapse of the Soviet Union should have terminated the endless struggle and in 1992 the UN supervised an election, won by the MPLA. Savimbi promptly reneged on the agreement and went back to war, funding his operations by control over Angola's rich diamond deposits. Diamonds, it turned out, could also be a terrorist's best friend, and for another 10 years Angola stumbled from crisis to crisis, outrage to outrage. UN representatives pointed out that if dealers in the West refused to buy Angolan diamonds, which were funding Savimbi's army, his power would have quickly melted away. UNITA's response was to shoot down UN aircraft carrying humanitarian aid.

Government troops finally managed to kill Savimbi in February 2002, which decisively concluded his long reign of terror. Angola is a Bad Land that just might be emerging from 30 lost years although unhappily the MPLA is hardly corruption free. I made a brief visit to Angola in 2005 although I didn't venture out of the capital, Luanda. In 2006 the Angolan football team qualified for the World Cup in Germany, an event that for the first time created a real feeling of national unity. Angola's economic boom continues apace, making it one of the world's most expensive countries to visit.

Surely Latin America can produce a competitive Bad Land? Argentina might have qualified during the generals' rule, but the little squabble with Maggie Thatcher over the Falklands/Malvinas scrubbed up that country. Kicking the Argentineans out of the Falklands in 1982 not only converted the Iron Lady's shaky political position to the solid control that allowed her, for better or worse, to comprehensively overhaul the British economy – it also terminated Argentina's military dictatorship.

Colombia definitely has Bad Land potential and will continue to face problems as long as the demand for high-quality Colombian marching powder stays strong in the West. Want to sort out Colombia's problems? Well, forget about stamping out the drug trade and just legalise the stupid stuff is my suggestion. Sure you'll have some new addicts who wouldn't have been addicts before, but they won't have to turn to crime to fund their addiction and Colombia (and other drug-producing countries like Afghanistan and Burma) won't have their own internal problems as suppliers. In fact let governments handle sales and marketing and cocaine and heroin could easily lose their forbidden flavour and become boringly mundane.

So I'll leave Colombia off my extended Bad List, move north into the Caribbean and put Haiti on instead.

I visited Haiti in 2008, less than two years before the terrible earthquake in January 2010 that devastated an already struggling nation. Of course, my visit was nowhere near as 'difficult' or 'dangerous' as popular opinion would have you believe, but this is certainly a country with a huge range of question marks over why it has ended up as such a basket case1.

Now there's a nice failed state – all that beach paradise potential, some of the world's best naïve art, French as the national language and total bloody chaos as the end product. Looking at Haiti you wonder how Fidel's Cuba ever deserved to be a Bad Land.

Check the stats. Infant mortality? In Haiti it's around 100 deaths per 1000 live births (among the worst in the world); in Cuba it's less than 10 (right up with First World standards). National income per person? It's only about US$3000 for Cuba, even when adjusted for the low cost of many subsidised essentials, but that's still two to three times the amount the average Haitian has to live on. Literacy? Close to 100 per cent in Cuba; more like 50 per cent in Haiti. Life expectancy? If you're born in Cuba, you can expect to live to your late 70s, just like Americans and other First World citizens. Haitians are lucky to see their 50th birthday. Government? Well, Haiti does hold elections from time to time, even if whoever gets elected never manages to stay in power for more than five minutes. That must be the reason Haiti has not been subject to economic sanctions and attempts to destabilise their government for the past 50 years, unlike neighbouring Cuba.

How about the Pacific – any Bad Lands there? Unfortunately there's lots of potential. The Solomon Islands, Papua New Guinea and East Timor have been labelled Australia's 'arc of instability': three countries that cannot get their acts together and in recent years have all needed outside assistance to try to clean things up.

Papua New Guinea, a vast and colourful nation with huge economic and tourist potential, is probably the biggest danger simply through its size and, therefore, the size of the problem. The great colonial carve-up of the island was strictly on the map – none of the colonial powers actually explored the territory where they so nonchalantly drew borders. First a north–south line was drawn in 1824 to separate Dutch territory to the west from British territory to the east. In fact Britain took virtually zero interest in their holdings until the Germans appeared and an east–west line was hastily drawn to separate German New Guinea to the north from British Papua to the south. It was nearly 50 years later before the first explorers, arriving in the New Guinea Highlands by air, discovered the border had been drawn not through an uninhabited wilderness, but through the most densely populated region of the whole island. By that time the Germans had lost World War I and the British had handed over management to Australia.

The Dutch retained their half of the island even after the rest of the Dutch East Indies became independent Indonesia in 1949. When independence came for Australian Papua New Guinea in 1975 it should, logically, have joined with Dutch New Guinea to create an island nation. Instead in 1962 the Dutch half had been handed over to Indonesia in what was seen as a US-pressured attempt to placate Soekarno, who was leaning heavily towards the USSR. Soekarno's control only lasted two more years, but the Indonesians have stubbornly held on to what became Irian Barat, then Irian Jaya and now Papua, despite ongoing resistance from the Papuans who are ethnically and culturally totally unrelated to the Indonesians, but closely related to the citizens of Papua New Guinea.

Since independence, democracy has had a tough time in Papua New

Guinea because allegiance is directed towards one's tribe, not towards the country as a whole. Constantly shifting alliances make for regular changes of government and high levels of corruption. Ongoing local violence, driven by low employment and fuelled by tribal machismo, has led to large slabs of the country falling into the control of quaintly named 'rascals'.

So we'll add Papua New Guinea to the Extended Bad List and move north to a tiny nation that is Sad Land as much as Bad Land: Nauru. The tiny equatorial island had the misfortune to be deeply covered in phosphate, aka guano, aka bird poop. For the best part of a century the phosphate was dug up and shipped out, a bounty that briefly made the citizens of Nauru among the wealthiest in the world, right up with the Arab oil states. Then the phosphate ran out, the birdshit investments turned out to be, well, shitty, and Nauru went bankrupt. Even their Melbourne skyscraper, locally known as Birdshit House, was repossessed, and for a spell poor little Nauru depended on half-hearted money laundering and a role as Australia's own Guantánamo Bay. Just as the USA used its Cuban enclave as a prison far from the reach of lawyers and the eyes of journalists, so did Australia, under John Howard's government, use Nauru as a place to closet away would-be refugees arriving from real Bad Lands like Iraq or Afghanistan as part of the 'Pacific Solution'.

Back in Asia, Pakistan is a strong contender for Bad Land status. After all, this was the only country that really supported the Taliban apart from Saudi Arabia. Any terrorist event in India is likely to be blamed on Pakistan (and with very good reason) and it was also the conduit for all those dollars heading to Afghanistan's mujaheddin warlords. A large slice of that weapons money leaked out of the pipeline and ended up supporting a roll call of Pakistani ne'er-do-wells, from international terrorists to local gangsters. Plus, and it's a big plus, Pakistan today is probably home for Osama bin Laden, if he's still alive.

In the Middle East there's no stronger candidate for a Bad Land listing, from the US perspective, than Syria. It's the conduit between Iran

326.

and the Hezbollah militia in Lebanon, it's done some terrorising off its own bat, it was Saddam's best pal before his downfall and it's not been very nice to its own citizens. It also has extraordinarily friendly people, good beer and wine, great food, wonderful Greek and Roman ruins, fascinating reminders of the early years of Christianity, Crusader castles and a positive passion for beautifully restored old American cars. The dry desert air ensures that Syria's fine collection of antique Detroit iron is in far healthier shape than the better-known relics in Cuba. You cannot, however, cruise down the Biblical 'Street Named Straight' in Damascus in an elderly Chevy. It's pedestrian only. Sending a US ambassador to Syria in late 2009, after four years without one, hints that the country's Bad Land status may be under review.

Last, but far from least, there's the combo that is arguably the baddest Bad Land of them all. For what would Iran have to rant and rave about or Al-Qaeda to mount terrorist attacks over if Israel/Palestine didn't exist? If it wasn't for the ongoing death, destruction and unhappiness, the Israel-Palestine or Israel–Arab-world conflict would look uncannily like the equally never-ending struggle between the cartoon characters Tom and Jerry. Jerry, the troublesome mouse, taunts Tom, the fat cat, until Tom, aka Israel, loses his temper and sets out in mass destruction mode to destroy Jerry, aka Palestine (or Hamas or Hezbollah or whatever part Jerry is playing this week). Tom never manages to flatten Jerry, who inevitably pops up to continue the game next time round, but he certainly smashes plenty of vases, furniture and anything else breakable along the way.

Or think of the Palestinians (or Hamas or Hezbollah) as the obnoxious drunk hassling the pumped-up bouncer until, predictably, the bouncer flexes those steroid-enhanced biceps and beats the miserable little troublemaker to a pulp. The winners and losers are utterly predictable, but it's equally unsurprising who wins the sympathy vote in many of the next morning's papers. Bouncers should have some self-control, one paper will editorialise. Drug suppliers shouldn't be nonchalantly handing out steroids to bouncers, another will accurately observe. Of course, some papers will, correctly, point out that obnoxious little drunks should learn better behaviour. Yet as soon as he's off his crutches he'll undoubtedly be hassling the bouncer all over again.

Sadly some things never change. In late 2008 the next instalment of the ongoing Tom and Jerry tale unreeled in Gaza as 'Operation Cast Lead'. Once again a lot of innocent bystanders paid with their lives, once again Israel won the battle, once again the Palestinians overwhelmingly took home the world's sympathy vote. If I was going to add just one more Bad Land to my main list, Israel/Palestine would have to be it.